These Strange Stones

By Christie Lietz

Cover photo: "Jia"[Home], painted by MaPing

Note for Librarians:
A cataloguing record for this book is available from Library and Archives Canada at
www.collectionscanada.ca/amicus/index-e.html

ISBN – 978-0-9939949-0-6

Printed in Canada
♻
on recycled paper
FIRST CHOICE BOOKS

www.firstchoicebooks.ca
Victoria, BC

10 9 8 7 6 5 4 3 2 1

About the title:

When a riverbed dries up, or the water level goes down, some Chinese like to collect "QiShi" [strange stones] -- those stones that the river has smoothed and shaped in unique and artistic ways -- as decorations and conversation pieces for their home. When the Israelites crossed the Jordan to enter the promised land, God told them to collect 12 stones as they crossed through, and place them on the other side as a reminder of how God had dried up the Jordan to allow them to cross over, *"...so that all the peoples of the earth might know that the hand of the LORD is powerful and so that you might always fear the LORD your God"* (Joshua 4:24)

As we look back on the ways that God has led us, provided for our needs, and kept His promises (especially the promise that if we have left brothers or sisters or father or mother for His sake we will receive a hundred times as much) during the last 20+ years of working in China, we want to collect some of these strange stones and lay them out as a reminder to our children, and hopefully others, of God's faithfulness and power.

Note on Lisu names:

You will notice some ambiguity among the Lisu names. Like, "Why are there so many "AKe's"? Lisu refer to each other as "First son", "Second daughter", etc. Sons (in order) are named APu, ADe [De sounds like "di" in "dirt"], AKe [like "a key"]. Daughters are ANa, ANi, AQia, ADu. So the children of one family can have the same names as their neighbours. As there's often ambiguity, they will add some defining characteristic, like "lame AKe", "curly haired APu". So we often use the preferred name for our Lisu "brothers or sisters or fathers or mothers" but sometimes use a pseudonym to avoid confusion.

Contents

Contents

The Vow

Well, I made a vow, and now I have to start my book! My testimony, really, and the ways that God has dealt with me. What initiated this book was a birth. A dreadful birth - the kind of birth I try to stave off by prayer every time I am called up to attend.

We live in the lower section of a Lisu village, the half which moved down to be near the road while the rest stayed on the mountain slope. I had noticed that a couple of the young women we had seen married last year were now evidently expecting. I make a practice of asking these first time mothers if they're afraid and if they'd like to learn about prepared childbirth because they otherwise receive no helpful instruction, and generally have not put aside so much as some clean cloths or something to cut the cord. They always say yes!

The only Lisu women who don't give birth at home are those who are in desperate straits, and who live through the arduous process of being carried down the mountain by bamboo stretcher and then by motorized trishaw to the hospital in town. The hospital where .... more about that later.

Anyhow, one of the expectant moms showed up on the day we'd arranged for the prenatal class and told me the other young woman had gone into labour already that morning, (Lisu women tend to be so tiny even in advanced pregnancy, and almost never know when they're due, either) so she couldn't make it. Instead, I had to go up and try to give her a crash course between contractions, in my pidgin Lisu, minus the help of a translator. She was stiff, frightened, and withdrawn; not very enthusiastic about any of the measures I suggested to strengthen contractions. I think she would have jumped at the offer of a drug to stop them! At that time I had birthed six children of my own, and could relate, but it would have been far better if she'd cooperated.

On my first hike up to her house, I submitted to being sniffed and barked at by all the village dogs, meanwhile praying for God's protection over her and the baby. I asked for an uncomplicated labour and for the baby to turn to a good position; for a safe delivery and a strong, healthy baby. By that night, her labour was still just niggling along, so I reminded her to eat, drink, and alternate resting and walking. The next day I went up to see her, and she was tired, hadn't taken any refreshment and didn't want to be examined. I warned her that she needed to do the things I'd said to keep up her and the baby's strength, but she said she was nauseated now, and only halfheartedly tried the other measures while I was there.

The next morning they excitedly told me that she had a little desire to push. She was fully dilated, but the head was still high and to one side, so we got her alternately squatting and pushing and walking. . . I asked her mother, various grandmas, aunts and friends who had gathered, to join me in prayer that God would deliver her and help that baby to slide into a better position. I also phoned a midwife friend and tried everything she could think of. After five hours of this, she finally submitted to another check - The baby had not come down at all, and her contractions had not become any stronger. At that point I strongly suggested that she be moved to the hospital for IV fluids, and labour augmentation before it got dark. I had also not once been able to get a fetal heart tone with my stethoscope. They discussed it and decided that if there was still no baby by day four, they would go to the hospital! One of her good friends told me she'd been in labour for three days as well and had a terrible time, but her baby had been fine. I tried to believe that maybe this would happen with this one as well. There wasn't anything more I could do, and I wasn't inclined to coerce them to take her to the hospital. The one time I did take a labouring tribal woman to the hospital it was horrendous. She needed a caesarean, and she didn't get one. I still can't bring myself to describe what happened that night. Suffice to say that I understood and shared their reservations. With a heavy heart, I left them my cell phone and told them to call me if they saw the baby's hair.

All this time we, the kids, and a widening circle of friends had been praying for God to please help this baby come out! We weren't praying for an easy labour anymore - just that the baby would somehow make it. I had also used some of the tedious hours that afternoon to bone up on infant resuscitation in a non-hospital setting.

At 3 am, the phone rang, and I was blasted with a string of excited Lisu. Of course, once again there wasn't a translator handy! This time, headed up the steep, steep path in the pitch black, I was so thankful for the other trips which had allowed me to make friends with all the dogs, who with the advantage of the slope could otherwise bark and snarl right in your face!

When I came panting up to the house, a pack of newly energized friends and relatives told me that she had just lost some more amniotic fluid! No hair. Inwardly groaning, I went about getting everything laid out for the delivery, and did what I could at that point to show them alternate positions for her to push in. As things had become more intense, they had slipped back into their traditional ways. The girl's eyes were closed, damp hair held back by the traditional checked kerchief, her body hanging limply from numb, field-hardened hands.

Labour in Lisuland is terribly hard work. It is the role of the older women to either jam a pole across a corner, held up by cracks in the rock walls, or to hang a strap for the labouring woman to grasp. From her first labour pain until the baby is born, the old women remind her to hang on and push. When she becomes too exhausted, they sit behind her and press down on her swollen abdomen. They don't understand the need to wait for the cervix to dilate, and to save strength for what should be a one or two hour period of pushing effort. Also, because of poor nutrition, they tend to bleed a terrifying amount. Most of the birth process happens discreetly underneath her oldest, voluminous, black skirt, and flipping that soggy, filthy thing out of the way (while keeping your gloves sterile!) to try and get a glimpse of how things are progressing isn't one of the nicest parts of attending these births!

Thankfully, there was one electric light bulb hanging above her corner, attracting moths, but unlike some families, they hadn't even laid out a rice husk mat on the dirt floor for the baby to be born onto. Realizing it was going to be a crisis birth, I insisted that they put down a mat so that she could be laid flat after the birth.

Finally, after two more hours of pushing, there was a little bit of hair...and then a little bit more, and then a bloody crown. (Why was she bleeding? Cervical tear? Premature placenta separation?) I knew a healthy baby's scalp would be pink; this one's was dark purple. Frantically, we pleaded with her to push harder. Her father and husband had long since abandoned their traditional detached role and had added their strength and encouragement to the cluster of people crowded into the corner. Now her parents started shouting at her, commanding her to really push, and she delivered their grandson. Perfect, steaming, maroon-coloured, lifeless. Everyone stared at him, stunned, and I heard the grandma grumble, "GaBa" [Wasted] somewhere over my shoulder.

Working as quickly as I could, I rubbed off his face, head and back, then began breathing for him, see-sawing his legs up and down and rubbing his back. Nothing. After a couple of minutes which felt like years, suddenly, he made a sound like a dying fish! Could it be? Or was it just air coming back out of his stomach? Galvanized into even more frantic efforts, I continued puffing air into his little nose and mouth for a few more minutes. I sat back for a moment and was rewarded by another gasp! I picked him up, and moved him onto his mother's stomach to keep him warm, while using the weight of his body to compress his mother's exhausted, flaccid womb. She was bleeding...I kept breathing for him, gasping between-times, "Talk to him! Call him! Wrap him up! Rub his back!" He was breathing! Raggedly, unevenly, but pinking up a little and opening his eyes! He was coming around! Murmurs of astonishment and thanksgiving started rising around us. He never did cry, but gradually life moved from his torso out to his extremities and he was breathing normally.

I quickly prepared an injection to control bleeding and gave it to the mother. Still bleeding,..another shot. I cut the umbilical cord, wrapped the baby better and, still holding him, used one hand and my teeth to unzip the hood of my down parka to cuddle down over the baby's head and help conserve heat. A few minutes later she delivered the placenta, and the family stood her up and moved her towards the bed, but there was still blood running down her legs and soaking into the floor -- another injection, another plea shot heavenwards. Finally, both mom and baby seemed stable, and as dawn broke, I washed my hands and started down hill towards home.

I was rejoicing, wondering, sore, wrung-out, still worried that there had been brain-damage, that she'd start bleeding again as soon as the medication wore off. Shucking off my dusty, blood spattered clothes, I crawled into bed beside my husband, Dave, and committed them to the Lord one more time before I fell into an exhausted sleep.

Two days later, the baby's grandma sidled diffidently into the yard and told me in a low voice that the baby wasn't crying, and hadn't nursed yet. Uh, oh. Could I please go up and check on them? As soon as I could free myself, I hiked up once more. It was true - he couldn't nurse, or cry; just look around with his big black eyes. He could swallow, however, so I got them a bottle and taught her how to express milk. Four days after the birth, my heart sank to see the grandma again shyly coming into the yard. Now what? He hadn't wet even once yet. I knew a healthy, well-nourished infant would be urinating several times a day already, would have a rooting reflex, would suck, instinctively seeking to nurse, would cry when uncomfortable, would "startle" when moved suddenly - he didn't have any of these basic reflexes.

With a heavy heart, I made my way up to see him one more time. He was so tiny, so thin and wrinkled. How heart-breaking. "Why, Lord? Why have me be a part of this? Wouldn't it have been better for him to have just died at birth rather than this drawn- out sorrow and anxiety? Please heal his brain, Lord. (but You could have kept his brain from being damaged if You'd answered just one of the many prayers I lifted up on his behalf during labour...)" Late that night, Dave felt me sobbing and discovered my wet face. He encouraged me to trust the Lord, and to pray for healing. I couldn't pray, just lie there with the tears seeping into my ears. I just could not drum up any more faith and told the Lord I felt like Mary and Martha must have before He showed up and raised Lazarus from the dead. That was exactly it. "If only You'd been here, this baby wouldn't be dying. Why, oh, why didn't You answer our cries for help? We asked you urgently, trustingly. How hard would it have been for You to just turn that baby a little bit?" This was the Lazarus story, only with no resurrection.

At the same time, I knew there was an element of pride in my offence and discouragement -- because I had tried so hard, I had expected Him to do His part as well. If I was going to be brought into this scenario, and be allowed to resuscitate that baby, then I wanted the outcome to be better than if I'd known nothing about it and things had just taken their course.

Dave had no patience with my silence. His ever-practical attitude about prayer is that 'you have not because you ask not'. Once the matter has been committed to the Lord, the outcome is His business, but up until then, we have an obligation to at least ask! "Well, if you won't pray, I will. God, please heal this little fellow and restore him to full health."

For the next few days, sadness continued to hang on me like a lead jacket, but I gradually came to the point where I knew that mature faith had to be content without miracles. God does allow illness, deformity, death and disaster. He does work in and through them, and can turn even the most crushing circumstances into blessing where they are accepted with trust. I knew there were many, many damaged children just like this little one in the world, and that He had used them to speak into the lives of people who were listening for His voice, open to His grace and mercy. I was humbled and moved by the attitude of this baby's family. They were accepting, even cheerful; caring for little Apu with the same love and gentle dedication they would have given him if he'd been perfectly healthy. In many other parts of China, babies are abandoned for being female, or deformed in some way, and I blessed them in my heart for their unconditional acceptance.

The next week, we had to travel out to the city for a week, and I mostly expected that we would return to hear of Apu's death. However, while worshipping with a group of other dedicated believers, I shared my burden for little Apu, and they all gathered around and pleaded with me in prayer for his complete healing. At that time, we were also privileged to hear the testimony of a doctor and adoptive parents who had seen the children under their care miraculously restored to complete health after devastating brain injury. These were people I knew - I had seen the children they were talking about running around outside, not realizing that they were miracles in motion! This time, tears cleansed my heart as I confessed my unbelief, and dared to hope for the impossible. In my heart, I vowed that if Apu turned out normal, I would start "my book".

We got home, to discover that Apu's family had been holding a prayer vigil of their own. Grandparents, uncles and aunts, pastors, elders, deaconesses -- they had gathered and prayed around the clock for healing. With her face shining softly, the Grandma told me that the baby was "Nursing just fine, thank God."

As I write this, Apu is 10 months old - a sturdy, cheerful little fellow, already toddling around on chubby legs.   He still doesn't cry much, but nobody's complaining about that anymore! He's not just normal - he's precocious! "Thank God", indeed!

Our son, Nathan, playing with little Apu

Entering the Promised Land

Before Dave and I were married, we got into a discussion about things which cause overseas Christian workers to give up and go home, even when God had clearly led them overseas. One of the issues I brought up was worry over "the children". For example, I said, a premature baby which would probably survive if born in a modern hospital in the west, might die if born overseas. The parents would be tempted to say, "If only we had gone back to our own country for the birth, this wouldn't have happened." Dave said, "But God *gives* the children, and it doesn't change the call on the parents. I was reading in the beginning of Deuteronomy the other day, and I came up to this verse where Moses reminds the people that neither he nor the fighting men who crossed the Red Sea were allowed to go into the Promised land. The people were unwilling to go in because they were afraid for their wives and children."

"Dave! I just read that verse, too, but I think it was in Numbers. Yeah, look, Numbers 14, 'I have forgiven them as you asked. Nevertheless, as surely as I live and as surely as the glory of the Lord fills the whole earth, not one of the men who saw my glory and the miraculous signs I performed in Egypt and in the desert but who disobeyed me and tested me ten times - not one of them will ever see the land I promised on oath to their forefathers. No one who has treated me with contempt will ever see it...As surely as I live, declares the Lord, I will do to you the very thing I heard you say: In this desert your bodies will fall -- every one of you twenty years old or more who was counted in the census and who has grumbled against me. Not one of you will enter the land I swore with uplifted hand to make your home, except Caleb son of Jephunneh and Joshua son of Nun. As for your children that you said would be taken as plunder, I will bring *them* in to enjoy the land you have rejected. But you - your bodies will fall in this desert. Your *children* will be shepherds here, suffering for *your* unfaithfulness until the last of your bodies lies in the desert.' "

We looked at each other, and agreed, "We need to never let fear for the children's safety cause us to pull back from what God is asking us to do."

"It's not like God was rebuking them for being unwilling to sacrifice their children in order to enter the Promised land. He was angry with them for not trusting Him to protect and bless their children if they obeyed. The children suffered in the desert for their parents' lack of faith."

"We don't have to try to protect our children from God's will."

"Yeah, I mean no. Obviously tragic things happen to people wherever they live, and it's not like we'll be immune. But I really do think, since God spoke these verses to both of us, that we had better be ready to trust God to take care of the children, wherever He takes us."

This conviction has been put to the test. We have faced many life-threatening illnesses, even living in the "TB [tuberculosis] capital" of China for ten years, in daily contact with TB patients. We have had people, strangers even sometimes, ask us heatedly how we can put our children in jeopardy by raising them in such remote places, or how we can justify not giving them a "proper" education or socialization.

All I can say is that by God's grace, the one birth where I truly needed expert intervention happened in a very good hospital in Canada. By His sovereign care and protection, we have survived many dangerous situations and illnesses, and our oldest children are now slipping into the Canadian school system, and doing very well. Not just academically; they are evidencing a great deal of wisdom and courage as they choose friends, priorities and chart their course. Praise God, He's faithful and has answered prayer, healed us and protected us up until now, and we look forward to His continued mercy to over-shadow us as we seek His guidance for the future. And how our family has been blessed with the unconditional love and godly influence of the many friends we have made overseas!   Mark 10:29-30, *"I tell you the truth,"* Jesus replied, *"no-one who has left home or brothers or sisters or mother or father ... for me and the gospel will fail to receive 100 times as much..."* has literally been fulfilled in our lives, and is part of our children's inheritance.

Romance

"What do you want to be when you grow up?"
"A pastor!"

As a child, Dave figured that a pastor was the only person who was truly close to God; everyone else was settling for a comfortable distance. So, naturally, he wanted to be one. Trouble was, he was terrified of standing up in front of a crowd, or even talking to strangers. When he was a young teen, there was an "I Found It" campaign in the city. You were supposed to wear a button that said, "I Found It", then when people asked you what you had found, you would tell them about finding salvation, or Jesus. Or, if you were too timid for that, you could just hand them an "I Found It" tract. Dave dutifully wore his button, and carried the tract, but prayed constantly that no-one would ask him about it!

As Dave grew older, he met pastors that dashed his stereotype, and many "ordinary people" who truly loved the Lord. So he began to modify his career plans. "What did God *design* me to do. I'll do that, and bring glory to Him, instead of trying to be a square peg in a round hole." He was, though, very bothered by the fact that in Canada everyone has a "Christian neighbour" -- someone in their circle of acquaintances who they can ask about the way of salvation, if they want to know -- but there are many parts of the world where this all-important information is simply unattainable. "I can't ever be a preacher, but I can be a 'Christian neighbour' where people need one." He decided to study engineering, with the aim of becoming a "tentmaker" witness overseas.

But where to go? He had no interest in going anywhere, except China. But there was the "Bamboo Curtain", and Christians couldn't go to China, as far as he knew. Then he got "The Call" to go to China. A long-time family friend had recently married an expert on China's minority people. He called:

"Hey, do you want to come to China?"

"I'll have to pray about it. {2 second pause} Okay, I'll come!" He wasn't ready to just "step out of the boat" and quit his job, though, so he asked for, and was granted, a one-year leave of absence.

Meanwhile, Dave and I met at choir in the big German Baptist church we both attended while we were doing our post-secondary education. By then, Dave was working as an engineer, and I was still studying nursing. We didn't really notice each other, though, and it wasn't until Dave overheard me tell another member that I might not be able to continue coming to choir because my ride was quitting that we really got to know one another. All of a sudden there was this deep voice behind me, "That's a stupid reason to quit choir. I'll give you a ride." I spun around, and it was Dave. I don't even think I knew his name yet! I soon got to know him and the "bro's" who all lived together at the "Bachelor Mansion" very well, though, because they invited me to join their cell group, and as a group started treating me very much as a younger sister. I could pretty much count on one of them being delegated to give me a ride to all the college and career events, and they also started including me in whatever they were up to. They'd borrow a girls' bike from somewhere and take me bike riding with them, or to the movies, or to play volleyball.

The only awkward moment was when they took me to their "Oma's" after church to be fed up along with the rest of them. She was happy to see me, but immediately asked with her German accent, "Vhich one of the boys are you with? Markie? David? No? Vhich one?" It took her awhile to believe I didn't belong with anybody, just with everybody! By this time, I had pretty much written off Dave as a love-interest, because I knew already that I wanted to serve God overseas, and Dave appeared to have settled into a lucrative career, worked out at the gym every lunch hour and drove me home every week in his red Mazda RX7. To me, that car symbolized a young man who was going to climb the corporate ladder and go for the kind of success the world measured things by. I had no idea about his plans to go to China, and that the car was a stop-gap measure: something with good resale value that he had bought after the seat of his last car fell through the floor and scraped along the pavement, shooting sparks while he was driving it! [1] So, when I heard he was going to China, and selling his car.... Well!

I wrote him a goodbye card, and promised to pray for him. And he wrote back. I had a fairly realistic idea of how challenging this first year away was going to be, because my parents had taken our family to Papua New Guinea when I was 15. It was an amazing year, but very stretching. I was concerned for him, and so I really did pray. That is a dangerous thing to do! We kept writing, too, sharing all about the amazing people and challenges we were experiencing. When Dave got anywhere with a post office, he would scribble several sheets onto hotel stationary, and he would receive answers written on spare lab requisition sheets during slow night shifts. And one day I sat down on the floor of my room, with a little red alarm buzzer going off in my head. I thought, "Now I've really gone and done it. I've fallen in love with him, and I don't even know if I'll ever see him again. What is it with you and unattainable guys, Christie?" Thus began a very long nine months for me, dreaming, praying, waiting for letters, hiding my feelings.

Meanwhile, on the other side of the world, Dave was getting some ribbing at the number of letters coming

---

1   Thankfully, like any good Canadian boy, he had a hockey stick in the back seat that he could use to prop it up so he could make it to work. For a while his boss had been insisting, "Get that piece of junk out of my parking lot! Don't I pay you enough?!"   The seat clinched it.

in for him from girls. He was vaguely aware that a "situation" was developing, but didn't really know what to do about it. He was in the process of surrendering to God's call to stay in China, and to his way of thinking, that could well also mean a call to stay single. Sometime in there, he also realized that he really loved me, but was so accustomed to thinking of me as a sister that it felt almost wrong or incestuous to think of me as a potential marriage partner. He prayed about it, asking God to change his feelings about me if it was His will for us to marry, and then he put it in a compartment to deal with later. Life was so full of adventure and overwhelming new experiences as he solo backpacked around remote parts of China, looking for China's ethnic minorities and taking pictures.

It was a year of growing in his walk with God too. Whether in times of serious illness, like dysentery, with no-one to help, or hearing, via letters from home, about disheartening situations -- like a friend being raped -- that he could do nothing about, prayer became his life-line. When his funds were running out, and he heard that the friend he had asked to sell his car didn't even have a "For sale" sign in the window -- he was just enjoying driving it -- all Dave could do was pray. So he did. A few weeks later, a friend of his cousin showed up at the door of the "Bachelor Mansion" with cash in hand to buy the car![2]

One evening, praying on a hill in the center of Hainan Island, Dave felt like he was being lifted away from the earth. As he rose through the atmosphere into space, he could see more and more of the world. Everywhere he looked, he saw people, small as ants, raking. They were trying to rake together piles of money, but, like leaves, it kept blowing away and floating off. He

---

2   His cousin had been talking with that friend about Dave being in China, and his friend asked, "What did he do with that little red car he used to drive?" "Dunno, but I can phone his brother and find out...."

realized then, that if he wasn't living connected to God, being part of His great purpose, that his life had no more significance than an ant's. In his heart he laid down his career plans, and purposed to do what he felt God wanted him to do: remain in China.

The next summer, Dave came home to settle his affairs and break it to his family that he was going back to China "for good". Thankfully, his brother, Mark, invited me along on a college and career canoe trip that he was helping to organize, and he put me in as Dave's canoeing partner! For three idyllic days, we floated down the Athabasca river, and talked. Dave saw me, and thought, "Wow! God, did you ever answer my prayer! Was she always so beautiful?" As for me, I was absolutely thrumming with pent-up feelings! What if he went back to China with nothing resolved between us? How could I possibly face going on indefinitely like that?

I didn't have to. Dave asked me to stay another week. My last night before I had to go back to my hometown and nursing job, there was a spectacular thunder and lightning storm. We went outside and stood in the shelter of the balcony to enjoy the full effect, awestruck. After awhile, though, I became so chilled my teeth started chattering, and that's when Dave put his arm around me and we confessed our feelings for each other. A few minutes later, we said good-bye, and he went back to the farm while I went into my friends' living room. I lay down on the couch and started weeping as I lifted up to God the anguish of having Dave go off to China again just as I learned that he actually did have feelings for me. I don't know how to describe what happened next except to say that God tickled me. In an instant I found myself giggling and weeping tears of joy. All grief at the parting was instantly and completely erased. Looking back, I think God just couldn't keep His joy at how He knew things were going to turn out entirely to Himself. I'll always be glad He did, because the next months were not easy.

When Dave got back to Hong Kong, he immediately dove into a one year intensive Bible and Discipleship training school headed by Roy Robertson. He was living in a big room with 8 other guys from the States, the Philippines, Indonesia, and India. They watched as God provided a fridge, beds, an air conditioner, even a piano; every day, something else they needed would just appear out beside the dumpsters, and they would bring it in. Within the first few days, Dave had been volunteered to do all the cooking for this group, and although only a few of them had adequate support or finances, they put all their resources into a common pot, and there was always enough. They studied hard, and then put it into practice among themselves (there were six cultures represented among them, and it could be a challenge to keep a spirit of unity in such close, muggy quarters!) on the streets and in the churches.

Dave was still receiving letters from more than one young lady, and finally decided it was all too much of a distraction. He sent both of us a letter of dismissal, saying he was not in a position to sustain our hopes. I only knew about my letter, of course, and grimly set about chopping down all my romantic hopes and disciplining my unruly thoughts and feelings. The next few weeks felt as bleak and barren as an arctic wasteland as I ruthlessly shut down every thought of Dave.

God was on my side, though, because the next book that group of young men studied was, "The Song of Solomon"! As they discussed the subject of choosing a wife, Barry Nelson, one of their happily married teachers, told Dave, "Don't ask yourself who you can live with. Ask yourself who you don't want to live without. You can't maintain an intimate friendship with a girl after she marries someone else." In his heart, Dave said, "Who I can't live without? That's a no-brainer. Of everyone I know, I'd hate most to lose Christie's friendship," and started regretting sending me that letter.

A couple of weeks went by, and then my dad phoned and said there was a letter from China in their mailbox. So much for carefully acquired indifference! I ran all the way downtown to fetch that letter!
It began, "Dearest Christie..."
I couldn't believe it!
I don't know what response Dave had hoped to provoke, but I was blazing mad!
I stomped and fumed, "What does he think I am, a flippin' light switch?!"
The letter went on to invite me to China, to explore whether or not I could be happy there, and join him in his life there. After that first stormy response, I wanted to go. I tried to answer Dave in the affirmative. I probably messed up 17 sheets of stationary and several days trying to tell him I would come, but there was a check in my spirit. Finally, I threw myself on my knees in front of my room-mate's floral futon and cried, "What, God? What is it? Why can't I say, "Yes"?
And God said, "Do you love Me more than these?"
I was overwhelmed. I thought he reserved questions like that for people like Simon Peter and Amy Carmichael.
But, really, there could be only one response. So I whispered, "Yes, Lord, I love You more. And if you want me to write Dave now and say, 'No', I will. It will break both our hearts, but You know best."

I waited. I waited for several days for the boom to fall, for the word which would crush the tender little thing budding between Dave and I. I waited in submission and with my soul on it's knees, but instead what came was a growing peace and confidence that like Abraham poised with his knife, both God and I had learned all that was necessary, without the killing blow. However, as I wrote Dave to tell him that I would come, and set about buying airline tickets and applying for a passport, I asked God to stop me if I was mistaken. I begged Him to keep me from following my heart into anything that was not His will for me. About that same time, God asked Dave basically the same question, and he also laid the relationship down until he felt assurance that God was blessing it.

There was one thing I didn't have to do, and that was to resign my job. When I first graduated from nursing, I wanted to go overseas immediately with some Christian organization. I quickly learned that they all wanted one thing that I did not have yet: nursing experience. Thanks to severe health care budget cuts which came down just as I started looking for my first job, there were very few jobs available. Most of my graduating class went to the United States to work, or into University for a higher degree. I sat down in my room with my Bible and Amy Carmichael's biography by Elizabeth Elliot called, "A Chance to Die," and told the Lord I was going to sit there until He showed me what to do. The job which God opened up for me was back in my home town -- the one place in all the earth I was most afraid of getting "stuck" in. At the same time, though, God gave me a picture of a number of beautiful teen age girls from my home church, most of whom did not have Christian parents, and shared His burden for them. I agreed to go back for their sake, but wrote in my diary, "Just for one year, though, Lord, and then You'll have to stop me from going overseas."

For a year, I opened my apartment up to the youth from my church, and did all I could to love and lead the girls God had put on my heart. A day or two after I had responded to Dave's invitation to go to China and was girding myself up to resign, my Unit Supervisor called me in and apologetically told me that the temporary position I had been filling was coming to an end because the nurse who had been on leave was returning! She was a little taken aback when I whooped! It had been a year exactly since I wrote that entry in my journal!

My heart was still a little anxious, however, because the day for my departure was drawing near, and my passport still had not arrived. "What if this is God's way of stopping me?" niggled in the background. Finally, I asked God directly for a word, for peace, for the knowledge that I was in His will with my preparations. A phrase came to mind, but I did not have a clue where to find it in the Bible. "Lord, I can't find it! Maybe I have a different translation?"

"Try 'coming and going'."

A happy glow filled my heart as I found the verse in Psalm 121.

> *The Lord will keep you from all harm --*
> *He will watch over your life;*
> *the Lord will watch over your* coming and going
> *both now and forevermore.*

At the same time, I just somehow knew that my passport would be in our mailbox the day I left.

I was confident enough of that to stand up in the little Baptist church I'd grown up in and drop the bombshell that I was leaving Canada for China, probably to get married to someone they'd never met, and that my passport would be waiting for me at the mailbox the day I left.

It was, too. We picked it up on the way to the bus station.

When I got off the plane, there was Dave. He was so afraid he'd be late that he'd actually arrived hours early. I'd dreamed of being swept up into his strong arms, but it didn't quite go like I'd imagined. I ran into his arms, and nearly knocked him over! He'd warned me that I might find him "a little bit sick", but he was pasty white and the exertion of helping me carry my bags to a friend's apartment left him sweating, with his heart knocking at a ridiculous rate. Nevertheless, it was a sweet, sweet reunion. Dave wept tears of joy and relief to find that I'd really materialized on that side of the world, and that we still *fit*. He has forgotten many things thanks to the number Typhus did on his brain a few years later, but he says he can still remember the moment he caught sight of me in the airport. After 18 hours in the air, I don't think I was turning any other heads, but he says I looked like an angel to him!

It turns out that Dave had been steadily bleeding to death from a duodenal ulcer, so that first week, a doctor friend of his from Hong Kong and I convinced him to go for some lab tests. We went for ice-cream while we were waiting for the results. The minute we returned, a team of nurses pounced on him, "Are you Mr. Lietz?!" They grabbed his arms when he said, "Yes," whisked him off down a hall way, and sat him down.

"Your hemoglobin is 6.2"

He turned to me hopefully, "Is that good?"

"Dave, I've seen corpses with higher hemoglobin!"

He was admitted immediately for blood trans-fusions before there was permanent damage to his organs. I watched helplessly as they tried and tried to get an IV started - his veins were just collapsing. Eventually they got one, and then it was time for me to leave.

Dave repeated the directions for me to find my own way back to the apartment he'd arranged for me to stay at, but I was so afraid! I have a terrible sense of direction, and HK was just so bewilderingly big and exotic as I stepped out into that humid evening. How was this girl from small town northern British Columbia ever going to find her way "home"?

"Lord, lead me, I pray. Just make me make the right turns."

I got on the right double-decker bus, got off it at the right station, made the right turns, found I was at the ferry terminal, got on the right ferry, and found my way back through the twisty little streets on PengChau island. It was amazing. I was so grateful.

After a jet-lagged but wonderful few weeks of getting to know each other in a "beloved" capacity in HK,

Dave took me on a 24 hour "hard-seat" train ride inland, and left me at a college where I would be studying Chinese for the next 3 months. I didn't know one word of Chinese and was the only foreign student on that campus! It was frightening, hard and wonderful all at the same time. That beginning was an honest initiation to our life in China...

The Bridge

"But Christie, you can't just bounce straight from courting in HK to expecting your first baby in the next chapter! What will people think?" So, in honour of my mother and her concern for our reputation...

We did get formally engaged in front of about 80 witnesses at Dave's graduation from his year of Bible training. Dave took me completely by surprise, and the look on his face was a study as he waited for me to get myself under control enough to answer him. After a respectable 6 month engagement, we got married on January 2, 1993, in Edmonton. It was only -20 degrees Celsius -- absolutely balmy compared to the -57 degrees it had been the day before when we drove down from Dawson Creek, BC. We nearly missed our own wedding due to the extreme driving conditions.

God Spoils Us as Much as He Dares

After Dave and I finished our year and a half intensive course in Chinese language study, it was time to find a job, and the job Dave landed was one he didn't even apply for! It never occurred to him to apply to teach at a middle school in a minority area of China, because such jobs did not exist. We had never heard of a foreigner receiving permission to teach English at anything lower than a post-secondary level.[3] He did apply at dozens of colleges, and did not hear back from any of them. We had two weeks until we had to move out of our apartment at the school we'd studied at, and we had no clue whether to pack our parkas for a move North to the Chinese equivalent of Siberia, or our shorts for steamy Guangdong just North of HongKong. Believe me, we were in prayer, and just to make absolutely sure, we asked God to keep it simple - "Just one invitation, Lord. Just let the school which invites us be the one you want us at."

Just days before we had to move out, we received a letter of acceptance from this middle school we had not even applied at (although Dave had visited, and prayed for, that town)! An acquaintance had applied there almost a decade earlier, and been rejected, so he started a company elsewhere in the province. Meanwhile, however, the school started preparing for him to come. When they contacted him to say, "We're ready for you to come teach," he was in no position to do so, but sent them our contact information instead. Sight unseen, they hired us. They also showed us a cute, brand-new apartment with big, sunny windows which they informed

---

3   Because of his experience counseling at summer camp, and teaching Sunday School, teaching at a middle school level was definitely Dave's preference. He had even prayed for this. But we had no reason to believe that it was a possibility yet in China in the early '90s.

us would be our new home, but then told us we'd have to stay in a room in the local government hotel for a few days while they notified the man with the key, and connected the electricity. Fine. Well, not so fine, since the hotel was being torn down, and for good reason. We nicknamed our temporary quarters "Rat Hotel" because you could see rats disappearing into holes in the wooden baseboards everywhere, day or night. They definitely owned the place! A "few days" turned into a month, we started moving stuff out of storage into our room, and I discovered we were expecting our first child.   The rats were gnawing away steadily at night -- on our bed, on our fruit, on our toothbrushes. My tummy was growing, too, and it was getting awkward to do all our laundry and dishes in the bathtub! And, the school officials were not getting around to applying for our teaching visas -- were they even going to keep us?

   We reminded them that our tourist visa would be expiring in a month, and asked if they were going through the proper channels to get it changed to a teacher's visa. Two weeks later we asked again. What was going on? Were they actually going to keep us on at all, or would we find ourselves without a job and without a home once our tourist visa expired? Once again, we found ourselves on our knees, pleading to be able to stay put and establish a home and a witness. I was so tired and morning sick; we'd been married for two years and not yet had a real home of our own.   The thought of having to cast around again for a new position was awful.

   We later realized they'd placed themselves (and the provincial and county foreign affairs bureau) in an awkward position, because they didn't have all the necessary permissions to invite us, and there was no precedent for anyone to follow either! In a western country, this would be quickly cleared up, but there, to just send us away would involve too much loss of "face".

So there were lots of big discussions and arguments going on behind the scene.

Deadline time, decision time. It took about 36 hours by train from where we were to the Hong Kong border. 48 hours to go before we would be in the country illegally, we packed our bags and caught a few hours sleep before flagging a taxi to take us out of town to the railway station.

The train from Chengdu to Guangzhou, just north of the HK border came through our little town at about 6 am. It would just stop for 5 minutes or so, and you could only buy "standing" tickets. If you could get on the train, you could try to find yourself a place to sit. If you were in luck and could find the right man, you might be able to upgrade your ticket for a proper seat, or even a sleeper (cot), but our Chinese friends assured us this couldn't be done without a bribe. There in the middle of the line, at a podunk place like Big Rock, the odds were slim indeed. To this day, the sound of a train whistle brings back the lonely feeling of standing in the pre-dawn cold and dark, waiting by the side of the tracks to see if we could squeeze onto the train. I was so concerned about the little one I was carrying. No-one even knew it was there except for us and God. For three days before we actually had to leave, I was urgently interceding for the safety of the baby, so anxious it actually doubled me over at times with stomach cramps. I felt sure that if I could not get a place to lie down for at least part of the journey, exhaustion, dehydration and being bumped around could well cause me to miscarry.

The train pulled in...but it was so crowded! Grabbing our backpacks, we joined the line struggling to get on the train, while a few passengers wishing to disembark fought the current, pounding on people's ascending heads and shoulders with their fists and handbags. Tempers grew so frayed later on in that train ride that I was asked to come help bandage two men who had attacked each other with broken beer bottles! Finally both Dave and I were squeezed onto the train, the doors closed, the whistle blew, and we were off. I was jammed up against the filthy metal door to the toilet, packed in so tight I could barely breathe. One hand was up above my head, and I couldn't even lower it to my side! Dave was further in, and we could barely shout to each other over the hubbub. Nearly in tears, I started to plead with God, "Just one sleeper, Lord, just one sleeper. The baby is never going to survive 40 hours of this."

Maybe twenty minutes later, the unbelievable happened. A young train official fought his way out of the far end of the compartment, pushing over and between the dozing forms layering the floor. He held up one finger and shouted at me, "We have one sleeper left. Do you want it?!" He had boarded that train in Chengdu, had already worked a full night shift, and for sure had people lined up trying to find him to bribe him for that last coveted bunk. I guarantee you that his coworkers were in the staff room with their heads down on their arms, making themselves as scarce as possible at a nothing stop like Big Rock. We upgraded our tickets for the normal Chinese price, rather than the usual inflated "foreigner" price, and were ushered into our first ever "soft sleeper" compartment. There were four wide bunks covered in soft blue plush. A small table in the middle was draped with a delicate white lace cloth. A decanter of boiling water for tea nestled into it's stand. The sliding door clicked shut, and all was quiet and peaceful. White curtains blew in the gentle breeze. I sank onto my bed and gazed through tears at the beautiful countryside gliding past in the light of the sunrise.

"Oh Father God. In the future, when hard times come and it feels like You're not answering our prayers, and are being hard-hearted or negligent about our fate, please help me to remember this miraculous provision, to remember that this is how you would like to always treat us.   So when You don't, it must be for a very good reason."

I mean, in the same way that God saved us one sleeper, couldn't, shouldn't He have saved Mary one room at the Inn? He could have, but He didn't. There must have been a good reason. A redemptive one. Hebrews says that Jesus was made perfect through what He suffered. It was His job description to be "a man of sorrows, acquainted with grief." It was God's will for Him to be a tiny refugee - and this meant hardship for his mother as well.

Part of what puts our heart on its' knees in absolute adoration is all about this -- that He came to identify completely with what it means to be human. No special treatment -- and there are times we have the privilege of being conformed to Him in this, even as we are very truly His sons and daughters, and heirs of all Christ's reward.

We were only in Hong Kong for a few days before the school contacted us to say, "We've taken care of all the paperwork. You can come back now." By then, I had seen a very good obstetrician for a prenatal check, and found out that everything was normal.   We arranged to come back to HK for this doctor to attend the birth, but discovered later that God had other arrangements in mind...

We returned to our school and our room in the hotel, until one morning when Christmas was just ten days away, I walked out into the hall and there was no more roof! They had been steadily demolishing the hotel around us to put up a new one, and thankfully at that point they finally "found" the key!!

Miriam

"Oh, Dave, what will we do?"

"Well, lie down for starters, and then there's nothing much we can do except pray. Are you timing the contractions? When was the last one?"

"Just a minute ago...they're not slowing down."

"Just take it easy. Deep breaths, relax."

"How many weeks am I? 27? 28? That's way too early. That's only about seven months. This is exactly like what I said when we were talking about the kind of situations that could make a couple leave the field."

It was also one of my worst fears. While we were still in language study, I had attended the birth of a Chinese friend in a hospital there, and had been horrified by the way she was treated, and the poor standard of care. I came out of that experience declaring, "I will never have a baby in China!" When I was actually pregnant, Dave broached the subject again, saying, "What if it's God's will for you to have the baby in China? What if that's a way He wants us to bond with the people here?" I was adamant: "I will never have a baby in China. Don't ask that of me." So Dave got permission from his school for a leave of absence to travel to HongKong when the baby was due. I didn't buy any baby clothes or anything, because all those sorts of things were much more available in HK than where we were.

Eventually the reality had to be faced: I was in premature labour in the little town of Big Rock. My "highly recommended" obstetrician in HK might as well have been light years away. No way would I be able to make the 40 hour train trip out. Big Rock had a dingy little "hospital", but when we arrived there with about half the local (Chinese) English teachers in tow, the prospects of delivering there were absolutely terrifying. The head of labour and delivery got me to lie down on a narrow delivery table in a bare, grey cement room with 3 other tables. There were no curtains, and the other English teachers trooped in with me, followed shortly by another woman in labour and her extended family. Under those conditions, the doctor had me take off my pants and roughly examined me . I was shuddering from head to toe with the winter cold, fear, humiliation and pain. We found out later that she was also the doctor who did all the abortions, so it wasn't surprising that she said to Dave, "What's the big deal? Just let the baby come out and die. You can always have another one. Are you worried about the inconvenience?"

Warm, small hands patted me here and there as the other women from Dave's English classes tried to comfort me. "The doctor thinks that you are in labour and will deliver your baby today." "Don't worry. This doctor is very skillful. My niece's baby was lying sideways, and she reached in and turned her the right way around and got her out." (Oh, God, a transverse presentation should be an immediate C-section, what kind of "doctor" is this?...)

"My baby was born here at 7 months, and she has turned out just fine. It will be okay."

"Oh, does that mean they have an incubator?"

"A what?"

"A box with a heater and oxygen to take care of the premature baby?"

"No. Nothing like that. If you went to Big Cloud, they might have one."

"Well, is there any way to get her to Big Cloud then?", Dave broke in.

"The school could probably arrange a driver..."

"They'll need money; they won't admit her without a deposit."

"The banks are closed..."

"We can take up a collection."

"Do you know anyone in Big Cloud?," one of the teachers asked Dave.

"Yes, there are some American teachers there who are our friends, and also an American doctor who is learning Chinese. If you could get us that far, I'm sure they would be willing to help us. If I could just borrow a phone, I'll try to call them."

"Is there anywhere I can lie down?"

Gratefully, I sank onto a cot covered with a bleached cotton quilt while the discussion continued above me. Dave's warm arms encircled me as I tried to relax. He put his head next to mine and quietly started praying. Tears flowed as we committed the whole situation to our Heavenly Father. We were so touched by the kindness and concern of the Chinese teachers at the school where Dave was teaching, and so afraid. We had only known them half a year, and had been praying hard for ways to reach them with the Gospel. What if this was part of the answer?

"Father, thank You for giving up your Son, Your only Son, for our sakes. We pray that You would mercifully intervene and stop the contractions, so that this baby can be born full-term and healthy, but Lord, we know You are good and that You cause all things to work together for good. It was so good of You to send Jesus, and if the loss of this baby is the way You're going to use to bond our hearts to the people here and bring them to a knowledge of You, then..."

Before too long, the official school car rolled up to the hospital, someone pushed a roll of bills into Dave's hand, and I was able to lie down in the back seat with my head on Dave's lap.

The trip took on an unreal, dream-like quality as the car purred through the night, until it pulled up to the hospital in Big Cloud, and the American teachers there stepped up and passed us a suitcase filled with everything we could possibly need for an emergency layette! The hospital admitted me and immediately started a drip with medication to stop the contractions. They also gave me some sort of strange pill which I had to melt under my tongue. Whatever it was, it worked. Before long, labour had eased off and we could try to sleep.

The next morning, our American friends showed up with fresh baking, fruit, yoghurt, and lots of laughter and good will. They were the only other foreigners we had seen in about three months, and it was inexpressibly cheering to be with them! After a week in hospital with me, Dave went back to his teaching responsibilities at the school, and I was discharged to the home of the American doctor and his family. They felt that I should spend a week there as well, to make sure I was stable before we attempted the trip back to Big Rock. Since their flat was at the top of a hill and about 90 stairs, it was truly a pretty good trial! I turned 26 that week; such a lonely week without Dave, and such a joyous reunion when he came back to get me!

I toddled out of the taxi at the train station, moving like I was 90, or made of glass, and tried to find somewhere to sit down while we waited. When the train pulled in, we were dismayed to see that all the seats were taken! Galvanized out of my usual aversion to preferential treatment by the thought of having to stand up and keep my balance for the next 3 hours, I button-holed an athletic-looking young man and begged for his seat. He got up courteously and with alacrity, and Dave smiled with relief as he turned from stowing our bags to see me safely settled.

As the train started off, an elderly gentleman in the same car stood up and offered Dave his seat. Dave politely refused. The old man insisted, "No, you are our honoured guest from afar, it is right for you to sit." "Sir, you are the same age as my revered grandfather, there is no way I can take your seat." Back and forth it went, banter, gestures, both of them standing in the aisle, pressing each other toward the empty seat while everyone in the car enjoyed the spectacle and then...KA-CHUNK - the train hit a cow and stopped dead! The elderly man catapulted backwards towards the front of the car, with Dave windmilling right behind him!

Thankfully, they both landed more or less unhurt, and when the shock wore off, it was just too funny! Everyone just roared as the red-eared debaters made their way back! The elderly man took the seat.

We got back to our home, and I went to bed.
I stayed there for six weeks.
We had no phone, no TV, no computer.
The glass in our bedroom window had a flaw, which divided the grey sky and skeletal tree tops in a lop-sided way. As the days passed into weeks, the misaligned trees grew more and more annoying. I watched the mold growing on the flower baskets on our walls in the damp cold of early spring, the dust bunnies accumulating in the corners, and the minutes ticking before Dave got back from work. I fretted because I still did not know what medication I was on to keep the contractions at bay, only that a local doctor thought it was "strange" and didn't think I should be on it more than a few days...

Finally, I reached 36 weeks gestation, got up, packed and went off my medication.[4] We got on the train and headed back to Big Cloud. I went to bed in the desolation of winter and got up in the balmy breezes and bright flowers of spring. The small team of foreign Christians there drew us into their Easter celebrations. Joy!! From isolation to Communion, from an unvaried diet of bok choy, tofu and bean sprouts (all that was

---

4   When we finally found a sufficiently comprehensive dictionary that had the name of the medicine, we discovered that it was just Ventolin! It relaxes the bronchial muscles for asthmatics, and also has the "side effect" of relaxing uterine muscles.

available during the winter in our small town) to a wine and cheese party! From long, anxious days to fun and laughter and the anticipation of Baby!

Early Easter Monday morning, I went into active labour - and didn't do anything to stop it!

The hospital had undergone the same sort of amazing transformation as everything else. While I was in bed, their staff all went to a WHO conference on Labour and Delivery. They came back decades further advanced in their ideas and practice, and immediately renovated the ward. Cute private rooms with lamps and decor reminiscent of a hotel replaced the drab white walls and cast-iron cots.

Even more astounding was the change in attitude. They were in "learner-mode"; deferential, and interested in everything I had to say about how I had been trained. They cooperated with my request that Dave be allowed to attend right up to and including the birth, allowed me to get up and walk around in the garden, and didn't make me lie flat to push. Two months before, they were adamant that none of those things would be permitted. I was delirious with relief! Mid morning, after we'd done many, many rounds of the hospital grounds, our American Dr. friend showed up. "How are you doing?"

"All right. Do you have a band-aid by any chance?"

He gave me a quizzical look. "Uh, sorry, I don't."

"I've been in bed so long, my feet are as soft as a baby's, and I'm getting the worst blisters on my heels!"

After awhile, they admitted another woman to the bed next to me, and she immediately seized onto the bed rails and screamed with every contraction. She was being induced and was already into her second day of pain. Between contractions, I started to coach her in relaxation techniques, "Watch me and do what I do. You can breathe the pain away, and it will actually help your labour progress much faster." Sure enough, as she started to cooperate with her body, things moved right along and the nurses pronounced her ready to be moved to the delivery room. Family members each took a leg, a nurse took each arm and they hoisted her across the hall like a sack of potatoes! Apparently they didn't have a gurney.

A few minutes later, another young woman was admitted to that bed, where she proceeded to thrash and scream. This time, Dave took the lead, "Excuse me, if your wife would just watch my wife and do what she's doing, she'll have a much easier time of it..."

An hour or two later, she was also carted across the hall hand and foot to deliver. We were getting good at this, but the waves of pain were becoming really intense, and so close together it seemed I would drown.

A nurse finally appeared in the doorway, "Could you please just step down the hall to the scale? We don't have your weight down yet..."

"Uh, she's really in a lot of pain now. Could you just wait a minute? Actually, could you maybe examine her and see how far along she is?"

"Two centimeters."

"TWO centimeters?! That's all?"

"Well, this is your first baby, it often takes a lot longer than this."

As she left, Dave and I looked at each other, aghast.

"There's no way I can do this for hours longer. No way."

And then, "I have to push."

"You can't! It's too soon! Pant! Pant!"

From somewhere in the tiny space at the top of my skull where all remaining coherence had been compressed, I thought, "My body's gone berserk. First it tried to have the baby two months early, and now it's making me push way too early." I panted, but it didn't do any good. In God's impeccable timing, our American doctor friend came back just then to confirm that I was actually fully dilated and "good to go". There are no words to describe the relief of that pronouncement!

So, Miriam Ruth was born Easter Monday morning, swaddled up like a little sausage, placed in the arms of her ecstatic parents, and described as "The most beau-ti-ful baby Ah've ever seen -- and Ah've seen a lot of babies," by a dear friend with a great Southern drawl. When we phoned them, both sets of grandparents wept with joy and relief as well. Dave's dad was from a family of five boys, and then had three sons. He had waited a long, long time for a little girl in the family! "The Lord, my Deliverer" took on a whole new wealth of meaning for us. He had allowed us to face a deep fear, He had led us into deep waters, and then shown us that He could faithfully bring us through.

Living on Love

Living on love when God is in the mix is actually a very practical way to live. You don't have to worry about anything except keeping close to Him, and doing what He asks of you. He really takes care of the rest! When Miriam was about a year old, we learned that our Canadian health care would be terminated if we did not return to Canada soon. This gave me a strange, lost feeling. I felt exiled. Even though Miriam had been born in No-where's-ville, China, with complications, by the grace of God she was still born safely and a healthy 7 pounds. Everything had turned out all right, and my confidence in God's ability to take care of us increased dramatically. But I still felt kind of cheated of the whole celebration aspect. There had been no prenatal visits, no doctor I could trust, no baby showers or ecstatic grandparents and doting Aunties. I wanted all of that the next time around, but there was no way we'd be able to afford to deliver in Canada once our coverage lapsed. I decided the thing to do was to get pregnant right away and go home to have this next baby while we still had coverage. A couple of months later, I conceived and we booked our flights and told our family we'd be coming home to have another baby!

Well, by the time we got off the plane in Vancouver, I was starting to bleed. Our second day there, I went for an ultrasound. Between the cramping and a bladder which contained about a Super-big-gulp too much urine, it was an anxious wait. The technician was very aloof and evasive. Then the doctor, not looking at me, and without any preamble, said, "The baby's dead you know." I *hadn't* known. It echoed in my head. I couldn't believe it. My heart utterly rejected it. We had rearranged our lives around having this baby. I had known from the bleeding that I needed to take it easy, take some measures to *keep* from miscarrying, but it had actually never occurred to me that it might already be too late. In fact our little one had been dead three weeks already and they assured me the best thing to do was just to have a D&C.

My throat closed up as I tried to tell the receptionist about the procedure I needed to be admitted for, and she at least had compassion in her eyes. I kept it together until we got "home" to our friends' house, and then I cried all night. Psalm 62 says "Trust in Him at all times, O people; pour out your hearts to him." I really did. Every doubt, every complaint, every grief -- I spelled it all out to Him, and as I did, He took them. By morning I was all done. I really and truly was no longer carrying the grief myself. I had vowed I would "never have a baby in China" and I had tried hard to organize everything so that Miriam could be born in HongKong. Well, that didn't work. Once I went into premature labour, travelling anywhere was out of the question. Now I had lost the baby we'd come to Canada to birth safely. Right then, I swore that I would never again rearrange our lives around having a baby.

When we arrived in Vancouver, we were a little sobered to realize that we had just $1000 in the bank. One week and $270 later, Dave was calculating that at this rate, he would need to find a job mighty soon. We both came from hard-working, self-sufficient immigrant and pioneer stock, and had used our own savings and wages to live in China up until now. We had never done any fund-raising, and recoiled from the thought. God had answered many prayers for us, but when it came to our finances, we were used to relying on hard work and thrift to make ends meet.

The church in Big Rock (where we'd been living for the past two years) was composed almost exclusively of octogenarians who had survived the Great Leap Forward and the Cultural Revolution under Mao. Dave and I, and then baby Miriam, were the only young people. Our friends' church in Vancouver had a Chinese congregation meeting there as well, so we attended. What a surge of joy to see young people, so many young people, enthusiastically praising the Lord in Chinese! Oh, to see that happening in China as well! After the service, someone invited us to attend their mid-week prayer meeting, and we gladly agreed.

We borrowed a car and drove out, and as we entered the house, a lady said "Oh, you must be the special speakers." "Uh, no, no - we just came to pray." Well, we were wrong - we were the special speakers! Although impromptu, it was so encouraging to be with that group of people. They were so sincerely interested, asked great questions and encouraged us not to give up. A Taiwanese man shared how fifty years before, the foreign Christians who came to Taiwan were despised, persecuted and hindered in their work, but that recently he'd seen the President of Taiwan honor their contribution on public television. Through humble perseverance, they had built schools, hospitals, and the Church of Christ to the everlasting benefit of the Taiwanese people.

Afterwards, one of them stood up and said, "I'd just like to pass a hat around so that we can bless this brother and sister and help with their expenses." We squirmed and protested, but he insisted, and finally prevailed by putting an arm around Dave and saying, "Brother Lee, please just let us do this." A few minutes later, he took the handful of counted money and said "Brother Lee -- it's $270." In the car heading home, Dave and I were jubilant and yet near tears, because we understood that God had just clearly communicated that He was going to meet our needs. He did not want us to worry about money.

When our time in Vancouver was over, we took the bus up North to visit my parents and then settled in

Edmonton, living first with Dave's parents and then with his brother Darren in Oma and Opa's [Grandma and Grandpa's] house while they were in Hawaii for four months. By this time I was pregnant, and due in April. That was when Oma and Opa would be back from Hawaii, and also when our friend Mel would need her car, which she had so graciously lent us while she was in university.

By this time, however, we were getting the hang of this 'living by faith' thing a little better. Some time after we set up house in Edmonton, Dave started looking for a job. This seemed the expected and responsible thing to do, but he was in for a surprise. Dave co-managed a landscaping business when he was in university, had done construction, studied auto-mechanics and engineering and worked as a waiter. He was willing to do anything; and he could not get a job. It was crazy. He finally got work for one day as a "swamper" -- strapping loads on trucks going up north to the oil field. The next day the weather changed, the ice roads up there melted, and they were done for the season. At that point, we decided we were being dumb and disobedient, and stopped wasting time looking for paid work. Dave had a number of things on his heart that he believed God wanted him to volunteer for, so he committed to those things. He started reading the Bible to people at a hospital[5] and teaching English at a Chinese church in the north of the city. As a couple, we hosted and encouraged a couple of cell groups.

The next week, his uncle in Calgary phoned with an offer. He had just been asked to find a computer engineer for a $10,000 contract - it would only take a couple of months, and all we'd have to do was move to Calgary. God's provision, right? After praying about it, we felt not. The Bible says "Let your yes, be yes, and your

---

5   These were people in long-term care who couldn't read for themselves due to blindness, multiple sclerosis, etc.

no, be no. Anything else is of the evil one." We really felt that God wanted us to stick with the commitments He'd prompted us to make, and to take them seriously even though they wouldn't pay the bills, and this contract would. We thanked Dave's uncle, but declined the job. Our house was right by the church we attended, so we would often have people drop by. Three or four sets of company a day was not uncommon. Twice a week we would host the cell groups, and cook supper for everyone. We bought stuff on sale or second hand and did what we could to keep costs down, but we weren't stressed about it. With no job income and no committed "support", we lived in Canada for a year, hosted almost constantly, travelled and bought gas when we needed to - and never ran out of money.

We asked our parents point blank if they had been surreptitiously beefing up our bank account, but they denied it. To this day, we don't know who gave, or how the money came to be there. It was the "widow's bank card".

The baby I was carrying was persistently breech - from the first ultrasound at three months until she was born. I was experiencing a lot of contractions and was terrified of going into premature labour again, so I went up for prayer after an evening service. The people there sincerely lifted up my desire to carry this baby to term and not have to go back on bedrest. Bedrest before I had any children was hard enough, but Miriam was a handful. She was outgoing, bright, bubbly, rambunctious and strong-willed. I was getting bigger and bigger and tired all the time. Sometimes I would put her in the bathtub and have my "quiet time" on the toilet seat, or hold her hands and let her jump on the bed until she was a little more sedate. I couldn't keep up with her on walks. She read her first word out loud off a cereal box when she was 18 months. That's also when she "turned two". Getting her mittens on to go outside was a battle from then on, and so was changing her diaper!

One bright spot those days was a young nurse named Gayle who was volunteering at church. She got in the habit of popping by our house with some home-baked goodies or fresh flowers that winter. One day near the end of March we persuaded her to come in for tea, and as we started to talk, we were amazed to realize that we were in reciprocal dilemmas. Our problem was that we had to return Oma and Opa's house to them in April and had nowhere to go. Her roommate was going on a trip to China, and Gayle was afraid she was going to have to give up her house because she couldn't afford to cover the full rent by herself! We shared a holy chuckle and agreed on the spot to move in with her.

A couple of weeks later, we moved to her place and were overwhelmed to realize we were just a short walk across the park from the extendicare where Dave was volunteering! The next day we gave Mel her car back in perfect peace. The English class (which had required quite a bit of driving) was finished for the year, other members took over hosting the cell groups, since we had a new baby imminent, and God had provided for Dave to continue with the Bible reading! By this time, I was overdue, and actually had to be induced! This was a blessing in that we could easily pre-arrange a ride to the hospital, and certainly proved that the prayers of our friends that I would not go into premature labour were efficacious!

The labour, too, went smoothly. Three hours after I'd been admitted, I transferred to the delivery room where I actually had to wait for them to find a doctor! Holding off on pushing is no fun; I don't recommend it. Neither is the clinical aspect of having a breech baby. But the result was a healthy, beautiful, 8 pound 4 ounce baby girl: Karen Jeshurun. Jeshurun is God's "pet name" for Israel, and means "little upright one". She had a sweet disposition from the start and was easy to care for as we prepared to pack up our little family and return to China when she was two months old. So, that was the beginning of "living on love". It has actually been this way for over twenty years as I write this, and we have increased from three people to nine, not to mention the increase in the cost of living, global recession and all the rest. Apparently it is easy for God to support us, if we will seek first His kingdom and His righteousness.

Healing

*"Bless the Lord, O my soul, and forget not all His benefits ...
who heals all your diseases"* Psalm 103:2,3

During Dave's first year in China, his right ankle began
to swell. At times, it became extremely painful, but he
figured it was due to all the backpacking he was doing,
and should settle down when he stopped. By the next
year, when he was living in Hong Kong, despite his
comparatively sedentary activity of studying the Bible,
the pain was so intense that the only way he could sleep
was to do a couple of thousand leg lifts until the overall
muscle pain was overwhelming enough to mask the pain
in his ankle! His Filipino friend and roommate, Franco,
began giving him nightly ankle massages, and when I
came to HK, I inherited that job. Dave ate enough
Ibuprofen to give himself bleeding ulcers, and went for
numerous other treatments in HK, but nothing worked.

He and many others had prayed for his healing,
but one day as he was reading in James 5:14,15 [*"Is any
one of you sick? He should call the elders of the church to pray
over him and anoint him with oil... And the prayer offered in
faith will make the sick person well"*], he felt that God asked
him, "Why haven't you obeyed this?" So, shortly before
he left HK, Dave felt convicted to go to the elders of his
church there and ask them to anoint him with oil in the
name of the Lord for his healing. One in particular,
"Uncle Philip", was very glad to. He said, "I can pray with
faith, because I have witnessed the miraculous healing of
my son. He was diagnosed with terminal cancer, but is
completely well today in answer to prayer." The elders
prayed for him, but Dave was still on crutches when he
came out. He was a little disappointed, but mostly just

felt that he had obeyed, and what happened next was up to God. He had been on crutches for eight months before the doctors finally told him the only thing left to do was surgery. He couldn't afford to have it done in HK, so arranged to go home to Canada.

He was still on crutches when he met my parents, but shortly after that he was able to get in to see our family doctor, who trotted out the door to chat with an orthopedic specialist who worked in the same building. It normally took about four months to get in to see that specialist, but a cancellation right then allowed Dave to see him immediately! He was booked for surgery a few weeks down the road, and we hoped by some miracle this pain and disability which had dominated two years of his life could be cured.

Dave underwent surgery on his ankle by epidural anaesthetic, but all he got out of it was a whopping spinal headache. The specialist came by, shook his head, and said, "We took biopsies and had a good look, but I can't tell you what's wrong, or how to cure it." He got a diagnosis which was more a description: "non-rheumatoid inflammation of one joint." He went home with a "zipper" of stitches up the front of his ankle, and a drain which was literally pouring fluid. When I saw how much drainage there was, I thought, "The minute we pull that drain out and it seals up, his ankle's going to start swelling again." Instead, it got infected, and for a few days was draining pus. And then, it just got better. He was gradually able to put weight on it, and by our wedding, was actually able to leap off the platform, click his heels in the air and walk me up the aisle!

Why the delay? Dave thinks he can see two reasons. For one, being forced to return to Canada for surgery was the only reason he met my parents before we married, and could actually obtain their informed blessing on our union, and their ongoing support of our work once we went back. Another "fruit" was that most of the Chinese people in Dave's College and Career group in HK were convicted by the fact that this foreign guy with a crippled leg was constantly going over the border into the 'dreaded mainland' to share his faith! Within five years, most of them were also working over the border, discipling young people or doing medical missions in the mainland!

When Karen was six months old and beginning to learn to walk at our new school in China, something clicked as I was changing her diaper. As soon as it did, I knew I had been putting off this realization for a couple of months already, and ferocious grief welled up in me. How could I have blinded myself like this? How could I have been so stupid, so irresponsible as to have failed to get this checked out? She had a dislocated hip. Normally in the West, this is diagnosed during baby checks the first month, and treatment is really simple: wide diapers or being carried on the mother's hip. If it's missed entirely, as sometimes happens in the developing world, the child is lamed for life and goes through life with a wasted leg and a hitch to their gait. At six months, we were looking at either bracing or surgery, and I didn't know if a full recovery was even possible. If Karen never ran or never walked normally because of my self-deception, how would I ever forgive myself? For sure, the children of medical professionals should be assessed and treated by someone else. Objectivity is too elusive when it's your own family.

That afternoon, when hospital staff positioned her for x-rays, one hip was obviously out of joint, even to the untrained eye. The Department Head was a kind man who tried to reassure me, "Mei guanxi, [it's no matter] I have treated many children with this problem, and they are fine." We agreed that he would put on a temporary plaster cast which could be removed for bathing, while we arranged for a proper brace from a big hospital in the capital. He also agreed that it was a good idea for us to have her assessed by a specialist during our winter break in HongKong. Karen screamed while the doctors forced her legs into the "splits" and casted her in that position. She cried piteously most of the night, too. I could only imagine how it hurt to be forced into such an unnatural position, and then held that way with no respite, so I gave her an extra bath. After all, it *was* awkward to keep her bottom area clean since she was still in diapers.

The school we were working for rushed to get the brace to us, and I got busy altering her clothes and her bouncer so that she could still use them. A fleecy jacket someone sent us was turned into padding to cover all the hard, knobby parts of the new brace. Karen was at a stage where she wanted to be crawling about and exploring, and instead she was stuck in her brace. She couldn't even sit up, but had to be propped, and her braced legs were so wide that we had to move through doorways sideways. She wanted to follow me around the house, and protested loudly whenever I moved out of the room where she was. Miriam became a big help, patiently playing next to Karen so that she wouldn't be lonely. A few weeks later, we took Karen out to HK. It was a Saturday, and we were booked to see Dr. Timothy, a pediatric orthopedic surgeon, on Monday. On Sunday, though, we took her for healing prayer to the same group of elders who had prayed for Dave's ankle a few years before.

Dr. Timothy was a Christian doctor, with the gentlest, most compassionate eyes I have ever seen. It was such a huge relief to hand Karen over to him. He examined her carefully, and then said, "One doesn't like to disparage the diagnostic ability of our colleagues in mainland China, but I find no evidence of any laxity or dislocation in this hip." We gaped at him, and then I said, "but her hip clunked, and the folds of her buttocks were uneven, one leg was shorter than the other and she pulled it forwards kind of sideways when she tried to walk. And anyways, we have her x-rays which clearly show the hip out." Another moment while we took in what he was saying, "But, we did take her to be anointed with oil and prayed for by the elders of our church yesterday." He had a look at the x rays, and then said, "Well, all I can say is, 'Praise the Lord!' It's incredible that such a severe dislocation could have resolved so completely in just two weeks!"

We kept Karen in her brace until her first birthday, just to be absolutely sure, since we were so far from anyone whom I could trust to monitor her progress. But, we set her free for a birthday present, and it wasn't long until she was "rowing" herself around the house. She never crawled normally, but sat in the splits, rotated both legs forward a little and then scootched her bottom up even with them! Within a few days of her emancipation, I was carrying her around the neighbourhood, and she started fussing. Miriam looked up and said, "Karen wants to walk, Mommy." She was right! The only difficulty was that Karen's whole body was soft and out of shape, so when she stumbled and fell, she couldn't catch herself with her arms, but would fall right through them and scrape her face. She had a scab on her nose for months! But, Hallelujah, she did learn to walk, and skip and run and jump and dance!

Sit Car Go Home Eat Baicai

"through the mouths of babes and infants"

When Miriam was three and Karen one and a half, Dave was commandeered from our school to participate in the Spring Festival TV extravaganza for our province. They needed a foreigner who could speak Chinese well enough to participate in a two-man comedy routine, and someone suggested Dave. He agreed to go if he could bring his family along, and they were happy to comply with that. They put us up in the hotel run by the TV company, in the provincial capital. One day, when Dave was not required to be on the set, the four of us set off downtown. In order to do our errands more efficiently, Dave ran ahead and instructed me to meet him at a certain bank.

Well, I thought I followed his directions, and ended up at a bank, but he wasn't there. I retraced my steps and tried a different corner. Still no Dave. This was in the days before cell phones and I had no idea where I was or where he could be. After about an hour and a half of carrying Karen and dragging Miriam up one street and down another, I was ready to cry. It was past lunch time, both girls had had it, and suddenly Karen leaned forward over my shoulder and asked, "Mommy, where is it Daddy?"

"Oh, Karen, I wish I knew. I don't know where Daddy is."

"Mommy, Sit car, Go home, Eat bai cai![bok choy]" she said emphatically. I thought, "She's right."

I felt in my pocket and gratefully discovered just enough cash to catch a taxi, scrabbled in my memory and came up with the name of our hotel, and hailed a cab.

When we got out at the hotel, Dave was just running down the steps. He'd also made a quick trip home, to see if we had by any chance come back to the hotel, before he resumed his search downtown! We were so glad to see each other! The bai cai at the hotel buffet was all gone, but we had some good tofu, and I will never forget the day God spoke to me through my baby daughter!

Home

"There you saw how the Lord your God carried you, as a father carries his son, all the way you went until you reached this place. In spite of this, you did not trust in the Lord your God, who went ahead of you on your journey, in fire by night and in a cloud by day, to search out places for you to camp and to show you the way you should go." Deuteronomy 1:31-33

Jesus was born in a stable for there was no room for them in the inn

"Foxes have holes and birds of the air have nests, but the Son of Man has no place to lay his head." Matthew 8:20

"In my Father's house are many rooms..." John 14:2

"For I tell you the truth, no one who has left home ... for me and the gospel will fail to receive a hundred times as much in this present age (homes ... and with them persecutions) and in the age to come, eternal life." Mark 10:29-30

"Seek first His Kingdom and His righteousness, and all these things will be given to you as well." Matthew 6:33

"Store up for yourselves treasures in Heaven... For where your treasure is, there your heart will be also." Matthew 6:20,21

We are on the brink of going "home" to Canada, where we will be spending some time at Grandma and Grandpa's and Nana and Poppa's places: the homes where Dave and I grew up, and even helped build and care for during our teens. Home definitely includes the woods where I spent so many happy hours building forts, running "like an Indian", riding horseback, cross-country skiing and just being. It includes the lawn where we celebrated the seasons - rolling huge, leaf-stencilled snow balls for snowmen, raking the poplar "cotton" and flattened, wet, black leaves in the spring, the fragrant, freshly cut grass in summer, and the heaps of yellow poplar leaves in the fall. Also the garden where we helped dig up the soil, dig in the compost and manure from the horse paddock, mark out and plant the rows of vegetables, weed and weed, water and water, and then finally start to savour the fruit of all that labour: the freedom to go out and pick a sweet juicy carrot, or some pea pods, tomatoes or strawberries whenever the urge hit us.

We have never had our "own" home in Canada. When our family was still young and small, we lived with Grandma and Grandpa, or Nana and Poppa for a few weeks at a time while we visited them, and lived in Oma's place with Uncle Darren while she was in Hawaii. However, once every five years since then, we have needed a "home" of our own for the four months that we were in Canada. The last time we returned there, everyone assured us that it was going to be difficult or impossible to get a place. Vacancy rates were zero. The oil patch was booming, and people were begging to rent even barns, garden sheds and junky trailers from people so they'd have somewhere to live while they worked. Landlords were only renting to people willing to put two years rent down before they moved in!

Under the circumstances, it did not seem very likely we'd be able to find a house, and Nana and Poppa offered to move out into a dinky, hot little trailer on the Northern Lights College campus for the summer so that we could use their place. In our hearts, though, we suspected that they felt responsible for us - as though if they didn't take care of us, we would be left in the lurch. We specifically asked God to provide for us "better than we could ask or imagine" as a testimony to them that He is our provider, and we truly do not need to be concerned for tomorrow, or worried about any of our physical needs so long as we are truly seeking first His kingdom and righteousness.

We needed a place to stay in Vancouver for a couple of weeks, a house in Dawson Creek for two months, and a home in Edmonton for the same length of time.

Well, in Vancouver, some friends of Jeanette DeVries (my covenant friend from Bible school) went to Hawaii for two weeks, and they felt led to lend us their house in their absence. It was a big, beautiful home filled with children's toys and every appliance and amenity known to North Americans. And, they had a big yard, a big deck and a big trampoline! We thoroughly enjoyed our time there! In addition, some other friends of Jeanette who own a chalet near the Hemlock ski resort gave us the use of their beautiful facility for a few days retreat! It was mid-May and all the rhododendrons were blooming in Vancouver, but a few hours drive away, our children got their first experience of snow and winter sports like sledding up in the mountains. What beautiful memories we made those days, alternating between the breathtaking outdoors, cozying up to the big fireplace and playing in the loft!

In Edmonton, close family friends were realizing the dream of a lifetime by going on a backpacking tour of Europe. They were gone for two months, and gave us the use of their house. They had also raised 4 children on the outskirts of Edmonton, so we once again had a very child-friendly, spacious home, and the run of the pastures, saskatoon and cherry bushes, a trampoline, and tree houses! It was a reasonably short drive to Dave's parents' home, and his brother's home, and within biking distance of a great little supermarket. Quite simply - it couldn't have been better.

For our Dawson Creek stint, God provided a home on an acreage within easy biking distance of Nana and Poppa's. Some friends of my sister had gone to volunteer at Camp for the summer, and left us the use of their spacious home. It also came fully equipped with two bathrooms, many bedrooms, toys, deck, trampoline, sand pit and acres of lawn to romp on. Purely bonus were the deer which could often be seen feeding by the pond in the dawn or evening. It was perfect, idyllic -- and did I mention it was just past the horse and buffalo breeding ranch from my parents? I grew up horse back riding and biking on that road...

This time, "home" will be with Dave's older brother, Darren, in the house which his younger brother Mark bought so we would have a place to live when we're in Canada. It is just a few blocks from Mark's home, so that we can spend time with his family. It is in a great location, just a short walk from a library, a swimming pool, a playground and shopping.

Our time in China has not always been so smooth. We've often felt like pilgrims rather than dwellers. We've moved 11 times in our two decades here, and a number of those moves were not of our choosing. Leaving Big Rock was particularly traumatic.

Big Rock was Dave's first teaching appointment after our language study. The school provided a cute little apartment there where Miriam grew to be a toddler. We really bonded with the other teachers and were looking forward to returning once Karen had been born in Canada. When Karen was two months old, we travelled back only to find that the school could no longer welcome us because of our Christian witness. It would have been nice if they had given us some warning before we got there, but I suppose we would have had to come and deal with our stored belongings anyhow.

When we arrived it had been raining for a month, and all our belongings were either adhering to the boxes with mold, or shredded by mice, or both. In addition, the mother-in-law of the young teacher couple we'd let house-sit our place in our absence was a medium, and had apparently invited a familiar spirit to take up residence there. We felt like we would go mad our first couple of days there; the kids were screaming non-stop and we ourselves felt greatly oppressed. We basically fled to the fellowship of other foreign Christians in a nearby town to regroup. Together we exorcised our home, wept over our having been kicked out, and worshiped. During my quiet time then, the Lord clearly spoke from Isaiah 41, "*I will make you into a threshing sledge, new and sharp with many teeth...*". I didn't understand clearly what He meant, but felt assured that everything was happening according to His plan, and was deeply comforted. The authorities might be rejecting us, but God was not. We also asked for sunshine to deal with all the washing and drying we would have to do. When we returned, we had only to open the door to sense that it had been cleaned out spiritually, and we could peacefully get down to the work of sorting, washing, selling and giving away most of our belongings. We had blazing sunshine and a hot wind for the next ten days, and it only started raining again as we got on the train to leave!!

During those days, some friends in the capital phoned us and when we explained what had happened replied: " Well, now that makes sense. We were calling to tell you that Father had asked us to expect you as guests, perhaps for quite an extended time." So, that's where we went. The only room they had to offer us was their office with mats on the floor, but they gave us far more than that. They gave us an oasis, and I was truly delivered from self-pity and discouragement and once again found, "*In quietness and trust is your strength.*"

Our host was eager to share some scripture which had encouraged her in recent times of feeling isolated, and it was pretty exciting for both of us, because it was exactly what I had on my heart to share with her! The passage was from Genesis 26:2-6,14-33. For her the significance was the peaceableness and obedience of Isaac. He had been told to stay in Gerar, and did so, though he experienced hatred, jealousy and contention, as he was driven from place to place. He didn't fight for his rights or linger when the wells his father, Abraham, had dug were being disputed. And eventually he was given space (like Psalm 31:8 "*You have not handed me over to the enemy but have set my feet in a spacious place.*") and could prosper. His enemies finally even initiated a treaty! Abraham was a picture of Jesus, our wellspring of life. Though sometimes an enemy comes and fills our well with stones, and even hinders us as we seek to open it up again, we can leave it in His hands and move on. Eventually Isaac received not only water, but a personalized version of Abraham's blessing: "*I am the God of your father Abraham. Do not be afraid, for I am with you; I will bless you and will increase the number of your descendants...and through your offspring all nations on earth will be blessed...*" Our host was experiencing stalemate in her attempts to restore a relationship. We were literally being driven on from well to well. Both of us could leave the outcome in His hands.

While we were there, we realized that Karen had a muscular problem with her neck called torticollis, but even this was not permitted to be as stressful as it could have been. God sent along a physiotherapist to be the guest of another close friend, and she was able to show us exactly how to do the exercises to straighten Karen's neck. Also during that time, some other friends in the city did some asking around for places needing English teachers, and came up with three options. As soon as we heard them, I had a clear premonition that one of them, Mountainview, would be our new home, so I was totally prepared in my heart to go there when the time came about a month later.

Mountainview was our home for two years. I'll never forget when we opened the door, and saw the living/dining room area - it looked like something out of a magazine or off the TV. Everything brand new and gleaming; so much nicer than any of the teachers' apartments we'd ever seen in China. We felt so humbled and bedraggled - it was hard to believe it was for us! The local teachers, too, were so kind and welcoming and excited to have us there. The campus was outside the city on a sprawling hillside with a beautiful view, and we took every opportunity to go for walks in the nearby vineyards, flower gardens and countryside.

There were challenges, too, of course. Dave was teaching all 1200 students, and their teachers, every week. From our first day there, he was working long hours, and I was left to cope with an angry, confused two year old, a sickly baby and a completely new situation with no friends. Our belongings didn't arrive for about three weeks either. There were no other foreigners in our town, and the only other Christian had retired to his home province the week we arrived. And then we discovered that Karen had a congenitally dislocated hip in addition to her neck problems. I was full of self-pity and became depressed, even though God worked wonderfully to enable Karen to get the treatment she needed and granted her a full recovery. I would go around the house telling God "I need to overcome. I have to get a grip! I am doing so badly, and I can't sense You saying anything at all. Help me! I could really lose it." Finally I got an answer. God said something like, "You are so full of pity for yourself, there's no room for mine." By His grace, that snapped me out of it. I realized that I had been rehearsing my problems continually rather than presenting them to God with thanksgiving as we are told to do in Philippians 4. I had talked myself into a depression, so then I had to talk myself out of it! Praise,

Thanksgiving and Supplication -- those were the keys to overcoming in that spiritually dark place.

Our first year there, we asked God all the time to send us team mates. We were the lone light in a brand-new experimental school, established to demonstrate the superiority of Marxist philosophy. It was set up and run by the manager of one of China's largest wine factories. He virtually owned the town, with the hospital named after him and so on. Somehow he did not see the irony in this! The second year, two other families came to join us there. We had weekly fellowship, weekly meetings to intercede for the area, and weekly English corners where a number of us would go down and basically preach the gospel to the students. They lapped it up. The Christmas party that year was phenomenal. The school came up with the idea of having a huge bonfire in the middle of the playing field, with Christmas trees arranged in a circle around it. Each class gathered around one tree, but they all joined in the singing. I'm sure they saw the glow of the fire and heard the singing as far away as the town as 1200 voices belted out "Angels we have heard on high" in Chinese! We felt certain that that night anyhow, the forces of evil were not comfortable anywhere in that vicinity! Repercussions were not long in coming, however. Between that and the accidental bombing by the Americans of the Chinese embassy in Afghanistan, tension was pretty high as we drew near to the end of our second year.

At that same time, Dave began waking at 3 am every night with the Lord persistently asking "Will you go to the village for me?" He had all kinds of reasons why he felt that was a bad idea, but finally surrendered and told me what was up. I cried for three days! We had visited villages before, and always found it so difficult with the children. No matter how idyllic the setting, I could never wait to get back to running water, electricity, and some privacy. The kitchen in most peasant homes was usually the fire and maybe a smoke blackened cupboard, while the bathroom was often just a secluded (or not!) corner of the barn yard. To add to this, the area of China we were living in is home to many minority nationalities. All of our teacher friends were educated minority nationality people. When you get out into the villages, however, very few people actually speak even the heavily accented Mandarin that the townspeople speak. They have their own language, and wherever we settled, we would have to learn it. However, we had received our orders, and godly friends confirmed that they believed it was of the Lord.

"But what do we have to give? What could we demonstrate?" We should also have asked, "What do we have to learn?" We came up with all kinds of ideas: things we'd had some experience with which were part of a more abundant life, like health education, raising honey bees, carpentry, sewing, baking;   things we had no experience in but seemed to be a strong felt need in village settings, like micro-enterprise loans.   Then we learned about Sloping Agricultural Land Technology (SALT), developed in the Philippines, and the lights went on.   "This is fantastic!   It's exactly what mountain farmers need here!   Most of the "farmland" surrounding us would only be considered forestry, -- or ski-hill -- land in Canada, and the longer they practiced slash-and-burn agriculture in any one area, the more erosion was taking the dirt away, exposing the bare rock underneath. Some slopes only had little pockets of dirt, with a few corn stalks poking up, here and there among the rocks.

Settling on a potential occupation, though, didn't solve the problem of how to get permission to stay in a village.   Foreigners were kept carefully segregated from the Chinese at that time, and couldn't even visit poorer areas without a government escort.

Once we got our feet moving, however, God began to make a way.   He started by inspiring the Matthews family and Ed, a single, to join us. We spent six weeks in the Philippines at the Asian Rural Life Development Foundation, learning about sustainable agro-forestry for mountainous areas. Their SALT system uses deep-rooted, soil enriching trees, planted along contour lines and kept trimmed as hedgerows, to stop erosion, create natural terracing, and provide fertilizer and animal fodder. Crops are planted on the land strips between the hedgerows.

Dave studied all about goats and SALT while Miriam, Karen and I (and the baby I was carrying) enjoyed gallons of sweet goat milk and ice-cream produced on location. Every day we'd go for a circuit of the farm, visiting the barns full of cute baby goats, rabbits and guinea pigs. Other than being kind of hot for a pregnant lady, it was a perfect place to rest and recover in the peace and sunshine of that place. All day we could hear the local farm labourers cheerfully singing hymns together as they went about gathering goat fodder, and their basketball games were punctuated by hearty laughter. So very different from the suspicion and outright hostility we had experienced in China as the "American" foreigners at a time when the news was full of propaganda demonizing the States for their "unprovoked slaughter" and "lack of concern" about the Chinese delegates killed at the Afghan embassy. It didn't seem to matter that we were Canadian, and had nothing to do with the event, there was still a somewhat frightening, sudden change in people, who for two years had been kind and friendly to us. We were unwanted foreigners in a foreign land and it was suddenly easy to understand what the Boxer rebellion and "Paper Tiger" eras would have been like.

At the end of the six week agro-forestry training, we went to the airport to fly to Luzon, where we hoped to await the birth of our third daughter in the guest house of Philippino church planting friends, Restie and Cris. Unfortunately, the airline official decided that I was nine months pregnant, not eight, and refused to let me on the plane! In vain I explained that I was only 36 weeks along. He'd say "9x4 is 36 - you're 9 months pregnant - it's for your own safety, Ma'am". I'd say, "Full gestation is 40 weeks! According to your way of figuring, babies would be born at 10 months gestation! I'm only 8 months along and can safely fly." I presented my obstetric report from just the day before which stated I was in no danger of imminent labour. Unfortunately, the doctor had failed to stamp it with the date! Argh! Finally Dave and I just looked at each other and mouthed, "Pray!" We did, and the official agreed to phone a doctor and clear up how many months 36 weeks was. I smiled graciously as he finally let us board, and whispered, "Thank you, Lord!" as I collapsed into my seat.

Actually, the fact that we were at the airport at all was a matter for praise, because the day before we ran into two snags. One was that we could not withdraw money to pay for our accommodations or our airline tickets, even though we tried three bank machines. We asked God to please help us, and the next effort yielded just enough to pay our debts, and no more. The next problem was that when we went to the travel agent to pick up and pay for our tickets (no such thing as e-tickets back then!), there was a cardboard notice hanging on the door explaining that the office was closed due to a national holiday and would be open tomorrow, sorry for any inconvenience etc. Oh, no! As we were turning away in dismay, however, a young man came bounding up the stairs. He was our travel agent, and had come back to the office on his day off to take care of something else. He graciously unlocked his desk, gave us our tickets and settled accounts! Praise God!

When we arrived, we were met by our friends, Restie and Cris. They are the most lovely people. A childless couple with a tremendous heart for little ones, they had opened a "Lamb's Daycare" beside their home as an outreach to the neighbourhood, so Miriam (5) and Karen (3) could attend that with the local children and experience a lot of love and fun while I rested and had extended times of prayer and Bible study. As anyone with young children can affirm, time to soak in the Word and His presence are rare and precious, as devotions are often truncated by all sorts of domestic demands and crises. In addition to this, we had daily fellowship over meals, and could participate in the vibrantly alive Lakas Angkan [literally "power of the clan"] indigenous cell church which they pastored. After four years of little fellowship, this was exactly what we needed. I wept through every worship service for months! There was nothing I could do about it but hope people got used to it. I was basking in His presence, and just undone. One Sunday in particular, I was praying for Miriam, who was standing on a chair beside me. I asked God to somehow reveal Himself to her, to help her understand that He existed and that He loved her. I felt that all the changes had been hard on her in particular, and now we were expecting another baby in addition to being in complete limbo. She suddenly leaned over and whispered in my ear, "Mommy, Jesus is in this house." Of course, I cried some more!

We soon found that God had thought of all sorts of things which we had overlooked. Our friends lived just outside the university in LosBanos, which is the agriculture university for the Philippines. Every "big name" organization in the Green Revolution and sustainable agriculture was represented, and we fellowshipped side by side with professors in all the specialties Dave was trying to learn about. Beyond that, when our parents (both sets) came to see their new granddaughter, (Constance Marie), the accommodations we had lined up for them suddenly fell through the day before their arrival! Restie prayerfully drove around the campus, and felt led to stop and ask at a beautiful big home overlooking a gorgeous ravine. The owners had just finished it and had not even put up a sign or started advertising yet, but their guest suites were perfect for our needs. And, serendipitous little detail, the proprietor, Tito, had been the overseer of UN community development projects in Asia for 20 years prior to his recent retirement! He was also a brother in the Lord, and we had some very helpful discussions with him before we travelled back to China.

Actually, the most helpful thing he said was, "To try to do a community development project the way you're wanting to in China is impossible. They won't even look at you. You need to join a big organization like the Peace Corps."   Dave being who he is, and sure that this was not our own idea but God's, took this as a challenge, and to the Lord! Our conviction was that God wanted to take us into the village in an unprecedented way as we simply moved forward in obedience. We didn't want to see if the Peace Corps could get us in there - we wanted to see God part the Jordan. For Him to do the "impossible" by providing a visa for us to live in the village would be all the proof we needed that He was "going up with us" and that we were in the center of His will.   Remember what Moses said to the Lord?   "If your Presence does not go with us, do not send us up from here. How will anyone know that you are pleased with me and with your people unless you go with us? What else will distinguish me and your people from all the other people on the face of the earth?" "And the Lord said to Moses, "I will do the very thing you have asked, because I am pleased with you and I know you by name." We had absolutely no interest in going anywhere without that assurance!

Another thing Tito told us was this: of all the thousands of agricultural projects he'd seen, only a handful were successful in the long run. These were all projects where an extensionist (individual or family) went to live in a community and made a long term investment, combining practical help with a concern for the spiritual development of the people.

Shortly before we left, Boni Arzaddon, the leader of Lakas Angkan Ministries, gave us a verse He felt God wanted to encourage us with. It was Isaiah 41:15-16 *"See, I will make you into a threshing sledge, new and sharp with many teeth. You will thresh the mountains and crush them, and reduce the hills to chaff. You will winnow them, the wind will pick them up , and a gale will blow them away. But you will rejoice in the Lord, and glory in the Holy One of Israel."* This was the same verse God had impressed me with as we left our home in Big Rock three years before! I was gradually starting to have an idea of what our "ministry" was, and could even give it a name: rock picking. It seemed our role was to move into new situations and set a precedent, opening the way for others, and through prayer and perseverance, picking rocks and roots to "prepare the way of the Lord." It seemed we would only be given enough time in any one place to prepare the ground a little, perhaps sow some seeds, and then we'd have to move on and leave the nurturing of the seeds and the harvest to others. I can't say I liked the job description that much. It involved a lot of uprooting our home, leaving our friends, facing opposition and language challenges in new places, and not getting to see the fruit.

Except once.

After we had left Mountainview, the majority of the students and teachers at our school had heard the message, and we had watered that area with urgent and united prayer. Yet there was very little response. Later reports from the area that filtered to us were discouraging: the national evangelists who had come from out of province had left, and the little group of a few believers, the only one that we knew of there, had been beaten and intimidated until they'd given up meeting together. But then, years later, we were delighted to hear that a friend of ours, the former communist party secretary from the school we taught at, was now a fervent believer. But that's just the tip of the iceberg. There is now a church there and it is growing in leaps and bounds, regularly baptizing new converts. Prayer meetings are well attended and people are on their knees weeping, confessing sin and crying out to God to bring light to the darkness of that place. The believers are active in witnessing and giving out materials in the community, including the Jesus film. At Christmas they had an evangelistic message at which more than 100 people came forward to respond to the Gospel!

But as God kept moving us on, ours was the blessing of Psalm 84:

Blessed are those whose strength is in You, who have set their hearts on pilgrimage.
As they pass through the Valley of Baca, (mourning)
they make it a place of springs;
the autumn rains also cover it with pools.
They go from strength to strength
till each appears before God in Zion.
Hear my prayer, O Lord God Almighty;
listen to me, O God of Jacob.
Look upon our shield, O God;
look with favour on Your Anointed One.
Better is one day in Your courts
than a thousand elsewhere;
I would rather be a doorkeeper in the
house of my God
than dwell in the tents of the wicked.
For the Lord God is a sun and a shield;
the Lord bestows favour and honour;
no good thing does He withhold
from those whose walk is blameless.
O Lord Almighty,
blessed is the man who trusts in You.

"Home" would have to be a location of the heart, rather than a place; an inward abiding with the Shepherd of our souls even as He moved us from pasture to pasture.

However, at times I was truly envious of those swallows who had a nest for their young! (Psalm 84:3 *"Even the sparrow has found a home and the swallow a nest for herself, where she may have her young – a place near Your altar"*)

Dave at the minority nationality market

Home, part 2

From the Philippines, we came back into China on a tourist visa with Miriam (5), Karen (3), and baby Constance. My parents were opposed to this. They wanted the children and I to wait with them in Canada while Dave "explored the land". I felt strongly, however, that we had to "stick our toes in the Jordan" by going back together. I guess I hoped that if we took some risks, God would mercifully extend His mighty arm and show that He was for us. He really did. The first thing was our temporary digs back in Mountainview. The rest of our "Agricultural team", Ed and the Matthews, met us there. They had found a new three storey apartment building for rent with one apartment for each of us. We had just moved in and taken our belongings out of storage at our previous school when the local police decided that they did not want us on their turf, and commanded our landlords to kick us out! After six months of being on the move, and with a new baby, this really felt like a low blow. I went to my knees and fumed at God. "God, you knew this was coming! The least you could have done was warned us, or somehow prevented us from having taken all our furniture and stuff out of storage -- now what are we going to do?" After a few minutes, however, I felt very convinced that the next thing God wanted me to do was praise. So, we did. We danced and sang, "God is good all the time," around the apartment. The next day, the police were back at the door. They came in, looked around, gruffly said "Well, you're going to have to get bars put on those windows." and left! We looked at each other and asked, "Does this mean we can stay?".

It did, for the moment. However, we had made a powerful enemy of the factory owner when we left our former school. When we went to the Foreign Affairs office to have our visa extended (usually just a formality) they at first refused, and then said they'd give us three days, just enough time to get out of the country. Ruby Matthews and I stepped outside the door and had a little talk with God. Our husbands were already travelling in a different part of the province, looking for "the village" where God was going to give us a home, and where they could set up an agricultural demonstration site. When we came back in and explained that our husbands weren't there, the authorities relented a little and gave us a whole ten days to get out of the country! When the men phoned later, we told them, "All right, you've got a week to come up with a new visa!"

Now, to get a visa processed in those days was always a dicey, lengthy affair, even if you were settled in at a school and were just renewing. Foreigners were considered a somewhat necessary nuisance by the authorities. The value of the technical skills and English we had to offer just, just outweighed the political and religious and moral pollution they assumed we represented. To walk into a new community and convince them to give us a visa so we could teach them something they'd never heard of and had no felt need for in just a week was so impossible. Three days later the men phoned again and said they'd found the place, and the visas were in process! Miraculously, although permission had to come from the local, prefectural and provincial government, they had visas in hand within that next week!

Then there was how they found "the place". They started out every day in prayer, confessing their sins, and asking God to show them "the needle in the haystack" which would be our new home. This is not something Dave has shared very often, but one night he had a dream. They were driving along, and he clearly saw two pillars on either side of a little road leading off to the right, and it led to our new home. The next day as they went by in the bus, he said, "That's it! That's the road in my dream!" When they followed that little road, though, it led to an unfriendly Miao village. Discouraged, they walked back to the main road. Just across the little creek on the other side of it, however, a friendly Buyi man welcomed them with a huge smile and invited them to live in his house. He was the "man of peace" that we'd asked God to direct us to. As we asked around that village, named Little Rock, for a place to build, they offered two lovely sites - one for the Matthews' and one for us. The Matthews' chose the site at the end of the village, leaving us a site up the hill and across the road and the creek from them. It looked ideal, but Dave wondered out loud how we would get the building materials from the road up the steep hill to the building site. "Oh, that's no problem", his guide offered, "there's a road just a few steps up behind us here." Sure enough there was, and guess where it exited? At the road with the pillars! When they first walked it, they hadn't noticed that steep little fork to the right.

All this was pretty exhilarating stuff. "Wow, when you stick your toes in the water, God really does dam the river!" was the gist of our thoughts and letters. In the meantime, though, we were all crammed into the temporary housing that local officials had found for us -- a tiny, sweltering apartment in the little market town of Creekside -- and could not seem to get permission to build a house in the village. We prayed and fumed and finally tuned in to the growing conviction that perhaps we were asking for the wrong thing. "Maybe God doesn't want us to live in our own house just yet. Maybe He knows it would be better for us to live with a local family for awhile first." We kind of hoped not, but had just finished reading a book on cross-cultural bonding. Surely living as the guests of a local family, which is what the book recommended, couldn't be that much worse than that apartment, where sixty to eighty people packed into our two tiny rooms to gawk at us every market day, and all the tap water had to be filtered through a sock which quickly turned green! Finally getting really honest with God, I wrote a "short list" of our rock bottom absolutely essential needs. It included things like: our own source of drinking water, two bedrooms, something to cook on...

Then Dave went back to the authorities to ask if we could live with the family of the "man of peace" who had first welcomed us to Little Rock. Dumbfounded, he came home a couple hours later with permission for us to move into the village! It was that simple!

We were so glad that God's wisdom prevailed, and that He did not immediately let us succeed in our very natural desire to build ourselves a home. We lived with the Lee family for 9 months, and although we had nothing in the way of convenience, we gained something far better. We really bonded with their family. We loved them, and they loved and took care of us, even though we could not even communicate with most of them at first. The grandfather of their family, Gonggong, had worked for the forestry bureau his whole life, so took a real interest in the agro-forestry Dave was trying to do, and was one of the few Buyi neighbours who could also speak Chinese. He was a gruff old man and scared the kids for the first few weeks, but once he'd taken us into his heart, he was a strong and honest friend. Unlike most Asians, he would tell us when we'd committed a faux pas, and was willing to guide us as we immersed ourselves in the Buyi language and culture. He'd tell us which neighbours we could trust, what to do when we were invited to a wedding and so on. Invaluable.

Our hostess , Mrs. Lee, the kids called "The Short Lady" because 6 year old Miriam was almost as tall as she! Her husband was a good match; he was almost as tall as I was, at just over five feet. Like most countryside women, our hostess was accomplished at many things. It was her job to raise the pigs, cows and chickens, to tend the garden, plant the fields, sell the produce, feed her family and to make their clothes. The Buyi still make their own hand-woven, hand-embroidered and hand-dyed cloth. They dye it a deep blue with indigo root, and their hands in the process! We were very curious about the colour of some of our neighbour's hands until we learned this. Since we did not have our own garden, the short lady took us into her field of Chinese cabbage and told us to help them eat it. To our surprise, we discovered that the best eating was once it had shot into flower stalks. We weren't able to do much for them in return, but they were delighted with us when we remembered to add the water we'd washed our rice in, or our left overs to the pig slop. They never failed to grin once we learned how to answer their greeting in the evening, either. It made us all grin, actually, because we had to say, "Goofy Rat Din" [I haven't washed my feet].

Our neighbours had a baby water buffalo, and the kids loved to sit on it and fondle it's long, droopy ears and look into it's soft, lash-fringed eyes. We bought a sweet puppy, too, and delighted in playing with her. As we were bathing her the first time with an herbal lice shampoo, and watching with satisfaction as the fleas fled from her fur, the local teacher walked by and said, "You'd better watch out. Those fleas bite like crazy, and they itch much worse than mosquitoes." Unfortunately, she was SO right! In Canada, fleas may be host-specific, but in China, anything warm-blooded goes. We scratched ourselves to distraction for many months until my mom did some research and came to the rescue with flea collars for us, and a non-toxic, natural insecticide called diatomaceous earth.

For nine months we either washed our clothes and diapers in the creek, or carried them back and forth from town. We used their "outhouse" - a huge wok positioned beneath two slippery boards, *partially* screened by trees. We ate meat on market days only, and several times ended up serving local officials a meal of just vegetables eked out by peanuts when they caught us on a "between" day.   Since they absolutely expected to be served a meat dish, we finally bought ourselves a rooster against the next official visit.   The only trouble was that for some reason he was the only rooster in the district, and spent his days speeding back and forth from one flock of hens to the other. We nick-named him "the Roadrunner" and never could catch him.

We ate fruit and vegetables in season, and sometimes ended up carrying our basket back the 5 km from town because buses were few and far between and we couldn't always catch a ride. Essentially, we lived as they did.

Finally, we were given permission to start building our own house, and the first loads of bricks rumbled up the back road to be dumped at the house site.   For some reason, the bricks available the day our contractor went to get them were a sunset pink with cream and black accents rather than the usual "brick red". I loved them. The kids and I would climb the hill every day to watch the walls grow, and when the walls were tall enough that they had to put in the window and door frames, I said " I finally believe this is happening". The wood they used, too, was a gorgeous cherry red while the floor was a wonderful collage of odd-shaped slabs from the nearby marble factory. The marble there was a beautiful mixture of black shot through with green swirls. Remnants were free, so we got that floor for the price of the transport.

Our home was designed very like our neighbours' houses, with a peaked tile roof and wide front door opening into the main living area, but where they had an idol shelf on the back wall, we had a big window opening out on a forest of maple trees.   We took a fierce and mischievous joy in that window! Our neighbours did not approve, but they did not understand the anguish we had suffered, looking up at that idol shelf in our adopted

family's home. At New Years it had been particularly
hard, as we had returned home to find the living room
floor (where we ate our meals) covered in blood. They'd
sacrificed their pig before the ancestor shelf, and now the
head and tail were presented in a bowl on it. They asked
us to share in the meal, which of course we could not do.
Knowing we were doing a very offensive thing culturally,
we still had to leave them to their festivities and walk the
5 km back to the market town apartment in the dark. The
next morning, we walked back, and were so thankful to
be sheepishly and warmly welcomed by our "family".

I can only think of one other time when living with
them was a real hardship emotionally, and that was when
our hosts' TV worked. We just felt that we *couldn't* share
the living room with the awful things they would leave
playing on it. Our children were young, and sensitive to
ugly, brutal, violent scenes and sounds. We really prayed
that God would deliver us from that influence, and He
did. It was one of the fastest answers to prayer we have
ever experienced! One minute it was blaring, and the
next it was on the fritz. Gonggong swore and thumped it
and finally unplugged it with a bunch of muttered
imprecations. A few weeks later, we saw him headed to
town with the broken TV on his back.
Shoot!
We watched with bated breath as he brought it back from
the repairman and plugged it in.
It worked.
We were guests and there was nothing we could do about
the situation but pray some more. Once again, the ugly
Ninja, KungFu, bloody tortures and levitating, battling
shamans disappeared into a welter of static! Gonggong
was totally disgusted and gave it up as a bad job, and we
praised God, our Redeemer and Deliverer!

One of the first things we did once we'd moved in
to our new home was to hang a swing in those maples
behind our house. For some reason, China has a dearth

of swings, but our kids had a dandy! The ropes were a good twenty feet high, and they could back up the slope, and then swing far out with a view over the whole valley.

The other strong memory I have connected to those maples is waiting for them to burst into flame and immolate our house in the blaze as well. Most of our neighbours did not have flashlights, or the money to buy batteries, so if night fell while they were still on the trail, they had the interesting habit of torching the mountain side to get a little light to see by! The forestry department was not really keen on this practice! Neither were we, especially the day a forest fire came over the top of the ridge behind our house and started relentlessly picking it's way down the steep slope towards us. I spent the whole day trying to decide if I should be hanging diapers or packing our baskets with things like passports and blankets for evacuation! I was feeling so strained by evening, but our neighbours calmly bided their time until the fire slowed down at the back road, then put it out with shovels. Over the years I have become very familiar with that feeling of subdued panic, and have perhaps become better at keeping my eyes on the Hand of the Lord, biding His time. He has delivered us from so many threats to health, safety and security. When He has allowed us to go through the fire or the flood, He has also fulfilled the other half of Isaiah 43:2, so that we were neither burned nor swept away.

Our time in Little Rock reads like a series of crises, and I haven't told the half of it! But when I look back on that time, it feels like the sun was always shining. My memories are suffused with radiance and warmth. How can that be, except that God's Presence was our light, our ever-present help and comfort?   Our first fall there, just after Constance recovered from whooping cough, [more on that in the next chapter] our family went out into the fields to "help" bring in the rice harvest. Our neighbours were very welcoming and very patient as we did our best to cut the stalks with their curved hand scythes, beat the rice into a large wooden box, and tie the straw into stooks with another strand of straw.

As we came home one evening, Dave said, "Something stung me when I grabbed a hand full of rice -- look, there's the hole and my thumb is all swollen." It was very swollen, and a little purplish. None of our neighbours could think what he might have encountered, so we just hoped it would get better. A few days later, however, his whole arm was swollen, red and unusable, the puncture was draining pus and the lymph nodes under that arm pit swelled up to the size of grapes. He went to bed with a high fever, malaise and headache, and I put him on some antibiotics. That seemed to do the trick, and for three weeks he was fine.

Unfortunately, a herd of cows broke through the scrub oak fence we'd put up around the agricultural demonstration site our team had planted, and Dave exhausted himself chasing them out. That night, he relapsed and I began to look in our medical manual under "Relapsing fever". I was on the right track, but did not have the experience to guess that it was Typhus. It didn't actually matter, however, as God's safety net, the Body of Christ was about to kick into action. I helped Dave get dressed, and then asked Ed, who has a background as a hospital orderly, to evacuate him out to the nearest hospital. Feeling very thankful to know Dave was in competent hands, I dressed the kids and caught a ride into town to send out an SOS from the office computer. That was all I could do, beyond waiting and praying. The local hospital didn't prove to be any help, so after three days, Ed strong-armed Dave onto the bus for the long, dusty, nauseatingly twisty ride out to the capital city. By that time Dave was feeling so badly he just wanted to curl up in a corner and die, but as Dave always explains, "Ed was bigger, so he got his way." The city hospital diagnosed pneumonia and tried to put Dave on the same ineffective treatment as the county hospital.

Thankfully, they ran into one of the American teachers at a college there who was a friend of Ed's, and a fully qualified lab technician. She irritated some people by her insistence, but ran her own tests on Dave's blood, which she described as "toxic". She recommended that they immediately head for HongKong before it was too late. At the same time, an American doctor who was running a Village Doctor Program in a neighbouring province read my SOS and contacted her, saying, "This sounds like Scrub Typhus. Put him on Doxycycline immediately. No excuses, please." She did so, but two days later Dave was grey, could barely stand up, and could not really understand what was being said to him, or reply coherently. So, with a prayer in his heart, Ed began trying to get Dave out to HK. Thankfully, the foreign affairs office came through with an instant visa even though it was right before closing time, and the airline still had seats for that evening, but Dave and Ed had no money to buy them! It had not occurred to them as they left the village that they would need more than local bank cards. As they were sitting slumped over a table praying about what to do, another acquaintance of Ed's walked by and noticed them. He was an Irish manager of a tire manufacturing company there, and he took a look at Dave and said, "Hey, you look like you're in pretty rough shape. You'd better get out to a hospital in HK or something." He peeled several thousand yuan out of his wallet, and offered it to them, saying, "If you get a chance to pay me back, fine, but don't worry about it. You just get on that plane." So, they did.

When they arrived in HK, the same doctor friend who had helped Dave with his bleeding ulcers met them at the emergency department of the hospital he worked in, and immediately admitted him to the "Observation Unit". He could stay there for free for three days while they tried to treat him. Six months later, the definitive blood cultures finally made it back from a lab in America so we could say, "Wow, Dave survived Epidemic Typhus, which has a 20 % fatality rate!"   But in the mean time, our friend agreed to presume Typhus, and the foreign manufactured Doxycycline he gave him finally knocked it out. The Chinese manufactured drug had done diddly[6]. About that time, I finally made it out to HK with the kids, assisted at every turn of the way by the goodness and kindness of other Christians. I couldn't believe it as I made my way around the last corner with kids and luggage in tow to see Dave riding a bike towards us! It had been two long and anxious weeks since I entrusted him to Ed out in the village. That night, as we enjoyed a sumptuous meal at the home of some new friends from church, our host chuckled and asked Dave, "Does she always look up at you so adoringly?"

Once Dave had fully recuperated, we travelled back to our new house in the village and picked up where we'd left off. Ed went back to Canada for a year, and then the Matthews were forced to leave. After many months of working on our own, Dave began to suffer from tormenting obsessive thoughts.   Unable to sleep, he became so weary of fighting it that one day as he carried a heavy basket of groceries the five kilometers home (no ride as usual), he seriously thought of stepping in front of a logging truck. He could only think what a relief it would be. Thankfully he did not act on it.

At that point I insisted that we needed to leave China for a time of "retreat" in a place with Christian fellowship. We went to "The Juniper Tree," named after the tree where the Lord found Elijah lying exhausted from his flight from Jezebel, and ministered to him. As our two wonderful weeks of resting in that lovely and

---

6   We found later with TB drugs as well that drug quality in China can be very hit-and-miss. Some brands have little or no efficacy, others work well.

consecrated place came to a close, Dave was better enough to agree that it had been the right, possibly even life-saving, decision to come. The place we were working was so dark spiritually, we were so isolated, Dave was doing the work and decision-making of three men, and trying to come to grips with the realization that Typhus had left him with a brain injury. He could no longer multi-task and having to focus on more than one thing at a time "fried his circuits". In addition, he had lost a lot of memories, (like our wedding) and his "photographic memory" and short term memory were also impaired. I kidded him that he was finally joining the "normal" world where people had to use lists and coping mechanisms, but it was still a big adjustment for him. From that time on, we started making family holidays a regular practice.

One strange thing about our new house was that it had centipedes: foot-long, red, hissing, rubbery, poisonous centipedes. The bite from those was like a scorpion sting to an adult, but could be fatal to a child. We killed at least eight of them, though we had never seen one the whole nine months we lived in our host family's mud brick home. Why they should prefer our high, airy, clean, new house was rather a mystery. Our neighbours were all animists, and felt that the centipede invasion was definitely a bad omen. Because of that, we took the matter to prayer, and never saw another one.

Planting on the demonstration site

Gently Lead, part 1

Remember my vow never to rearrange our lives around having a baby again? Isaiah 40:11, *"He tends His flock like a shepherd: He gathers the lambs in His arms and carries them close to His heart; He gently leads those that have young,"* has been a precious, precious verse to me as I carried our next five children through another often tumultuous and challenging decade and a half.

Our third daughter, Constance, I conceived while we were contemplating leaving the "well marked path" of teaching English in China and our secure, now-familiar, comfortable position at the school.   When we boarded the plane for the Philippines -- to study agro-forestry in preparation for moving to the countryside -- I was almost seven months pregnant, the same stage at which I went into premature labour with Miriam, and had to have contractions stopped with Karen as well. However, God gave the faith to do it, and thankfully, premature labour was not an issue at all. In fact, when Dave's parents arrived in the Philippines "to see their new grandchild", that child was still stubbornly "on board"! My due date came and went and I started having to see my obstetrician every four days because the amniotic fluid was dwindling.   Grandma and Grandpa also started counting down the days and giving not so subtle hints about having to leave before the big event.

Finally my doctor gave the ultimatum "No baby by tomorrow morning, and we induce." I was not keen to do that. In my experience, induced labours were far more painful, and could often lead to the need for pain control measures which in turn interfered with the effectiveness of the birthing process, which in turn led to C-sections. Dave interceded for me, and took me for a walk. He told me afterwards that he'd had the sense that his prayer would be answered that night, and it was. Constance was born about the time I would have been coming in for my induction.

She was a very alert and strong newborn. She made eye contact immediately, and seemed to regard us with a sweet recognition right from the first moment. She was lying cuddled on my shoulder with her face turned in towards my neck at one point when Dave spoke from the side. She lifted her head right up, turned her face towards him and looked at him! Pretty impressive for a baby a few minutes old! However, Constance was colicky, and screamed every waking minute for the first month.

During that time, Dave and Miriam also became really sick with a very sore throat, high fever, no appetite. I wasn't sure how contagious they were, so would change my shirt and wash hands every time I went from caring for them to caring for Constance. Thankfully, after about a week and a half, it occurred to Cris, our hostess, that perhaps they had contracted Typhoid.[7] Dave did the blood test and came up positive, so then he insisted they test Miriam as well. The doctor didn't want to do it. "She isn't acting nearly sick enough to have such a serious disease." Dave said "Believe me, she's acting sick!" Miriam never admitted it when she wasn't feeling well, and was energetic and active even when she was really sick. That week she just sat around, wanting to cuddle . Sure enough, she had Typhoid as well.

Once they were both on antibiotics they made a pretty rapid recovery, and I was able to relax a little knowing that Constance and Karen and I were not going to catch it through the air or casual contact (it's fecal/oral transmission).

The other challenge Constance faced was that the humidity made her umbilical stump start to rot before it

---

7   Not to be confused with Typhus, transmitted by a combination of fleas and rats, which just about killed Dave later on, in Little Rock.

fell off, while her skin turned into one big red heat rash which turned into blisters which melded together and made her skin come off in sheets. Poor little munchkin! Thankfully her doctor knew exactly what to do, and the lactic acid soap she recommended healed it up quickly.

When Constance was about a month and a half old, my parents came to visit. We drove out to Olongapo to visit an orphanage for street kids there. It's called "Jireh Home" - and truly the Lord has provided for that place! Three amazing stories I still remember 13 years later had to do with what happened when Mount Pinatubo erupted near there. So much ash was thrown into the air that it buried the entire area several meters deep. They did not see the sun for many days. All their crops and gardens were covered. Many buildings collapsed from the weight of the ash, but their orphanage had been built by an American contractor with "wastefully" thick steel struts in the roof, and it withstood the test! The other immediate need was for food, but God was ahead of them there as well. As they prayed about their need, they realized that a large refrigerated transport truck had become stuck outside their gate. The driver waded into the yard and said "Help yourselves! This food is all going to go bad if you don't eat it - I'm not going anywhere!" So, they had lobster and ice-cream and all kinds of gourmet food to eat up while they waited for the roads to be cleared! However, as they looked out at their rice land and gardens, still buried a meter or more in white ash, they could have despaired. They grew all their own food. How could their land become arable again? They chose instead to pray. Some weeks later, the Commander of the nearby American naval base volunteered his troops and equipment to help them clear the land. They had bulldozers and dump-trucks and it did not take long at all to have the fields scraped back down to dirt.

From Jireh Home we headed to the coast and spent a week at a little resort, just resting and visiting with my parents. And then it was time to board our plane and head back to China. We stayed for three months in a little apartment back in Mountainview, in the town rather than out at the school. One day, a couple of weeks before we headed out for our first home in the village, we dropped by the home of some Chinese friends of ours, then went out to enjoy the spring sun along with many other families in the housing complex green space. At one point one little girl with a runny nose and watering eyes toddled over and tried to play with baby Constance. I kind of fended her off, but not as quickly as I would have if I'd realized what she was ill with!

Two weeks later, a truck was on the road with our furniture, and we were following by train and bus. By the time we got settled into a cheap little hotel in the provincial capital, we were all feeling queasy and spent the night being violently ill. No sooner had we recovered from that than Karen came down with a high fever. She was so hot she was hallucinating and begging us to get the monkeys off her bed because they were biting her toes! Two days later, the mystery illness declared itself as the glands in her neck started to swell. Mumps! Well, that wasn't the end of the world. We decided to go on with our plans to take the bus out to our new home anyways. That next day on the bus, Karen was basically prostrated on my lap, Constance had started coughing, and then Miriam had a seizure and was screaming out in a strangled voice from her seat several rows back. It was nuts. In my heart I just thought, "The Devil knows my greatest fear about moving out to the countryside is that our kids will get sick or badly hurt out there, and we'll be too far from a doctor to help them. He's trying to get me to back down and give up right at the beginning. If I don't see this through right now and take this ground, we're licked."

We made it to the tiny apartment that Dave had rented in Creekside, and set up basic housekeeping there. Within a few days all three girls were coughing, but then Miriam and Karen recovered, while Constance was getting worse and worse. Finally, she started strangling on thick, shiny gobs of mucous and whooping when she finally coughed it up. She had Whooping Cough! She had been immunized once at 2 months, but not since, because we had not been settled anywhere for me to access public health care. We told my mom, and she did a little bit of research and got back to me all in italics and capitals: "GET THAT BABY TO THE HOSPITAL NOW!" So, I did. Just two weeks after our big venture to "the village" I was on the bus headed back out with a baby who was threatening to quit breathing at least once each hour. We checked in to the Pediatric hospital, where I tried to convince the young doctor that Connie probably had Whooping Cough. He told me very nicely that that was highly unlikely, and put us in an eight bed ward! I waited until the night staff came on and tried to explain to the next doctor that my baby probably had a very contagious disease, and maybe they should check if all the other kids in our room had been immunized. He started to put me off as well, until Constance went into one of her spasms. Then, he got a little excited, and the next thing I knew we were transferred to the Communicable Disease Hospital with the TB and AIDS patients!

After ten days, she was finally better enough for us to go "home" to the rest of our family. I felt so grateful for her life, and so thankful for the kindness we'd been shown that I took a basket of fruit to the nursing station, and asked the Head nurse if there was anyone in the unit that I could help financially. She closed the door, and with tears pouring down her face said, "I'm so sorry. I am just so touched that you would ask that. We often have people who need more help than they can afford, and although we do our best, and sometimes even cover their costs out of our own wages, we can't save all of them. In fact, there are two children on this unit right now who are recovering from Meningitis. They must have several more weeks of treatment if they are going to recover, but they are already in debt to the hospital and will have to be discharged. If you wanted to cover their costs, we would all be so grateful." I extracted the cost of our bus tickets from the money I had, and put the rest down on those patients accounts. I was walking on air as I gathered up my baby and our gear and made my way down the steep, mud road to the bus station.

Just one more thing to do...I went back to the fruit stand where I had purchased the fruit for the nurses and bought a big box of luscious peaches to take back to our family and the Matthews; we never saw any fruit like that out in the countryside! The best our neighbours could produce seemed to be caustically sour pomelos, oranges filled with little spring-loaded, jumping orange worms and lumpy, little watermelons. Those peaches looked like something from the Promised Land to us!

When I was seven months pregnant with our next child, Nathan, we had just moved into our new house in Little Rock. My parents were very concerned at the thought of me trying to deliver a baby "out in the middle of nowhere" and pushed for evacuation out to Thailand or Hong Kong or *somewhere* for the birth. And they didn't even know that he was breech yet! I did, though, so we were praying fervently for direction as I moved towards the deadline of when it would be safe and feasible for me to still travel the gruelling eight hours to the capital and take a plane from there. The thought of uprooting us all from our new home, and the work which was in full swing, to go wait in a city for three months was not appealing. The thought of leaving Dave (who had just recovered from Typhoid, Typhus, what had looked like a heart attack and a severe bout of Giardia already that year) by himself while I took the girls and went to live on my own until the baby was born was even more appalling. Finally I took the bull by the horns and prayed, "Lord, you know all things. You know how this birth is going to go, you know my parents' concerns, and how hard it would be for them to forgive if we didn't take precautions and things went wrong. You also know this baby is breech. If it is your will for us to stay here, carry on, and deliver in a local hospital, then I pray that this baby would turn the right way soon." That night, the baby turned!

With great peace and thankfulness, we settled back into our life "on the ranch" and did what we could to get ready. God showed us great kindness through the faithfulness of our friends, the Nelson's, at that time. Their whole family of seven came from HK out to the village to watch our girls when Dave and I went to the hospital. Several days before they arrived, it seemed that labour was imminent, so we basically greeted them and then got on the bus right away for the county seat, which was about three hours away, and had a small hospital. We were there for *ten days* before Nathan was born, and a few days to recover afterwards as well! He was our biggest baby, and I was so ready to have him by the time labour started! All the joints in my body had loosened to the point that I felt like a marionette when I lay down, and every day the Nelson's would call, hoping for news and offering suggestions on how to hurry things along a little. It was, nevertheless, a sweet time for Dave and I of being freed up from all our other responsibilities. All we did other than eating and napping was walk and talk! We walked miles and miles every day, so I was in fantastic shape by the time my pains started. And labour went so quickly that we basically just had time to walk to the hospital and be admitted before Nathan was born. We couldn't believe he was a boy! I also couldn't believe they expected me to climb down off the delivery table and walk down a lengthy hallway to my room, but I supported my baggy stomach with my arms and made it, while Dave followed with the baby! It was fun to go back to our hotel room that afternoon, baby in arms, and let ourselves back in as if we'd just come back from a morning of shopping.

A Brick Oven

Our first winter in our newly built house in Little Rock, we thought it would be great to have a wood-burning brick oven. We'd seen them in Dali in the pizza joints, and thought that it would be a lovely appropriate technology to have in our own home, especially considering the frequent power outages and lack of central heating! With a new baby arriving just at the start of winter, I really hoped to have a warm place to bathe and change him. There were sufficient bricks left over from building the Matthews' house to do it, so we arranged with a friend who owned a "trucktor" -- a dump truck bed attached to a small cab, with a hoodless engine and drive-belt sticking out the front -- to transport the bricks. He was in bed with TB, so agreed to let A Bo, another young man in the village, drive.

On a sparkling fall day, Dave, with Miriam and Dale, a friend from Christie's home church, set off across the little valley which separated us from the Matthews' and the rest of the village. They cheerfully loaded up the trucktor with enough bricks for the oven, and then casually threw on a few logs which were lying around for fuel once the oven was constructed. The logs were long, so Dave poked them through the back window and along both door frames. "Your seatbelt", he joked with A Bo. Miriam had pleaded to ride in the cab, but Dave was a bit concerned about the jostling logs, so made her get out again.

As the load jounced past the house of the friend who owned the vehicle, Dave thought, "I'm able-bodied and can get more wood whenever I need to; he's laid up with TB," and he pulled several logs off the load to stack by his house, clearing the driver's side window. Further on, he and Miriam were stopping to admire A Bo's brand-new baby when a tremendous "CRASH!!" interrupted them!

They and the rest of the village ran outside to see what had happened, and saw the trucktor upside down in a rice paddy! It had gone off an embankment about four meters tall, and the cab was crushed completely flat! Imagine Dave's relief when he saw A Bo circling the crushed vehicle in a daze! His next thought was, "Thank God Miriam is with me, and not in that cab!" When they asked A Bo how he'd gotten out, he could only remember sort of rolling forward, but he must have dived out his open window (or been plucked out by an angel). Dave was so glad he'd listened to his conscience and removed the logs which would have trapped him in there! He laughed and laughed with relief and said, "Thank God! Thank God!" And our animist neighbours joined in! As for the bricks, we hauled them the rest of the way in back baskets, and the owner of the truck was grateful that we could pay him for the damage.

The only sad part of this story is that we never did get a working oven out of the deal! Dave carefully followed the directions from a "sustainable technology" DVD someone had given us, but that thing would never draw and always filled the house with smoke. Trying four different styles of stove kept us busy and distracted until spring, though! And we did learn something which has stood us in good stead - never promote a technology you haven't personally proven!

The trucktor

Suffer the Little Children

[A letter written from our new home in Little Rock]

A week after the fire behind our house, Miriam ran out the back door to wash some veggies for supper, and then started screaming for Dave. A large green snake was meandering along the cement foundation skirting. There are times that kid's leadership skills and vocal cords come in handy! It took her about three seconds to have Dave arriving on the run and the six or so kids playing in our yard all corralled well away from it. I am SO thankful it was her and not one of the younger children who happened upon it! When Dave went after it with a hoe, it reared up, flared out the red portion of it's neck and hissed. A postmortem examination revealed the poison fangs, and a neighbour said even the meat of that kind is poisonous. Don't know if that's true.
I later learned that it was a red keelback, and very venomous.

We had a terrific thunderstorm last night, with hail and loads of rain. Thankfully the hail did not last long enough to pummel people's painfully nurtured beans into the ground just before they were ready to sell the first picking. We had hail falling on our bed, though, because for some reason although the rain sheds properly, the hail fell straight through. Strange to be moving our bed to a less leaky spot in the middle of the night and have ice stuck to the bottom of my socks!! Finally, the end of the drought, and hopefully of the "water wars" between neighbours trying to submerge their rice fields. The two kilometer long water line which Dave pretty much single-handedly put in all the way from the spring to our side of the village has been chopped up numerous times. Farmers whose land it crosses keep digging it up and cutting it so the water will run over their crop land. We would be fine with them doing that at night when people aren't using it, if they would make some effort to keep the downstream end out of the muck. As it is, it's completely contaminated and plugged up when Dave goes to reattach it, which is probably why we have diarrhea. And of course, it means we have no water a lot of days.

Today at least 16 kids who come down to school from the high villages showed up at noon, asking our kids to give them this and that and hopeful for an invite for lunch. Of course it was muddy, and so were their feet. Since it was still drizzling, we let them come in. What would you do? There was absolutely no way I could feed them all, and the din and chaos while I was trying to feed the baby and get lunch on the table -- well, you can imagine! Miriam was gone on an errand for Dave, but Constance fled outside, and Karen took refuge on the stairs. Nathan got trundled back and forth in his little chair by six kids at a time. Actually, that was quite cute, and he loved it. Of course, I had to wash his chair afterwards because they blow their noses with their fingers and don't wash their hands, and he chews on it when he's bored. I really want to make the most of this opportunity to receive the little children and bless them, and yet hate how I actually feel inside about how they're impacting my family.

Next day:
I just wanted to let you know that His grace is sufficient. I had a good time with the crowd of kids today, and it's because I had a long talk with God about it last night. Told Him exactly how I felt, and how I wished I was, and that He would have to make up the difference.
I had just mopped the floor when they arrived today, and Miriam was up on the site with her dad, so I told them they couldn't come in while the floor was wet and Miriam was gone. Then I brought a basin of water, soap and a towel for them to wash their hands before I brought out

the leftover breakfast, which I always double in preparation for their visits now. They did a great job of washing their hands and proudly showed me. I asked them if they knew how to say "thank you" in Chinese. They said yes. I said I didn't believe them, 'cause I served them food every day and had never heard them say it. They quickly remedied that! Then I brought out a colouring book and some felts, and helped them choose a picture and a colour. I think it was a first for them. They were afraid that if they shared their pen with someone else, they wouldn't get it back, so they were all colouring with just one colour. I encouraged them to share, and eventually little groups of two and three started cooperating with colours. They also returned everything when they were done, which I hadn't really expected. Miriam was home by then, so she handed them the felts back as a gift. She is so good with situations like that. She directs big groups of kids with no intimidation and lots of common sense. While we had our lunch, they voluntarily used the time to water our garden. Wasn't that sweet of them?

Some time later:

My knees are all green from falling on some rocks while chasing some goats out of our garden. They were in the process of finishing off what the neighbours cows had left from the day before. They ate all the beans from the seeds you sent us. Grrr! I did rescue one good meal of them off the ground. Also they ate the cauliflower and broccoli, the peas and cabbage -- basically everything we were on the verge of being able to eat for ourselves. So, we will be dependent on market days and the goodness of our neighbours for awhile yet. They are being good to us, though. We have four big sweet pumpkins as well as sacks of sweet potatoes, little green melons and bok choy.

I got back from chasing the goats off and trying to rescue the garden, all winded and muddy and bruised, and all Dave, who was sick in bed, had to say about it was, "Do you think anyone saw you chasing them?" I looked down. I was dressed in pink long johns and my rubber boots!! It could have been worse. I at least took the time to change out of my fuzzy green slippers!

Did we ever tell you that Dave had to bury a baby a few weeks back? Our helper came in one day and mentioned that there was a baby's corpse near the road. She was so afraid to walk past it in the dark, early mornings that she'd started to take the bus to our house. Since we're the only ones not afraid of ghosts around here, it became apparent that if it was ever going to be buried, it would be up to us. Dave knows "us" in these kind of situations means him, and he's gallant enough to spare me these kinds of things. What we were told was that the parents had taken the baby to the doctor, but that they couldn't save it. For some reason they abandoned it either dead or dying on the way home.

Leaving

Part way through our first year in Little Rock, the Matthews had to leave for awhile. They asked Gonggong to sleep at their house as a night watchman. When I met him on the path a few weeks later he casually asked me if I had ever seen a ghost. He said that the Matthews' house was haunted, but that he'd had a lot of experience with ghosts over his long life, and wasn't really afraid of them anymore. I told him that I was a Christian and had no need to fear ghosts. When the Matthews came back however, they were somewhat unnerved to find that their house was indeed "haunted": footsteps at night made by invisible feet, things moved around by invisible hands, the kids screaming with nightmares night after night. So, once again we gathered in prayer and asked the Lord to do a spiritual house cleaning. That was the end of the problem, but it directly contributed to our decision not to ask anyone to stay in our house when, after two years in Little Rock, we went home to Canada for four months.

In the weeks leading up to our departure, we heard disturbing rumours that some rough characters in town were boasting that they were going to come at night and rob us. Our neighbours were really worried about it, and wanted us to get a big dog, or some weapons. Their fear was kind of contagious, and we were quite isolated up there. Our nearest neighbour was an old opium addict -- not much help or protection. One night, when Dave was on a trip, my stomach was literally in knots, so I decided to take the issue to the Lord. Should we be buying a big dog, reinforcing the doors, preparing to protect ourselves? I honestly couldn't think of anywhere in the Bible where this issue was addressed, and asked God to show me as I opened His word. The Bible fell open to, *"Run, tell that young man, 'Jerusalem will be a city without walls because of the great number of men and livestock in it. And I myself will be a wall of fire around it,' declares the Lord,' and I will be its glory within.'* My eyes crossed the page and read, *"This is the curse that is going out over the whole land; for according to what it says on one side, every thief will be banished ...The Lord Almighty declares, 'I will send it out, and it will enter the house of the thief ... It will remain in his house and destroy it, both its timbers and its stones.'"* (Zechariah 5:3)

So, we did not get the big dog, and when we went to Canada, we just closed the house like we were leaving for the day, with a prayer that God would give His angels charge over it as a witness to our neighbours, who all thought we were crazy. Stealing was such a part of their culture that they could never leave their home empty. Even if the family was invited to a wedding or funeral, one person stayed home to guard everything, from the livestock to the dishes or the strip of meat hanging over the fire. Otherwise, they would return home to find themselves cleaned out. I had been so blessed by those verses, however, that I almost felt like inscribing them on a rock as a warning to anyone who would be foolish enough to try to rob us! When we returned, we listened in satisfaction as our neighbours told us, "We just don't understand it! No one went near your house! They were all scared of it for some reason..." Seriously, the only loss we suffered was from rats. The rats had really made themselves at home in the kids' clothes drawers!! And, a few months later we were forced to leave Little Rock for good. That was a loss, definitely a loss...

We had a vision for the Buyi. They were so hospitable. Work teams for the electric company or road crews did not need to worry about where to lay their heads while they were in Buyi country. The locals would welcome them in and share meals with them free of charge, even for several months! At the agricultural training center in the Philippines, farmers had to live in little huts on the compound with their family while they studied. We thought, "When farmers from other areas come to study agro-forestry here, they can live in our neighbours' homes. If some of our neighbours come to trust in Christ, not only could they show hospitality, but could share the love of God around the cooking fire." It was hard to see that vision die.

So, why did we have to leave? We could certainly blame circumstances: a friend of the Matthews came to visit them, and was aggressively evangelistic, and confrontational towards the officials. They were denied visas shortly afterwards, and had to leave. The family who sold us the land to build our house was regularly complaining to the officials that our demonstration site was no good; if they tried to plant that way they would starve to death. Meanwhile, they were telling the other villagers, "If the foreigners ever have to leave, and you buy their house, we'll come every night to curse you." Clearly they were hoping for a free house out of the deal. There had been a pseudo-Christian cult in the area a few years before, causing locals to view our faith with suspicion. To top it all off, the Falun Gong explosion happened at that time, so anything religious -- and we were openly Christian -- was potentially dangerous.

But, circumstances aside, I think there was one more factor to our having to leave, and that was that we allowed ourselves to get too focused on outward success, on vindicating ourselves as bona fide agricultural extensionists to the local officials. Ever since the Matthews had to leave, we had felt ourselves "under the gun" and having to prove ourselves in order to stay. Family devotions slid under the pressure of getting out to the fields to do the work of three men before it got too hot, and of trying to keep up with garden, housework, and four young children. (Nathan was born while we were there and was a colicky newborn). Those were our excuses. You just can't do that if you're trying to establish a spiritual beach head. You have to keep spiritual warfare a priority, and we did not. We had little to nothing in the way of fellowship with other believers, and should have been aggressive about praise, worship and intercession.

Dave had worked like a Trojan on that SALT (Sloping Agricultural Land Technology) demonstration site - it was clean of weeds, covered in neat hedgerows of various leguminous trees and interspersed with thriving young fruit trees and soil-enriching ground cover. In the arid winter months, it was the only green spot in the whole landscape. That postage stamp of verdant life across the valley was the last thing we saw as our bus laboured around the last switchback, leaving. Our neighbours were tough, stoic. They'd tell you that their child had died, and then laugh to show it didn't signify. But they gathered at the bus and wept as we left. We asked God to remember their tears, and to send them a continuous stream of witnesses in our stead.

One of the things that struck me, reading through letters I wrote back then, was how *nice* God was to us. Although we experienced anguish while "in limbo" afterwards, I am really encouraged and touched to see how I did not experience our time in Little Rock, or getting kicked out, as *hard* at the time! I had kind of forgotten that. I truly had supernatural joy and peace and companionship throughout that time:

"It's been an interesting time! I believe we've hit new levels of lessons in patience. Maybe 301 instead of 101. Lots of times where I could just hear Mom saying, 'Oh, good grief!!' Ridiculous things. Disheartening things. And yet, here I am in the middle of it all, and so very happy. I am THANKFUL for this time. I am so thankful that the comfort and presence which I started out petulantly demanding, "At the very least, I thought we'd have some sort of special GRACE considering all You're letting happen," has really been given. This time has been good for us. I think both Dave and I are walking closer, and I am receiving constant affirmation, like an inward hug every time I turn my eyes up. "I'm here. I hear you. I see you. I'm with you. I'm for you. I'm for these people. All is not in vain". Something like that. I feel very surrounded and very safe, even at night, with Dave gone. My heart is at rest, and though I miss Dave, I am not at all lonely. I have been reading Luke, and so many of Jesus' instructions with how to deal with the opposition of people are so very straightforward and applicable. It boils down to where your treasure is and what you're trying to protect. It boils down to believing that things asked for in secret are in the process of coming to pass, though as yet unseen. And that we are playing our part, with repercussions in high place, though how it all works together is obscure to us. Well, I just noticed that there's a poopy diaper waiting to be rinsed out, and a pile of muddy sweet potatoes to scrub in time to be put in the oven for supper, and two beds waiting for sheets which are probably dry and needing to be brought in before dark, so..."

"It would seem that embracing or accepting the situation we find ourselves in, with it's duties, challenges and joys liberates a great deal of energy which would otherwise be occupied with "if only's". We can make an offering of the things we wish we could do, and entrust those good desires to the One who knows of what we're made, and orders our days. It encourages me to know that there are seasons in our life, and things which I would love to do now, and simply can't -- due to being a busy mom -- that I may well be able to do later, with the added benefit of the seasoning and maturity which will happen in these intervening child-rearing years. I need to be first of all a tree planted by streams of water which continues to bear fruit in drought time. Ministry comes to people who are like that, because there are precious few with that deep calm and strength and integrity. When Dave gets home one of these days (we don't have a phone), I'll find out whether or not he's found somewhere for us to move to. The people in charge here are just itching for us to go, and our visa runs out in 16 days. We are welcome in other provinces, but the place he is now is the last shot at this province. However, the romance of this life is that He has never yet failed to come through, albeit usually at the last minute. We are learning, definitely, to wait on Him, and are completely leery of any solutions which smack of man's effort or contrivance. As the years pile up and there is nothing to show for this style of following, I sometimes wonder if we're mistaken to go at things this way, instead of by 'leaning on our own understanding' and picking a place and work which seems best suited to our strength and temperaments. But then I remember Moses, herding sheep until he was 80 years old, John in the desert, and Jesus in the carpenter's shop until he was 30 and I still believe that it's the hidden things that count, and the waiting times which prepare us for what comes next. To all appearances our work over the last two years has been completely wasted and what we hoped might remain is being systematically destroyed. It seems we've been completely vanquished, and then I remember good Friday. Are deeper purposes still being served by all this? We still believe so. Psalm 84 has become my petition, and John 15 my aim."

Abiding

{telephone static} "Wei, Hello..."
August, 2002
"We're wanting to expand the work of Project Grace into your province in China, and as our Board has been praying about it, your names keep coming up. Would you be interested in heading something up?"
Dave's thinking: {Seriously??!! We're on our own trying to do this huge agro-forestry demonstration site at the moment, still working hard at learning the Buyi language, and just had our 4th child!}
"Umm, we're a little busy at the moment -- not looking for new projects to start -- but we'll pray about it"

"Christie, I just had an interesting phone conversation with Project Grace. They're wanting us to work with them. How can people feel led to ask us to work with them when our plate is already so full?"

weeks later
"Hi Dave, it's Ed. I hope you're sitting down."
"Why, what's up?"
"They're not renewing our visas. The local government is canceling the project."
"What?! They can't do that! We have a seven year contract, and it's only been two years!"
"They say the project is not successful."
"What do you think? Is that the real reason they're shutting us down?"
"Probably not. I'm guessing it's because we're Christians. We already know some of the officials have a problem with that."
"Well, we could challenge their verdict on our project. That way we'll know if it's the real reason. If it's not, they'll come up with some other excuse to get rid of us."

September, 2002

As we prepared to return to China from Canada, we knew we were in for a battle. "Let Your will be done on earth as it is in Heaven, and let Your will be for us to stay at our home in Little Rock," was the gist of our prayers. The officials assured us that they would accept the recommendation of an agricultural expert if we could get someone to assess our project.   A professor in the Chinese Academy of Sciences, who was a highly respected expert in the type of agro-forestry Dave was demonstrating on our site, was very sorry to hear about the difficulties we were up against, and agreed to inspect the site and send in an official report.   In it, he unequivocally stated to the authorities who were trying to oust us that this was the best demonstration of SALT that he had ever seen in any of the countries he had worked in and visited.

In spite of all our pleas, our visas were not renewed, and we had to leave it all behind: the beautiful home we'd built, the agricultural site Dave had toiled to build up, our village friends, and the other "foreign" friendships we had built up over almost a decade of work in that province. We were very truly heartbroken and completely crushed. Most nights, the tears would run into my ears as I prayed about it all. We begged God for another chance. We begged Him not to "bench" us indefinitely. We told Him that if He ever gave us another chance at ministry, we would know it was because of His unlimited mercy and grace towards us. We took away some valuable lessons, though:

(1) Abide in the Lord. Nothing can be allowed to take priority over that. Be a worshipper of Jesus Christ, and do our work as unto Him.
(2) Take time to enjoy one another, as a couple, and a family. Take breaks.

(3) Faithfully teach and train the children. Bring them on board with what we're doing.

(4) Ask in prayer for the housing situation Father wants to give, and accept whatever is offered by the locals. Live as close as we can to their standard of living.

(5) Present the technology or the project in such a way that farmers immediately see and own the benefits. Train the farmers to do the SALT technology on their own land, rather than on a demonstration site.

(6) Have a little plot of land near our house, easily managed by just ourselves, for experimental purposes.

(7) Settle somewhere that the farmers are already intensively using their sloping lands and will value them enough to keep the animals off, and to put in the work that's necessary to establish the hedgerows. Once the hedgerows are established, their work will actually be decreased because the mulch suppresses the weeds and fertilizes the ground for them.

(8) Introduce the animal feed potential of the trees at the beginning and plant those species which grow fast, to compete well with weeds and produce results by the end of the first year.

(9) Be sure to submit progress reports to the local authorities regularly.

(10) Avoid becoming a "big boss" or someone who dispenses favours.

(11) Avoid giving loans.

(12) When we run into difficulties, find solutions which our neighbours could emulate.

January, 2003
  I had just discovered that I was pregnant with our fifth child, while we were in total limbo, house-sitting in an apartment in Kunming, and had no idea what we were going to be doing or where we would be going. Exile. To top it all off, my face had broken out in a painful and

disfiguring rash, and the medication I was on to cure it could not be taken during pregnancy.

I cried through every church service, too. We met in the top room of the old, concrete four storey "Three Self" Church. The other three floors and all the stair wells were full of our Chinese brethren as they met to worship. Upstairs, God met with me very specifically two times.

The first time, He said, "You're kneeling in the ashes." My heart acknowledged that that was very true. Every word He speaks is just so true. He doesn't mince words, or waste them.

The second time He said, "Can I abide with you?" I nearly burst into ironical laughter right there in the middle of the service! "With me, Lord? With *me*? I hardly even know where *I'm* living!" I had been begging Him to help me abide with *Him*! I felt like such a ragamuffin, such a refugee, such a mess; hardly hostess material! Finally, hot tears flowed as the incredible condescension of the Lord sank in. Of course I knew that He had come into my heart when I was a small child and had asked Him to forgive me and come into my life, and He had been with us in unmistakable ways ever since. In a sense I suppose I could have wondered why He was asking me that. But it just touched me at the core of my being. I wasn't purposely shutting Him out, but I had just been consumed by such a sense of unworthiness, such a feeling of having been reproached and cast away. That all went away as I finally just responded to His invitation, and slid onto His lap. A few days later I realized the rash on my face had healed spontaneously, and it never came back. God is just so kind.

And the invitation to work with Project Grace was also a timely reminder from Him that He was in control of our situation, even as we sat in the ruins. Now it made sense. We had no idea that our work in Little Rock was coming to an end, but He did, and wanted us to know that He was already preparing a new assignment. The day before Ed phoned, during my quiet time, I was suddenly strongly impressed that Isaiah 54:13, "*All your sons will be taught by the Lord, and great will be your children's peace.*" was for us. I was grateful, but as we were faced with the task of telling our children, "Um kids? You know how we promised that we were only leaving our home in China, and Patches and Stripey for a few months? Well, we're not actually allowed to live there any more." those words of promise took on incredible significance. I still cling to them today.

We have another reminder, hanging up in our bedroom, that God was not silent at that time. On January 2, our wedding anniversary, we went to eat at a nice hotel called the Sakura. On the second floor they have a western buffet, central heating, and inviting, cozy decor. It was coming in out of the cold in many ways! When we got off the elevator, we were pleasantly surprised to see that an artist had an exhibit on that floor as well, and strolled around looking at the pictures. One picture just outside the restaurant entrance stopped both of us in our tracks. It was a beautifully executed painting of a little minority child in brightly embroidered traditional dress, crawling up over the door lintel of a rough village home. A quartet of chicks cheered the baby on. It made us so homesick! It could have been any of our neighbours' homes in Little Rock. The price tag, however, was 1500 yuan, which certainly put it out of our league. Nevertheless, it had touched us both, so as we sat down to eat and celebrate ten years together, we bowed our heads in prayer, and just asked the Lord if He wanted to give us that picture. We agreed on an amount that would be affordable to us, and asked that they would be willing to sell it for that. After we finished our special meal, we went back out into the hall. There was a sweet-faced young Chinese woman sitting there now, so we went over and told her a bit of our story, and how that one picture had touched us. We also told her that, regretfully, we could not afford it because we had four children and no fixed income. She said, "Mei guanxi [it doesn't matter], just tell me how much you could afford to pay for it, and I will ask my sister what she thinks. Really, it is more important to her that her work goes to people who appreciate it. She has even given her pictures away at times." So, we told her the amount we had in mind, and then went out to let her phone her sister in private. When we came back in, she smilingly told us that we could have it for our price. When she took it down to wrap it, we saw that the picture had a name. In pencil on the back was the title, "Jia" [Home]. {front cover photo}

Home, part 3

After having to leave Little Rock, we arrived in Kunming, the capital of Yunnan province, just in time to attend a conference put on by Project Grace, who had invited us to work with them. We went to the conference feeling so alone, so pushed to the fringes of things. Our desperate prayer was that God would help us to meet the people He wanted us to be involved with, and help us discern what the next step would be. We were in a lovely hotel, surrounded by a multitude of wonderful families, with several interesting seminars being offered each day, and both Dave and Nathan came down with fevers, vomiting and diarrhea. They were so sick that I basically couldn't leave them. Why, oh, why were we having to miss it all? I mean, the hotel was a nice place to be sick and all, and for once there were lots of physicians around to consult with, but that wasn't why we were there! Little did I know that God was helping us narrow things down a whole lot.

The organization put us in touch with people who could help us find what we needed in Kunming, like a place to stay after the conference, and maybe some cheese. Cheese may seem like a funny priority, but we hadn't had any for months. The person who took pity on us and went way out of her way to help us was May Liu. She noticed the hand washed laundry draped over the lamps and every other available surface and took the rest of our dirty clothes home with her, showed us where to do our shopping and just encouraged us with her energetic, cheerful presence. We were blown away to find out that not only was she Canadian, she had grown up not 10 miles from Dave's parents' farm, and Dave's dad had been her school vice principal! Even on our first day together, we decided that we would love to work together with the Lius. They shared our vision of doing community development work somewhere in the countryside. Shortly after that, they found out that a place was available in their neighbourhood which we and "Uncle Ed" could rent if we wanted. It was perfect for our needs, and just around the corner from their family. This was our home base for the next six months, actually. We had hoped it would be much shorter -- Dave, Ed and Ming Liu all felt God had prepared for us to move to Riverbend county, in the Salween river valley (Lisuland), but then SARS[8] hit, and Riverbend was quarantined for their own protection for several months until the epidemic was under control.

So there we were stuck in the city with our quaint, hand-made countryside furniture, our countryside kitten, and our countryside puppy. The animals were parting gifts from dear Buyi friends, and we had four kids who knew how to plead their case! By the time we actually pulled out for Riverbend, I was seven months pregnant and did not care that I was turning my back on "civilization" and decent hospitals! We had had it with concrete, with trees the kids were not allowed to climb and "lawn" which they were not allowed to walk on, parks which were closed to the public and squads going around beating to death any dogs which were found outdoors (one way the city government tried to prove that they were on top of the SARS prevention situation). And we could not convince our puppy, Patches, to defecate indoors. She simply wouldn't do it. Being very intelligent, she also virtually stopped eating and drinking as well so as to decrease the need to go. The situation was ludicrous. No prisoners planning a break kept closer tabs on their guards than we did on the security guards of our complex! We'd watch out our windows until they went around the corner on their beat, then rush downstairs with the dog and skulk in the bushes, admonishing her to "hurry!" and do her business so we could flee back

---

8   Severe Acute Respiratory Syndrome

upstairs! One day, the dog got away from Karen, and went romping through the compound and frisking past the gate guard. Thankfully it was the one guard with a sense of humour; he laughed and turned his back while she and the rest of the kids frantically corralled our errant puppy!

One sweltering morning when I was about six months pregnant, I looked out of our high rise window, and saw a patch of green. Far in the distance, through all the concrete buildings, there were the tops of trees. Desire to just take the kids *somewhere* green and natural, to soak in the peace of a park or garden and let them run free gripped me with sudden, painful intensity. We were so homesick for the country! With a sob, I prayed "Lord, please just help us to find those trees. And I pray that we'd be able to actually go in to whatever that is." I quickly packed a picnic lunch, got the kids shoes on and started herding them in the direction of the trees. An hour or so later, we were all sitting on the curb, baking in the heat and thinking maybe we'd have to eat our lunch right there to the accompaniment of air compressors and metal being hammered. Joy. We had walked miles of concrete sidewalk past stinky gutters, auto-body and tire shops, and as far as we could see was more of the same. Once again I lifted up a plea for help in getting to our oasis. A woman walked past, and I had a sudden compulsion to follow her. She turned off the main road uphill on a dirt road lined on both sides with tufts of tall weeds. The sun blazed down. Finally I caught up to her and diffidently asked if she knew where there was a place with some trees anywhere near. She said "Yes! Just up ahead at the power station." After a few more minutes, we could see a veritable forest at the crown of the hill. What a find that place was! What a bountiful gift from a loving Heavenly Father!   The power station was organized in the old commune manner with comfortably ivy-overgrown brick apartments and courtyards full of gardens. Little concrete tables and stools which looked as if they might have just been vacated by dwarves or elves nestled under towering evergreens . The manager of the power plant turned out to be a hobby botanist who had turned all the barren land around into a miniature paradise. A clear stream with bridges meandered down the middle of a small valley, while all the plants and trees had been carefully selected and were labelled with their Latin names! There was also a huge greenhouse where I was able to purchase an Aloe Vera plant -- another thing I'd been trying to find for it's medicinal properties before we moved out to a village.

The actual move was mercifully easy. Dutch friends with 12 children and a 15 passenger van put us, the animals and the luggage we would need immediately into their vehicle and drove us out. It only took 14 hours instead of the usual 18 on the bus, and we didn't have to argue with the driver about where to put the dog and cat. Our first view of the Salween canyon was awe-inspiring. It was June, and the water of the Salween river was at a record high, licking away the road in places and tossing white spumes of water 15 feet in the air wherever there were rapids.

The road twisted along the canyon bottom, following the river through shadows cast by the precipitous walls, and past terraced deltas, sun-drenched only at high noon, or where there was a rift in the surrounding peaks. As we drove north, plantain bananas and sugar cane gradually gave way to native vegetation checkered with small corn "fields" clinging to the near vertical slopes. The patchwork of fields looked more like a black diamond ski run to us, and extended right to the top ridges of the nearest mountains. We tried to imagine having to climb up there to work the land, then realized that the villages were actually above the fields, and that the villagers came *down* to work their land -- unbelievable! Down by the road, life was dominated by the roar of the river and had a moist, temperate climate. Life at higher elevations was very different. I'll never forget the first time we climbed high enough that the river receded to a narrow azure ribbon, and then disappeared. All of a sudden the only sound was the piping of birds, and there was nothing to block the sunshine. It was so peaceful -- a world apart. We could see why the mountain Lisu loved the life up there in spite of the hardships and deprivations and colder winters.

There were two possible housing options which Dave had come up with on his first trip in. One was on the road side of the river, and the other was across the turbulent river over a long, rail-less, plank suspension bridge. As I heaved my pregnant self out of the van and took two of the four pairs of hands which would need to be held, the decision seemed pretty simple. We lived for a year in a little three room cinder block house next to the basketball court in that town of Bridgeford, which was about half-an-hour from the town of Riverbend, the county seat. In some ways it worked well; there was a small market near by and the kids could play away from traffic. In some ways it proved to be very difficult. Every one of our rooms had a window, and every day curious noses would be pressed up against them, watching our every move. We also had to come out of our house to get from the kitchen to the bedrooms, used the disgustingly dirty public pit toilet and had no bathing facilities. Basketball tournaments were a big part of village life there, and were fueled on Coca-Cola.[9] The later it got, the louder and more cantankerous it got. By 3 am it would seem half the shots were ricocheting off our flimsy roof! More sinister was the discovery that two of our near neighbours were burnt-out alcoholics and pedophiles. Our nerves were strained to breaking from the lack of privacy, and not being able to let the kids out of our sight.

---

9   The losing team would buy everyone a round of pop, then they'd start another game. After 5 hours of this, everyone would be pretty wired.

When our neighbour started building a three-storey house just ten feet in front of ours, completely blocking our sunlight and our view, it was the last straw. We began to pray earnestly that God would provide us with another place to live. At this time, we *really* had to take to heart the commandment not to covet our neighbour's house! Every trip to town, I was ogling houses, hoping that maybe this one or that one would be available to rent! It was important to us that any rental agreement we got into would be mutually beneficial. In other words, we did not want to rent any house which already had a local family living in it. Many people were willing to move out of their new house back into their ramshackle old one in order to obtain the rent money, but we were not comfortable with that. We were also really hoping that our new neighbours would turn out to be good ones. Villages in the countryside are made up of clans - sons grow up and marry and bring their wives to live in their village. Different clans have different character. We trusted that God would provide a new home, as He always had, but we had to be patient. He still had a few things for us to do before we moved from Bridgeford...

Along the Salween river

Angela

One morning after breakfast, the kids came running in and said, "Mom, there's a crazy lady out there!" They were right, there was. She was young -- maybe in her early twenties -- and quite pretty, except for her matted hair and filthy face and clothes. She was perched on a couple of cinder blocks, watching the children with evident interest, interspersed with loud, perturbed streams of gibberish aimed at an invisible audience. What might she do? Was it safe to let the kids play out there? Our house was truly tiny, however, so I decided to let them play in the yard while I kept a close eye on the situation.

That evening, she wandered off , and I heaved a sigh of relief. Next morning, however, she reappeared! I started to feel convicted about her needs, so I took a bowl of food and some chopsticks out to her. She thanked me, ate it up, and brought the dishes back when she was done. A neighbour lady watched this disapprovingly, and told me in no uncertain terms, "Don't feed her and she'll go away. If you keep giving her food, she's going to start living in your yard." I thought, "You're probably right. If you don't want a cat, don't start feeding a stray." But that was immediately followed by the thought, "Do not forget to entertain strangers, for by so doing some people have entertained angels without knowing it." I decided we would keep feeding her, and we started referring to her as "Angela" between ourselves. Day after day, Angela hung out in our yard, unless there was something going on at the church -- then she would rush up and sing along with the best of them. Where was this girl from? We started praying for her, and that we could restore her to her family.

We did not have a bathroom in our house there, so I washed the kids in a plastic baby bath in the yard on sunny days and we all washed our hair under the hose which Dave had stretched down from a pool in the creek above the village. One day we saw Angela dousing her hair under the hose, and obviously trying to clean up a bit. I decided to try to help her, and tentatively brought out the shampoo and the de-lousing solution. She let me help, and it was both a satisfying and revolting job! The lice were dying by the hundreds or thousands, and I had to keep flicking the bodies off my hands as I tried to work the lather into the matted clumps of hair. I also collected a bit of an audience, as it seemed every passer by had nothing better to do than watch the crazy foreigner washing the crazy woman! When we were done, I gave her a comb and saw with satisfaction that she remembered how to use it, and she didn't stop until she had a neat braid.

That evening, the village official knocked on the door. Apprehensively, I opened it for him. He was civil to us in public, during the day, but it seemed he only came to see us at night when he'd had too much to drink and could no longer repress his feelings of hatred and antagonism towards all foreigners. Every time he'd come to our house, he'd been very rude and hostile. This time, however, it was to ask me what on earth had possessed me to help a crazy woman get rid of her lice. I told him it was because God wants to show His love through our lives. He shook his head and said, "I didn't think people like you existed." And that was the end of any hatefulness from that quarter!

The longer Angela lived near us, the calmer and more responsive she became. She frequently smiled at us now, and sometimes answered our questions. She couldn't tell us where she was from, though, and Dave had asked everyone he could think of if they knew where she lived. No one seemed to have a clue. Finally, he ran into a man at a nearby market ....

"This girl you describe would be about 19 years old? And she's always turning to look beside her at someone who's not there, and tell them a bunch of unintelligible nonsense?"

"Exactly!"

"She's from our village, across from Sandbanks, then 5 hours hike up the mountain. I'll tell her father when I go home tonight."

Sandbanks?? That's 4 hours walk down the road. And then another 5 hours? How on earth did she find her way to our house?

Sure enough, though, the next day, a thin, middle-aged man with tattered clothes showed up with his teen-aged son. The boy had the same aquiline features as Angela, so I knew they must be her family. They were so grateful to have found her, and as they rested in our yard and took some refreshments, our house helper translated their story for us. In the past couple of years, they had been stalked by tragedy. His oldest son died from a fall off a mountain path. His wife died from what sounded like TB, leaving him to care for 5 children. Then his oldest daughter[10], Angela, fell off the back of a truck and hit her head, leaving her crazy and prone to wander. Then their house burned down with everything in it, and finally his own health had become so poor that he couldn't work their fields, and they could only harvest the amount that his next three oldest children could plant. Salt in the wounds was his neighbours' attitude toward his Job-like experience. He said that when others were in difficulty, he had done what he could to help them, but lately the church had become very divided and isolationist, and nobody had reached out to help them in their time of need. He told his neighbours, "Don't worry, God will take care of us somehow. It doesn't matter that you aren't helping us, I know He hears my prayers." We

---

10   She was actually "ANi", the 2nd daughter. "ANa", the first, had died young.

were quite touched that he counted the little we'd done as an answer to his prayers. I wondered what else we had that I could give them, and thought of a warm, colorful wool throw which I had purchased because it looked so cozy. I hoped that the bold colors would infuse hope and courage even as the blanket kept them warm. Before they left, he pressed Dave to come visit them soon, and Dave promised to do so.

A couple of weeks later, Angela's dad came to lead Dave up the arduous trail to his village. Dave's legs were shaking with fatigue by the time he made it home that night, and he was pretty impacted by the degree of need he'd seen. "They're sleeping on the dirt floor, Christie: no beds or furniture. They've eaten nothing but corn with a little salt for months now, and are almost out of that. None of the families have enough to eat, but Angela's family are the most pathetic. It's actually the poorest village I've ever seen. What has compounded the situation is that because the village has accepted cult teaching, they will have nothing to do with other congregations, refuse aid from the government, will not take medicine, and who knows what else! Also, Angela's dad was coughing so hard on the way up, and had to keep stopping to rest. I think he's got TB."

"Well, do you think he'd come down to do a chest x-ray? If he would, and has TB, maybe we could help him with treatment. If he could get his health and strength back, he could start providing for his family again."

"Yeah, that would be the main thing."

"How can we get hold of him? Will you have to hike all the way up there again?"

"I think so. He doesn't have a cell phone. I doubt anyone in their village does. In fact their village doesn't even have a name. It's so high up there that people just call it A Ga [Up There]"

X-rays and sputum tests showed that Angela's dad did have TB, so the next step was to find someone who could observe his treatment up there, to ensure that he took the full course. He had to do this or risk spreading antibiotic resistant TB which could wipe out most of his village. There is another village, Dorfli, about a third of the way up, with a saintly 66 year old pastor and considerably more hope and cooperation. It was the most recent village to be included in a Nubian goat project, and Dave had been there to help them plant nutritious fodder sources. So he arranged a date with the pastor from Dorfli and our friend, APu, the goat project manager, to go with him to Angela's village. That morning Dave got up early, with a raging head cold and trudged up the mountain in the rain, claiming Isaiah 40:31 (*"Those who hope in the Lord will renew their strength... they will walk and not be faint"*). In his back pack he had the TB medication for Angela's father, and some protein-rich food, which he had to get to them before he went off on a trip to the Philippines at the end of the week. He came home in the evening, exhausted but rejoicing because of what he saw happen. His companions were full of joy as they came down from the village and told him that this was the first time the people there had opened up and been willing to receive them and listen to them. Angela's uncle, who had cut off relationships with her family because they had begun associating with the people of Dorfli, was there with his whole family, as was her grandfather and many other neighbours. There was a lot of good humour exchanged, they all prayed together, and the pastor's exhortation to love and help one another was received thoughtfully, brokenly. A number of people in the community have committed to make sure the father keeps on with his medication. The pastor has also committed to go up two or three times a week and check on him. He's actually thrilled at this chance to re-establish contact with someone from this "splinter-group" congregation. He also agreed to help bring up eggs, beans, oil, and whatever else we could get to him to improve the family's nutrition.

So, Angela's dad was the first of many TB patients. A couple of years later, our team was joined by a Singaporean psychotherapist named FangFang. Her first thought was to help counsel orphans who were showing signs of post-traumatic stress disorder, depression and so on. However, when we introduced her to Angela, she became her first psychotic patient and the beginning of her village based Mental Health Care project. Since Dave had begun working for the goat project by then, it was also possible to help Angela's village through that. Angela's brother, ADe, received the little buck which was to service the area's does. He took great care of it, and it soon grew into an enormous billy which he trained as a pack goat! It carried fire wood and other heavy burdens for his father or the old widows in the community. ADe was also a good learner. Of all the people who participated in Dave's training on how to do Sloping Agricultural Land Technology (SALT) planting, Angela's brother was the best at following directions. Dave was so proud of him, and the great results he got!

Isn't it interesting that all this much-needed help came to Angela's family as a direct result of her wandering to, and camping out in, our yard? God actually used her mental illness -- a situation which no good could conceivably come out of -- to fulfill her dad's hope that, "God will take care of us somehow."

It looked like their family was finally over the hump, but then Angela's dad came down with TB again and spent many months huddled in bed. However, by this time, Angela was on medication, much clearer and able to help, her younger sister had married a fine young man from their village, ADe had grown into a strong young man who could do the field work, and little ADu was old enough to do the housekeeping. When Angela's father recovered from his second round of illness, he was feeling well enough, grateful and rich enough (they still lived in the same bamboo hut with no furniture, but now had more than enough to eat) to take in two little orphans who had no one to take care of them! And so life and love go on.

Bridgeford

One night, my new house-helper and her family came over to share a video of the Easter celebration that we had all attended up the mountain from our little house in Bridgeford. It reminded me that April had been a month full of adventure and bonding. First, a lady we had sent to the Provincial capital for medical treatment asked me to come help with the birth of her first grandchild. As I prepared to do that, another neighbour came over almost pleading with us to go up the mountain to attend her sister's wedding. Dave had already committed to climb up to another village with an American businessman...Good grief, nothing happens for weeks and then all this before 8 am! What to do? We left Jessica and Nathan with the helper, Dave took the three older girls up to the wedding, having begged off his other engagement, and I went to see about the baby.

The young mother had been in labour most of the night and was now in such pain they thought the birth must be imminent. Unfortunately, no. The baby was lying diagonally and the head hadn't even engaged yet. Countryside babies are almost always birthed at home, and in most Asian cultures, male physicians (and husbands) are not allowed to attend. Our local village doctor assured me that he was never allowed in. I comforted myself with the thought that my being there couldn't help but be better than nothing and tried not to worry about having no back-up. Well, no medical back up. That little hut was surrounded with the prayers of Patriarchs and Matriarchs, grandparents and parents and aunties, and me.

By the grace of God, I managed to coax the baby into the right position, and keep the mother as comfortable, strong and calm as possible until late afternoon. It was hot, she was squatting on a mat on the floor, and the flies were crawling all over everything. But finally, finally she felt she needed to push. Two hours later she was fed up, discouraged, exhausted, and tired of doing what I told her. I phoned an American midwife friend in the capital and tried to get the young mother to try what she suggested. She was beyond cooperating, especially through an interpreter. At three hours, I convinced them to let in her husband (for whom she had been calling), and when I saw that they were coping well, I stepped out for a few minutes to nurse Jessica and to call my midwife friend one more time. She felt that the time had come for an ultimatum and a trip to the hospital.

With what wonder and chagrin I viewed the situation on my return! A beautiful, pink baby girl lying on the baby blanket, with the *village doctor* beaming and taking care of the cord, and the previously desperate young mother calmly slipping into her jeans in the bedroom! "Thank you," she whispered with a sheepish smile. "Well," I said, "if I'd known the baby was just being shy of me, I could have left hours ago!" They had run for the doctor when they saw hair, and he had arrived in time to take the baby from Grandma and do the baby care. Both mother and baby were perfectly fine. Isn't God good?

Later, this new mother was in the group watching the Easter video on our computer (as we don't have TV). Easter Sunday had dawned sunny and fresh after days of dark clouds and rain, and we couldn't help but sing 'psalms of ascent' as we climbed the beautiful, sparkling wet (and slippery) mountainside to the village which hosted this year's three day celebration of feasting, dancing and singing. Hundreds were gathered up there to celebrate the Resurrection, and at dozens of other "host villages" the length of the valley. It was awesome.

The next April event was the retreat we almost didn't get to. For weeks we had hummed and hawed about going, but finally decided that we could register, and if it was a mistake, it was a simple matter for God to stop us. Three days before we were to leave, someone stole our water line, and it started to rain.   I still managed to wash all the clothes we would need, and hung them optimistically on the laundry line. If we ever got any watery sunshine I would run to grab them all and move them onto the railing or wherever it was the sun was hitting directly, in hopes of being able to pack them in our back packs rather than plastic bags. Spring is the rainy season, and that means landslide season in the valley. The day before our departure, it was still raining steadily, and there was no traffic coming into the valley; a huge landslide had blocked the road. The next morning we heard that a rock the size of a small house had landed on the road between us and town, so we were cut off from both sides. Was this a "No"? They dynamited the rock out of the way the night before we had to go. We got down to the road the next morning to catch the bus .... and no bus! There was a flood over the road to the north of us, and another landslide to the south! Locals assured us nothing would get through for three days. We splooshed home, lined our back packs up, prayed, and started eating some of our travel food.

The sun came out a bit, so I unpacked some of the still soggy clothes and laid them out to hopefully finish drying. While I was doing that, I suddenly saw the roof-racks of a bus go by on the road below us! "A bus! A bus! I just saw a bus go by!!" Stuff the clothes, grab the bags, hustle the kids through the mud to the road...now what? Here comes a jeep! Flag it down, "How much do you want to catch us up to that bus which just went by?" "Oh, I know the driver, I can call him for you. Don't worry, we'll catch them." About fifteen minutes later we did -- at the "ford", which was now a raging river! Hallelujah! They still had exactly the number of beds we needed to get our family to Kunming -- and that driver was determined to get there. While we were transferring on, two more buses pulled up, and out hopped all the other members of our team, grinning! Our driver gunned the motor and drove through water almost up to the windows, with all passengers on board. Our team mates had to get out before their drivers would try it, and then walk over on a makeshift plank bridge which some enterprising soul had hastily constructed and was charging a toll for! Later we learned that those three buses were the only vehicles to get through for another four days. The Lord made a way.

We had a wonderful time of encouragement with Stewart and Jill Briscoe on the nitty gritty of getting the job done: You do it tired; you do it sick; if you're working outside your gifting and can't do it *goodly*, then you do it *badly* and *heartily* until someone who can do it better comes along and takes pity on you; you do it in His strength, and you never say you *can't* until you've *tried*. Pithy stuff like that! Since they are now in their 70's and have just begun a gruelling new ministry in the last three years, tramping all over the planet training leadership of infant churches in the Third World, they know whereof they speak! Since we have spent a lot of our last ten years sick, tired and relocated, it encouraged us.

Back here, in the Salween, among the Lisu, we have gradually been piecing together an idea of what's gone on since the era of the Cookes, the Kuhns and the Frasers. While tramping around in the mountains, looking for some native apricots to be used as root stock for better varieties, and seeing what other fruit varieties exist here[11], Dave met a young man with a clear, steady gaze who offered to guide him to any village and help in any way he could. He helped Dave find some figs which foreigners had introduced a few generations ago. Dave

---

11   In Lisu, plums are called "MaPa Sise" [Teacher/Pastor fruit], due to being introduced by the foreign missionaries. There are some amazingly tasty varieties scattered throughout the region.

took note of him. Later on we found out that he had been selected by his village for three sessions of Bible training. Although he was chosen for this training because he was an upstanding member of the local church, he first discovered the way of salvation through attending the training. We also found out that he was the grandson of an orphan whom Allyn Cooke had adopted, and who became this area's first ordained pastor!

This young man's mother and his three aunts are also people of staunch faith and loving kindness. They were kicked out of school because of their father's occupation when the Communists came in in the l950's. They were also "struggled against" during the Cultural Revolution, a time of intense persecution of believers throughout this region.   Thousands fled over the mountains to Burma.   People had to keep their faith under their hats until 1982 when the first church buildings were reopened.   His mother and aunts are eager to get involved in 'mother-care':   passing on training in things like godly child rearing, hygiene, nutrition and care of the sick.   There is a high infant mortality rate here, and there needn't be.   When asked what she perceived to be the greatest need of the area, however, his mother replied, "Our unsaved young people."   Although Sunday School is not permitted anywhere in China, if the parents learned how to 'story tell' the Bible, they could ensure that their own children could grow in their relationship to God.

But they're not there yet.   Dave was at a large gathering of Lisu *pastors* who all admitted that they had never read one entire book of the Bible (not even the one-pagers like Jude).   So how will they get to know their God?   We are afraid that there are many Lisu who will say to the Lord on That Day, "Lord, Lord, I went to church every time the door was opened.   I never touched a drop of alcohol and I gave whenever I was asked to," and He will say, what?   "Depart from me, I never <u>knew</u>

you." And even sadder, they never <u>knew</u> Him. "So let us know, let us press on to know the Lord. For as surely as the dawn He will come..." May revival come to the Body of Christ among the Lisu, and in us. May the Temple be completed on the good foundation already laid.

Our neighbours dancing at the Easter celebration

Valleyview

We found a two-storey wood and stone house in Valleyview, a village with a good reputation, and moved there from Bridgeford in June, 2004. After living in a "fishbowl" for a year, it was so restful to be able to go upstairs and close the door on the world outside!

Our new house was an amazing piece of architecture. Our landlord, one of seven sons, decided to build his only son a house on the piece of land right behind their farm cottage. His son was only nine years old -- not in imminent need of his own house -- but by building it, his father was laying indisputable claim to the land. The only hindrance was a huge chunk of bedrock jutting out right there. Not a problem. He and his brothers and work crew started chopping it up with chisels and sledge hammers, and soon had quite the pile of fairly uniform rock "bricks". The levelled remainder of the stone provided a "rock solid" foundation for the two storey stone house which was gradually raised there. That foundation was a source of considerable comfort when a big landslide started rumbling down the gully right beside our kitchen, and the swollen creek started sucking away at the corner of the house there! The walls were a good two feet thick, perfectly straight and all a uniform shade of mica -flecked gray. They did a beautiful job, and that house could probably stand a hundred years if they don't decide to tear it down and sell the rock for construction materials. When we came looking for a place to rent, it was basically finished to Lisu standards, but they were happy to accept a little less in rent in return for our putting in a concrete floor and front deck, plastering the inside walls, and putting in a floor and dividing wall upstairs.

Since we were expecting a new baby, we splurged and replaced the rickety scrub oak ladder with steps up to the second level. We also built a little outdoor shower room, and a bit of a roof over a marble table just outside the kitchen door. The marble table, a "reject" slab from the marble factory just down the road, was where we did most of our food preparation and the dishes. Dealing with the dish water was so easy! We'd just toss the basin of waste water towards the ditch, and then watch the Muscovy ducks clean up all the bits of rice and other scraps out of the mud. The only problem with that system was that sometimes the ducks would get a little hasty, intercepting the dish water and getting rather soggy as the dish soap stripped the natural oil off their feathers.

What I absolutely loved about this place was the front corn field. Well, it was a cornfield when we first saw it, but it was studded with big chunks of picturesque bedrock. The potential for a stunning rock garden was irresistible, and Dave indulged me. Every date became an occasion for me to choose a new flowering shrub, and the front garden soon became every bit as beautiful as I had imagined it. Before long, Dave had also planted peach, nectarine, plum and shade trees. Most villages are crowded together, with a view of the back of the neighbour's house and what's running out of their cow byre. What a feast for the eyes we had, in contrast, as we did dishes, kneaded bread, visited with neighbours and looked up from reading a story. Calm nights were a joy, too. With no light pollution, the stars hung thick and lustrous, and the moon made the river shine like mercury.

That front garden was steep, though, which caused me to worry for two-year-old Nathan. He had a big yellow Tonka truck from his grandparents which he loved to drive down the yard at full speed. One day I heard him crying from where I was in the kitchen, and came out to investigate. He was nowhere in sight, but I finally saw him way down on the path towards the road. I wondered how he'd gotten down there, but then noticed his shoe hung up on a bush halfway down on the drop off between the edge of our patio and the path! He'd gone tearing down the patio with his head down, pushing his truck, and shot right off the edge! It was a good 15 foot fall, so we really gave thanks that his only injury was a little blue bruise on his thumb nail! [12]

Another time, he was in our upper garden behind the house with the rest of the family, when I came around the corner and looked up at them. He smiled at me, and stepped towards me, right off the edge. Again, it was an eight or ten foot drop straight down. The worst of it was that we had stacked a number of tall, broken roof tiles right there. They are made of corrugated asbestos and concrete, and had very jagged edges. Standing there, they reminded me of huge ripple chip graters, and my baby fell face first right past them. I have never been more afraid to pick him up. I was terrified that those tiles had taken his face right off, or that falling on his head from such a height had broken his neck. Again, other than a nick on the tip of his nose, he was none the worse for wear. Nathan was always falling or cutting himself, but the only other close calls were the two times he happened into very close proximity with poisonous snakes. One of those was a "two step snake" [ie. after it bites, you can walk two steps before you keel over, dead], which he came nose-to-nose with while climbing our peach tree. He hopped out of there like a tree frog!

Our house blended in with everyone else's from the outside, but on the inside we made some concessions to the fact that I had not grown up cooking over a fire or

---

12 We didn't have a fence around our yard because (1) the drop-off was tame in comparison to most of the terrain around us, and it was better that our kids learn to respect edges where it would only injure, not kill, them, (2) there was a row of trees just below the yard, to break their fall, (3) the main path to some upper villages went right through our yard, so we couldn't block it, and (4) a fence that would keep Nathan in??!!! Hahaha!

washing our clothes in the creek! I was truly thankful for our fridge, because our attempts at gardening were an almost total failure thanks to our neighbours' voracious flocks of "free range" chickens. Our neighbours all had land further away from the village, out of range of the village fowl, where they planted their vegetables. We did not. So, the fowl got fat on our experimental crops of peas, beans, lettuce, strawberries and so on, most of which we were trying to grow from imported seed. After two or three years of this, we finally gave up on keeping the "wild jungle fowl" out; they could fly easily to the tops of tall trees, or over any kind of fencing you care to name. Neither booting or plucking pinion feathers seemed to leave any impression on the chickens, and our neighbours would not pen their chickens except for about two weeks while the corn was being planted. So, for a long time we gave up on educating either birds or villagers on the significance of boundaries or the advisability of chicken coops! Twice a week we would catch a ride into town and bring our food home from the market, and the fridge kept it from all going bad.

We cooked over two induction cookers, and baked with two toaster ovens. One time, we also got an extension cord and plugged in an electric frying pan. That was a mistake!! The occasion was the anticipated arrival of nine foreign guests. I thought, "I'll bet by this time on their tour, they are rather missing western food. I know, I'll make them a roast dinner with all the fixings to celebrate their having come all this way." So, there was a cake in one oven, a roast in the other, carrots and potatoes on the two burners, beans in the electric frying pan .... and an electrical fire above the kitchen doorway when they all trooped up to our house! It was a little difficult to invite them in for tea, with Dave up on a kitchen chair in the doorway, frantically putting out flames, pulling out scorched wires, and installing new ones. Once the electricity was back on, I could finish supper, but I doubt our guests will ever forget that we put on the fireworks for their arrival!

Our house with a view in Valleyview

Home, part 4

Our new home in Valleyview was truly God's provision, but we were still plagued with an old insecurity: how long until we would have to move again? When Jessica was born in Riverbend, the county seat, we had to set about the process of getting her passport and visa done from that remote location. Usually the embassy required you to present the baby along with the application in Shanghai or Beijing, but they were willing to waive this requirement considering the six to eight day travel ordeal that would put us through. When the passport came through, Dave took it to the prefectural foreign affairs to get her visa put in. The head of Foreign Affairs, Mr. B., refused. He said we'd have to take her back to Canada and apply for a visa from there! He refused to discuss how we were going to get a baby without a visa across the borders, and walked out on Dave.

Dave came home that night after 7 hours on the bus pretty worried and discouraged. We knew that the Foreign Affairs officer could issue the visa; Miriam and Nathan had also both been born in small towns in China, and their visas had been processed locally. Finally, Dave phoned the Provincial Foreign Affairs and explained the situation. They were quite irritated to hear this and promised to "sort him out". We knew it was a very risky move, to go over the local official's head like that -- especially since we would presumably have to keep dealing with him in the future -- but we felt we had no choice. It was his responsibility, and if he wouldn't do it, we were completely stuck. The next day Dave presented himself again, and although he had to listen to a lot of blustering, was able to get the visa! We were really concerned about Mr. B.'s attitude, though. He was "the" one who would have to process all of our team's paperwork, and he obviously didn't want us on his turf.

We really started praying for him. And we tried not to worry that we might have to move again so soon after getting settled where we thought God wanted us. Miriam, who was helping Dave plant the garden and some fruit trees, asked, "Why are we even bothering to plant these? You know we'll have to move before we ever get to eat anything from them." She was only nine, and already so cynical!![13]

Then it was time for Dave to try and switch our temporary visas for a work visa, since he had become the manager of the Nubian goat project. This should have been a formality; the company was well-established and had the right to hire a manager and provide a visa for him. Once again Mr. B flat out refused. Walter, the HongKong businessman who owned the project, tried to reason with him a little more, and once again Mr. B walked out. At that moment, Walter said, the conviction grew on him that the only possible 'banfa' [way] was through prayer. So, he just sat there in the little waiting room and prayed.

After a while, Mr. B came back in and agreed to process the work permit and visa!! He remained gruff and suspicious however, until the day Dave discovered that a flowering ground cover plant called Australian peanut, which he had been unable to locate or order from any of the nurseries he knew of, was growing outside the foreign affairs office! He was so excited and asked Mr. B if he could please have some. It turns out Mr. B was an amateur horticulturist, and when he discovered that Dave actually had some agricultural knowledge, he warmed up considerably. We could not believe the change in him the next time we had business! He came over, greeted us cordially, shook hands and said "What can I do for you?" What an answer to prayer! From then on our team had every assistance in managing our visas and work permits,

13   At the time, my dad, trying to be encouraging, said, "Well, I keep telling God, 'They have to live *somewhere*!'"

forgiveness for accidentally lapsed documents and advice in how to get the most economical visa "deal".

Before our move to Valleyview, we attended a retreat at which two significant things happened.

One was that a doctor friend shared how the Lord had opened up an amazing ministry for her among migrant workers in the city, most of whom were Buyi, and that a small but vibrant church was growing up. She truly felt that this was part of the Lord's answer to our prayers and anguish over the unreached people we had had to leave behind.

The other came from a slender, soft-spoken young medical student visiting from Singapore. After one session, she came over, placed her hand over my heart and said with absolute certainty [from Isaiah 43:18,19], "The Lord wants you to know that He is going to do a new thing in your life. Forget the former things." The hope which immediately sprang up was that this new thing would mean a change from the pattern of moving every year or two! I had been praying 'Oh Lord, grant us a spacious place where we can do your will and proclaim your word without hindrance and without being forced to move right away." Now, after 10 years in Lisu land, we have to say with such deep gratitude that He did indeed do a new thing. We got to eat the fruit from our orchard for six years and see a good deal of the work of our hands established for us. (Psalm 90:17 *"May the favour of the Lord our God rest upon us; establish the work of our hands for us"*). Our younger children got to grow up in a lovely community and a beautiful natural setting.

Those years were also the fulfillment of another prophetic word which had been spoken over me at a conference while I was still a nursing student. A young man came up and said that he'd seen me surrounded by a crowd of people who were being healed. I had actually been surrounded by crowds of people looking for medical help at our house for years before I even remembered that, and realized that it was coming true.

What were other blessings of being "at home" in the village?

It was the place where our kids were treated just like the other kids. They were rebuked, as Lisu kids would be, for climbing the neighbours' fruit trees or letting the puppy chase someone's chickens. A beautiful thing about the Lisu is that they give you your space; there was no grabbing and holding the kids, taking photos without permission, and other "little celebrity" treatment which the kids hated when we went anywhere else in China.

It was the place where we could count on catching a ride, and being allowed to pay after some protest. Travelling with a large family and all our bundles was never easy, but knowing the drivers, and being known, honored and taken care of by them in our neighbourhood was a nice feeling. We never took it for granted, but were continually touched and blessed by the people who would stop for us, make room for us, change their route for us, refuse payment, answer the phone and pick us up at some ungodly hour, or help us in our hospitality by transporting our guests with a kindness and warmth which no money could buy.

It was the place where our neighbours were our "security and surveillance". In the early days in the village, the other children would play with ours for the express purpose of snitching their toys. Anything which our younger children forgot to watch for a minute would disappear. Later on, however, once our role in the village was known and accepted, clothes and toys which our kids forgot out in the field would reappear in our yard, and our neighbours absolutely offered us the same "clan" protection that they gave each other. They told us that thieves would bypass their village, because it was known to be composed of about four big clans who would not hesitate to protect each other's lives and property with cudgels if need be. One miserable, rainy day, our family went into town to visit friends. Angela's father did not know this, so chose that day to come down from his hut in the mountain heights for one of his infrequent visits and health check-ups. He thought we might show up any minute, so got out of the rain by huddling in a corner of our veranda. He always wore dirty, worn out khaki army surplus outfits, so probably looked like an old tarp and fit right in with the hoes, empty flower pots and other gardening paraphernalia! While he was there, he suddenly heard breaking glass right above his head and ducked out for a look. He was just in time to see a pair of bare feet disappearing into the kids' second storey bedroom window! He ran down to the road and raised the alarm. The first we knew of all this was when one of our neighbours called us on his cell phone. He said, "We're surrounding your house. A thief broke in, but we think he's still there. What do you want us to do?" We said, "Call the police!" So they did, but it turned out the thief had actually escaped, by taking a risky and certainly painful leap out the 2nd storey back window down into the gully behind our house in his bare feet! He had taken off his shoes before he invaded our home! He must have realized he'd been discovered almost instantly, because he ripped the curtains in his haste, and left a hank of black hair caught in a sun-catcher ornament. We were truly thankful, because we had just taken a large sum of money out of the bank to pay for a little baby girl with hydrocephalus to have life-saving shunt surgery. If the thief had had time to snoop around and discovered that, it would have been difficult to replace. His shoes fit Constance, and she wore them until they wore out. I have to smile whenever I think of this. Isn't it just like

God to use the father of our "Angel unaware", the very least of the least, to save us from a disastrous burglary?

It's where we were accepted for who we were, and tolerated in our strange ways.

It was where we had treated or helped virtually everyone in one way or another, and knew everybody by their illnesses and crises!

It was where we could usually think of someone who could help us with our attempts to assist others, and were almost never turned down.

Our "kids" at home

Gently Lead, part 2

Oct. 2003

"Jessica! Come on baby, stay with us! Come on baby!"
My heart squeezed as I looked at her maroon colored
little face and glassy eyes. She was only breathing
intermittently - maybe 5 times a minute. I slipped the
suction tube down her throat again to try and keep her
from aspirating on the meconium she had suddenly
started vomiting up. She had been born just minutes
after we hustled in to the delivery ward at the local
hospital, and although the cord had been wrapped
around her neck, she had recovered quickly and seemed
just perfect. After trying to rest unsuccessfully on the
hard wooden bench outside the delivery room for a
couple of hours, we had felt justified in discharging
ourselves and going back to the hotel room where I had
done my labouring.

Her first eight hours had passed peacefully and
joyfully, but suddenly we were fighting for her life! We
had had no idea that she had swallowed the greasy green
guck which is a newborn baby's first poop. If she had
breathed any of it in, she was in big trouble and would
have been transferred to a neonatal ICU in a bigger
center. Here in Riverbend, 16 hours from the nearest big
hospital - it was basically up to us and God. Moving in a
blur, we grabbed baby, blanket and our shoes and rushed
down the stairs, out of the hotel and out onto the street.
It was about 11 pm, dark and deserted. "God, help! I
can't run! I just had a baby!" Wonder of wonders, the
sound of a motorcycle engine, and a motorized trishaw
came around the corner! We hailed it, clambered in and
kept an anxious eye on our baby's face. As the cool breeze
hit her, she blinked and although we couldn't hear
anything over the engine noise, and could only catch
glimpses as we passed under streetlights, it seemed like

she was coming around. By the time we reached the hospital, she was breathing regularly and had returned to a normal color.

Thankfully, there was a calm and competent young doctor on duty. He finished suctioning her, then listened to her lungs and pronounced her "very good". All our peace and contentment had blown up, however. We were still on red hot alert and took turns watching her all that night, and the next two nights as well. Every hour or so, she would start making little hiccuping sounds which preceded another episode of vomiting. She kept it up for three days. Thankfully, I was able to phone a pediatrician and ask his advice. He felt that the fact that she hadn't actually inhaled any of the meconium was due to the protective vagal reflex being stimulated by the suctioning. Also thankfully, about then my milk started to come in, and she started to be able to keep it down, as three days without liquids is a long time for a little baby.

Finally, we could take her home to meet her excited siblings. Miriam, Karen, Constance and Nathan all piled into bed with me to admire and fondle their new baby sister. Nathan was just barely two. He looked from the little bundle in my arms to my more or less flat stomach, and delightedly proclaimed "Baby Tum OUT!" A couple of days later he wanted to share some of his supper with his newborn sister, and I told him she couldn't eat that yet. The next time I was nursing her, I slyly asked him, "So, Nathan, what do babies eat?" He looked at me, got a huge grin on his face and confidently proclaimed, "Shirts!" One night after supper, I retired to the bedroom a little early to just lie down, leaving the baby tucked into the guest bed in our kitchen/dining room. One by one the others came into the bedroom to be with me until I suddenly realized that everyone was there except the baby...and Nathan! "Quick! Go back and check the baby and Nathan!" I was just a little too late, and we once again proved the vigilance of our children's guardian angels! Nathan had gotten up on the bed, picked Jessica up and tried to bring her down off the bed. He dropped her, but he dropped her right into a big basket full of bok choy! So, there she was, contentedly looking around from her bed of greens!

Oct. 2005

We need to be careful what we pray for! Unknown to me, my mom had been constantly praying during my sixth pregnancy that I would have "an easy and relatively painless labour". Once again, I was huge, overdue and so ready to have that baby! Finally I was wakened by the beginning of labour pains in the wee hours of Oct. 10. It was Thanksgiving day, 2005. By breakfast time, things were starting to intensify a bit, so Dave and I called the babysitter (Uncle Ed) and found a ride to town. We registered at the local hospital, did some walking and shopping, went for noodles and then decided to try and grab some rest at Walter's apartment while the contractions were still relatively easy. I ran a hot bath, and thoroughly enjoyed that luxury while Dave read some Psalms to me and sang.

Eventually I thought, "Well, this is very nice, but I've relaxed so much that labour has essentially stopped, and I guess I'd better get out and try to get this show on the road." By the time I'd gotten dressed, I realized that labour had been moving right along, but the warm water had been such an effective pain killer I hadn't even realized it! A few minutes later, I started to get that shaky, coming undone feeling I'd come to associate with transition, but the pain was still not anything like what I was conditioned to expect. Nevertheless, I told Dave we'd better make our move back to the hospital. I bent to put my shoes on. That did it! My water broke, contractions came on like a tidal wave, and I never did get my second shoe on! Dave very quickly decided that we were going to have to have that baby right there, mostly because the Lord had given him a word of knowledge while he was singing and praying for me. This was just a sudden very strong impression that *he* would be delivering this baby. I think if it hadn't been for that, he would have freaked out and Haven would have been born in the stairwell or by the side of the street as he tried to hustle me all the way across town![14]

I said, "We *can't* have the baby here - we have nothing to tie the cord with!" With a triumphant flourish, Dave pulled a small roll of dental floss out of his pocket! "Never leave home without it!" he quipped. "But what about cutting the cord - we don't have a razor, " I wailed. A minute later he'd rummaged some nail scissors out of our toiletry bag and thrown them in a pot of water to boil. At this point he was moving so fast he was skidding around the tile floor with his slippers flapping. I would have laughed if I hadn't been so busy! The bed was actually already covered with a big piece of plastic Dave had put on in case my water broke while I was resting, so Haven was born right there.

In some ways it was the most peaceful of all our births, because it was just the two of us, and we were cooperating perfectly. Usually while I was most in need of support, Dave was having to fill in papers, or put on scrubs, or protect me from all the out-dated birthing practices you run into in the developing world. Praise the Lord, everything was absolutely perfect. Haven was in great shape, and I was just fine as well. Once she was out, we kind of just sat there in shock. After a minute Dave picked her up and started to rub her off, then cut the cord, while I started to wonder what to do about the little lake I was lying in. That was the weird part of a "do-it-yourself birth" -- figuring out what to do with the mess! Eventually we got everyone and everything cleaned up

---

14   Dave firmly believed that obstetrics fell into the same category as brain surgery -- something best left to the experts.

and decent , and could start stunning our friends and family with the news that we already had a baby, and they could come see her whenever they wanted.

The first to show up was a Naxi friend of ours who adores babies and runs a restaurant in town. She arrived full of clucks and good will, carrying the kind of hand scale that you suspend bags of fruit and such from. We tied Haven up, stork fashion, in a pillow case, and weighed her in at just over 8 pounds. Then it was time to be fed all the sustaining traditional Chinese foods for postpartum moms. Eggs poached in fermented sticky-rice and brown sugar, chicken soup steeped with herbs and red dates, and the Lisu dish of free-range chicken braised in a kind of waxy grey oil they make from the berries of lacquer trees.

So, Haven's birth was really just one big celebration. But from the time she was a couple of months old until she was six months, she suffered from chronic diarrhea, sometimes coupled with vomiting. It was really difficult to keep enough fluids and energy going in to counteract how much was being wasted. At one point she was so thin and weak she just lay across my lap in whatever position I put her in, so I took her to the hospital for IV fluids and nutrition. With all of my children, there has come a point early on in their lives -- often even before they are born -- where I become very clear that their life is a gift, and I give up responsibility for keeping them alive to their Maker and mine. I reached that point with Haven near the end of that illness. One night, as I walked the floor with her ever-so-light and listless form in my arms, in anguish at the thought that she might actually die, I surrendered her up to His will, knowing that ultimately life is something He is completely in control of, and that He would do what was best and right. Thankfully, after that she recovered totally for quite a few months.

I remember one day we bought a baby walker and put Haven in it in the front "yard". Our yard was actually just a slim concrete patio which dropped off into our steep front garden. We noticed that she could move the walker, so we cleverly removed all the wheels to keep her stationary and safe. Next thing we knew she had "hopped" the walker all the way across the yard and over the edge! She and the walker did a complete somersault, and then got hung upside down in one of our hedges. When we recovered her, she was just fine, but very indignant about the dirt up her nose and in her mouth! Following that little episode, we got even cleverer and tethered her walker to a post!

The only other time Haven really caused us concern was the day she ate the mushroom. When she was about 18 months old, and Dave was up in the corn fields with the rest of the kids, preparing the land, he found a red mushroom and decided to make an object lesson of it. He picked it, handed it to Miriam and said, "Call the other kids. I want to show them this and explain why I think it's poisonous, so they'll never eat one by mistake." Miriam dutifully took it down to the house and sat down to await Daddy and the others. Haven toddled over, looked at the mushroom for an instant, and then lunged over and bit the cap off! She didn't even use her hands to touch it, and she swallowed before Miriam could react.

"Moommmyyy! Haven just ate the mushroom Daddy said should never be eaten!"

"You're kidding. Miriam, don't even joke about things like that!"

"I'm not kidding! She really did!"

"Well, make her spit it out. Quick!"

"She already swallowed it!"

"She can't have! Stick your finger in her mouth and make her spit it out!"

"She already swallowed it!"

Well, when a finger down her gullet produced lots of other stuff but no red mushroom, I rummaged for the hitherto unused syrup of Ipecac, which mercifully was where I thought it might be, and gave Haven a spoon full. We waited for it to produce the desired emetic effect, and waited, and waited. Finally, after about 15 minutes, I became afraid the toxins might hurt her before she vomited, so Miriam and I forced her to drink several big syringes full of activated charcoal. She was not impressed and fought just as hard as she could, spewing black stuff all over herself and us. And of course, then she started vomiting. Since everything she vomited up was now inky, we never did figure out when she rid herself of the mushroom, but she was just fine once we'd given her a bath. She never ate another thing that we hadn't told her she could eat! In contrast, her older sister Jessica had been a real gastronomic adventurer. One morning she found the parts of a rat the cat knew better than to eat, and finished it off for her. One of the older kids just saw the tip of a tail disappearing into her mouth! Another day they caught her fishing all the spilled seed out of the pan in the bottom of the bird cage and licking that up! In spite of this, or perhaps because of it, she was almost never sick and looked like a jolly little Buddha in the bathtub!

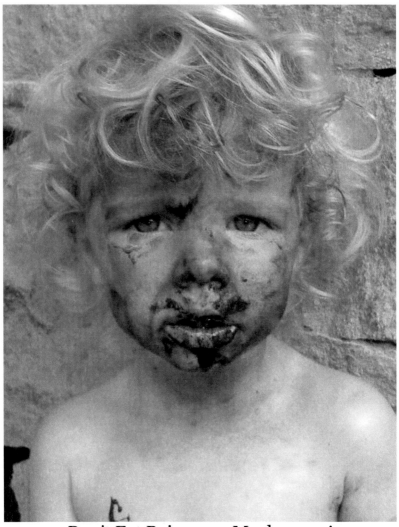

Don't Eat Poisonous Mushrooms!

The Big Snow

March 6, 2005 was already a cold, miserable rainy day, but then something happened which hadn't been seen in over 100 years - it started to snow![15] Heavy, slushy snow. At first the children were totally excited, and went galloping out to make snowballs and marvel at and taste the snowflakes, but with no mittens or heavy socks, they quickly became cold and wet through and retreated to steam by the wood stove. We were supposed to visit the Lius, though, so we dressed in our warmest clothes and walked over, since there were no vehicles coming through in that weather. The walk home was eerily beautiful: so strange to look at the hill tops just visible against the midnight blue of a winter's dusk and see the stands of bamboo bent double under the weight of a thick mantle of *snow*! I'd seen poplar trees like that, but never bamboo!

We noticed that the power lines, also, were sagging into deep parabolas and that people with single storey dwellings were climbing onto their roofs to scrape off as much snow as they could. Good thinking! What on earth could we do to lessen the burden of snow on our second storey roof, though? Not much, it turned out.

We had a funny house guest, a photographer friend-of-a-friend who was staying in our first floor guest room, so when we got home, we joined him in a hot drink, bundled into warm dry clothes and went to our various beds. Dave's and my sleep was uneasy, though, punctuated by the creaks and groans of the roof timbers. Several times we both woke up and worried in whispers, wondering if it would be wiser to move our whole family

---

15   In Lisuland it snows on the mountaintops, enough that the passes to Burma are blocked during the winter, but down by the river it doesn't.

downstairs where the upstairs floor would protect us if the roof collapsed.

CRASH!!!

Dave and I catapulted out of bed and woke up standing bolt upright on the floor, flooded with adrenaline and sure the anticipated had finally happened! But no, the roof was intact, and there was still a sound like a case of ball bearings rolling into all the far corners! What the...!?

The irritating "nnnn, nnnn, nnnn" of the phone off the hook attracted our bewildered gaze as we flicked on the flashlight. The phone was no longer on my desk, but apparently nailed to the wall up by the roof where the line went through the wall. Ah, ha! The phone line, which had just been put in two days previously, had apparently gone down, and tried to pull our phone through the wall after it! On it's flight off the desk, the phone had smashed into my "what not" shelf and sent a ceramic vase containing a couple of pounds of iridescent marbles cascading all over the floor! That had made a noise to wake the dead, and it was finally sufficient to rouse our slumbering guest!

I was sorry about the vase. On our last trip out to Hong Kong, some friends had treated us to a day at "Ocean Park" (the Sea World of HK) and we made the mistake of wandering into the gift shop. The kids all chose stuffies, but I was drawn to a beautiful ceramic planter made of the gracefully intertwined forms of dolphins. Dave had looked at me like I was crazy when I pointed it out, and patiently asked me if I was *sure* I wanted to try and fit that into my back pack and how likely was it to arrive home intact? Besides - where would I put it? I was having a stubborn moment, however, and rebelled at the thought of my ever-so-utilitarian life and home. How come all the other ex-pats I knew could have beautiful things, and I never could? We could build a special shelf for it, and then finally have a place for lovely shells and rocks and pictures, too. Well, it survived the trip home, and Dave built the shelf...I put what remained of the ceramic back up there as a little joke between God and I. Others' lives allowed for fragile, beautiful ornaments. Mine, rather emphatically, did not!

Well, that shattering moment galvanized us into decisive action. We gathered up all the kids and the bedding and spent the rest of the night with all seven of us on one mattress down in the school/storage room! At least we were *cozy*... and safe!

The next morning we woke to the clear white light of the sun reflecting off a world muffled in a foot of fresh snow!

We threw a rope over the roof of our house and spent the whole morning experimenting to find something which was both light enough to be dragged back and forth over the roof and heavy enough to actually push some snow. We finally gave up; it was about as heavy and sticky as clay. I doubt the kids will ever forget our house guest that day. He didn't want to get his last pair of pants wet and muddy, and would not borrow anything, so he wore shorts and sports sandals as he accompanied Dave through the deep snow. He kept insisting, through a volley of sneezing and sniffling, that he was warm and would be just fine!

As it started to thaw, slushy water started pouring through all the cracked and broken roof tiles, and the kids and I were kept busy trying to find a dry place for our desks, medical files, books, bedding and electronics. Thankfully, Dave was able to bum a ride into town and buy some new tiles before they were all sold out. That morning, we watched 38 avalanches come rolling down the steep slope across the river from us, and then a big chunk of the mountain on our side suddenly peeled off and came rumbling down the gulch right beside our house!!

Chunks of pine trees, huge boulders and a wall of mud came grinding past the kitchen window while the two-foot thick stone walls shook! I screamed for the children, grabbed toddler Jessica and hustled everybody out to the other side of the house and up the hill. The slide splashed the walls of our house with mud, but seemed to be staying in the gulch. We didn't have any windows facing the mountain side, so relied on the earth-shaking rumbling every few hours to know when to clear out. The nights were the worst. Over the torrential rain beating on the roof, thunder and lightning and the roaring of the stream in the gully, we strained our ears for the thunderous roar which was actually more of the mountain coming down. We went to bed fully dressed with our passports in our pockets and who would grab which children on our minds. When the roaring would wake us, Dave and I would hug each other tight and pray. The morning I realized that all those tons of mud and rocks had passed by without even taking out the strawberry plants in our garden was a turning point! The mud actually made a 90 degree turn at the end of our garden for no apparent reason! When I saw that, I said to myself, "God is hearing your prayers - you have nothing to fear," and we began to take comfort and sleep again.

Another thing which prompted our landlord to shake his head and comment, "Jesus really likes you guys," was the fact that when the power pole beside our house fell over, it fell right between the house and the water tank, and onto our rabbit hutch. However, it fell right down the middle and didn't hurt either of the rabbits!

Throughout the valley, there were few deaths, though many people lost their roofs to the snow, or their homes in land slides when it melted. All the church roofs had to be replaced; there was nothing but open air services for awhile! A group of HK businessmen came for a visit, and were so moved by the needs that they went back and raised enough funds to replace hundreds of roofs, including almost all of the churches. Up in the higher mountains, some villages had chest-deep snow and the cold and lack of feed killed a lot of young stock. The roads were closed for three weeks, and it was three months before electricity and cell phone service were restored! The town virtually ran out of things like propane and candles, because everyone was relying on them, and there was no way to bring in new supplies. Thankfully, spring and warmer weather was just around the corner! We cooperated with other ex-pats and locals to distribute relief rice, oil and blankets, and to bring in medical teams once the roads were passable. And our kids developed a very un-Canadian dislike for snow.

The Goat Project

"Go with the people. Live with them. Learn from them. Love them. Start with what they have. Build on what they know. But with the best leaders, when the work is done, the task accomplished, the people will say, 'We have done this ourselves'."
— Lao Tsu, Chinese Philosopher, 700 B.C.

Our second year in the Salween valley, Dave decided to connect up with Walter Chan's Nubian goat project. Walter had been working in the area for eight years already, but could only come to see his workers about three times a year. In between times, they were on their own. Without a knowledgeable manager "on the ground", the project was experiencing some difficulties. Quite a few of the expensive Nubian bucks had died of unknown causes, and very few villagers were compliant with the mandate to keep their goats penned, especially in the winter. Winter in the Salween is the dry season; the slopes turn brown and most of the vegetation dries up. It becomes virtually impossible to find enough fodder to "cut and carry" it back to the goats, so villagers let them forage for themselves. But goats browse very selectively; they just love to eat all the young growth, especially fruit trees and gardens! Other problems included indiscriminate breeding, spread of disease and parasites and animals going missing through theft or accidents on the craggy terrain. Those farmers who were trying to stick to their contract were feeding their goats large amounts of fern -- about the only green thing left in any abundance -- thus inadvertently poisoning them, causing the does to abort. With the only accountability coming from local workers, quite a few of the villages took their contract pretty lightly in other ways as well. Sometimes when the goat workers came by, there were no more goats in the village - "They all died." Then they'd hear from other sources, "They all died all right: were butchered and sold or eaten!" There was a critical need for someone to manage it "on the ground" for awhile to help solve these challenges.

At first Dave thought, "Well, I can give a couple of years to get such a worthy project off the ground. The main need is for them to learn how to plant enough fodder for their goats." He soon realized, however, that a lot more was involved than just teaching them the agricultural techniques he'd learned in the Philippines! Almost none of his fellow workers could really speak Chinese, and the upper mountain villagers even less. So, he'd have to learn Lisu. Then, the altitude was too high and the temperatures too cold to allow them to use the known fodder species which were being propagated in other places in the world, and which he had access to seed for. He would have to search out all the Nitrogen Fixing plants, local and exotic, which might survive in mountainous zones, and do some original research on how to propagate and plant them. Those first few years, Dave was "up the mountain" working with villagers all spring and fall, because those were the planting seasons. Planting seasons were also the wet seasons, so he would typically arrive back at sundown, muddy, exhausted and hungry, and often with stories to tell.

"Hi, Hon. How was your day?"
"Good. Thank God I didn't kill someone today."
"You're kidding. What do you mean?"
"Well, we were planting with this one village, and I just went to walk across the slope and this HUGE rock let loose straight for a young woman who was working below me."
"Oh my gosh! But it didn't hit her?"

"No, but she had to jump with the baby tied on her back and everything. The other villagers were kind of upset with me."

"Why? How could you have known that rock was going to move?"

"I dunno. But I won't be walking above any big rocks while they're hoeing up the field any more, I can tell you that much! Praise God what could have so easily happened didn't."

The rest of the time, when he wasn't sick in bed with diarrhea, he was busy training his workers, learning Lisu and working his own land, which served as the "control plot" for his planting experiments, and a bit of a seed bank for rare species. The kids were a big help with harvesting and processing seeds which could be divvied out to the farmers. Most of the nitrogen fixing trees bear their seeds in bean-like pods. The two we found most exciting were Velvet bean, which reminded me of Jack-and-the-Beanstalk, and an Indigofera species which would pop open with great force in the sun once they were ripe, shrapnelling harvesters and passersby alike. The Velvet beans grew enormous vines loaded with huge pods. One year we came back at the end of the summer and looked with both awe and trepidation at where we'd planted one bean at the foot of a power pole; the pole looked like it was on the verge of being pulled right over by the sheer mass of the vine! A handful of seeds can go a long way when the farmers are also trained to leave a couple of trees at the end of each row to continue producing seeds!

One exciting aspect of Dave's work was to recognize the assets Lisu people and villages possessed, and to plant the idea of sharing these gifts with each other. Sometimes it would be something like apples which one village had been planting and harvesting for a long time, while a village just across the way was asking

Dave for apple seeds! Another time the treasure would be a humble widow or the son in a destitute family who listened carefully, did exactly as they were instructed, and worked their little fodder nursery diligently. Their tremendous success revealed the real reasons that others in the same village failed in their attempts to raise enough feed to qualify for goats from the project! Careful questioning would reveal that the others had not watered, or had weeded carelessly, pulling up the seedlings along with the weeds. In those days, Dave's conversations were liberally sprinkled with stories of all the ways people had undone their first year's work!

"Today we learned to tell the villagers, 'When you're choosing the land to plant your fodder bank on, be sure and choose land which corn can grow on.' The village we went to today planted all their seed on a slope which only gets an hour or two of sunlight a day. It was too cold for it to germinate."

Or, "The villagers at the village we went to today said, 'That seed you gave us was no good. None of it came up.' So I went along the rows and found one here and there, but they'd buried all the rest when they planted their potato crop."

Season by season, year by year, Dave and his team learned, discussed and came up with strategies to help farmers succeed at this business of penning goats profitably.

Their farmer trainings became very thorough, covering everything from "how to build a pen which will keep a goat in", to simple vet care, breeding and genetics 101, simple record and account keeping, basic business practices, planting for an adequate diet (beast and human) year round and Bible storying. On the side, Dave learned, taught and developed materials for anything and everything he saw a need for: pruning and grafting fruit trees, composting toilets,[16] organic fertilizer, locally appropriate hedgerows to prevent soil erosion and enhance soil fertility (and a photographic hand book to help people recognize all the varieties), using goats for packing, and building simple chicken brooders. It is so funny! Dave has always hated chickens. Maybe the fact that when he was growing up the chickens always roosted over the back door and filled his shoes with their dropping has something to do with this. Anyway, living here with the neighbours' free-ranging fowl eating up everything of worth he's ever planted has not increased his fondness. We've even raised Muscovy ducks (which stay home and don't fly over 2 meter high fences like the local chickens do) and encouraged others to do the same. But now we have lots of people dropping by our house to see how to raise chickens scientifically. That's good, but it's the least intentional demonstration he's ever done!

Dave was so glad when his team of Lisu co-workers actually started implementing what they were learning on their own land, and in their own families. Once they were no longer just teaching hearsay, but what they were personally convinced of and successfully doing, their effectiveness as extensionists took on a whole new dimension, and the whole project suddenly started looking sustainable. When I did a one week training with Lisu women on "Abundant Living", covering the basics of nutrition, hygiene, and recognition and treatment of common threats to maternal and childhood health, I was able to take them to Dave's co-manager, APu's farm. Their homestead was such a delight! Their composting toilet was clean and odour-free, and he was able to show them a garden just bursting with a variety of healthy vegetables thanks to the extra fertilizer! Their traditional

---

16   MaPa [Pastor] John volunteered to translate Dave's composting toilet materials from Chinese into Lisu. Dave kinda choked and said, "Sure we can call it, 'Cleaner toilets by MaPa John'!" (MaPa is pronounced "Mop a")

Lisu corn was tall, with big, full ears, and he was quick to point out the advantages of this "ancient grain" over hybrid varieties: better taste, better nutrition, and viable seed which could be saved for next year. Their pens were full of healthy goats, and one spare pen had been turned into a chicken coop with fat Lisu chickens in it! They were feeding them their own corn and chopped leaves from the hedgerows, not the despised and expensive commercial feed. Those chickens were worth about 50 yuan[17] each -- twice as much as commercially raised ones -- and the women knew it! Furthermore, APu pointed out that by penning, the mortality rate was reduced to almost nil, whereas free ranging hens are only able to raise one or two chicks in ten to butchering size.[18] Plus, the vegetable gardens were no longer ravaged and the penned animals' manure could be used to fertilize the corn and other crops. Down by the house, he pointed out his sand and charcoal water filter, and explained how much their health had improved since they'd stopped drinking raw water, and how much less fuel wood they needed now they did not have to boil their water, or cook up pig food.

He showed them the Nitrogen fixing hedgerows between the corn rows, and explained how the shrubs actually nourished the crops, while producing easy-to-access feed for the goats and chickens. The sturdy, deep-rooted hedges also stabilized the land and protected their home from landslides. Once the goats had eaten the leaves and peeled the bark off the hedge clippings, the left over sticks provided most of the wood they needed for cooking. He said that while at first his wife had been skeptical and resistant to the idea of planting hedgerows

---

17   One yuan (RMB), the Chinese currency, is worth about 15 cents Canadian.

18   The chicks get stepped on, drowned in cess-pits and ditches, caught by cats and hawks, run over on the road, or succumb to contagious bird illnesses and rat-poisoned grain.

or getting rid of the cows and pigs, she was now totally sold and told him all the time how much easier the goats were!   He also said that he'd learned through all these years of working with family and neighbours who didn't want to cooperate with these "new-fangled ideas", that prayer was the most important factor to seeing them change and become cooperative. The ladies absorbed it all, and went home discussing which of the many wonderful things they'd seen that day they would start implementing in their own villages!

APu's relationship with his wife and sons also took a tremendous turn for the better when he started to read the Bible and pray with them at the start of each day. Discussing Biblical truth with his own wife opened APu's eyes to *how much* of what he and the other "MaPas" [Preachers] were saying was going right over the women's heads - and probably over a lot of the illiterate men's as well, not to mention the children.

Dave was teaching the goat workers to learn to "story" the Bible with him. Storying is simply becoming so familiar with a portion of Scripture, that you can tell the whole story, with all the significant details, from memory.   It's that easy, and that difficult!   (Try it!) However, for people who largely rely on oral history, it's a very natural thing, and by the time they can tell the story correctly, they really know it. It's also very natural to ask questions like, "So what do you think happened next?", or "How do you think God felt when the people did that?" or "If that happened to you, what would you do?" It's a small step, then, for them to draw out personal applications and truth for their own lives.   Lessons learned like that are there to stay. By contrast, most people can recount only a tiny amount of a sermon they've just heard the day before, even if it was one they enjoyed at the time, and brought all their western-trained faculties to bear on.   Most Lisu sermons involve extemporizing on and on about one verse, or are read from that year's Rainy Season Bible School notes. Generally, they are so much straw, not feed for the sheep. It is no wonder that so many young people are breaking out of the "pen" of legalistic restrictions and foraging for themselves on forbidden things.

When these Lisu goat workers started, most of them had never read an entire chapter of the Bible for themselves, and could only do it haltingly and with minimal understanding even when they did it together. However, over the weeks, their literacy and understanding levels increased rapidly, and so did their interest! Week by week they were astounded by what they were discovering, the discrepancies with what they'd been taught to believe, and the relevance and applicability to their lives! Dave taught them to approach the Bible with the assumption that God had recorded everything in His word for a purpose, and to actively seek Him for it. They learned to just read the story, to think about how they would have behaved in the same situation, and to consider the outcomes of the choices the Biblical characters actually made. What was there to learn about God's ways, human nature, faith, redemption and the power of choices? One by one the men were telling him that up until they'd done this, they had always considered themselves "Christian" but now realized they had not personally come to know Christ. By the end of their time together, all the core guys had made that decision and were using their time together to discuss how to walk it out, and hold each other accountable.

Dave's last couple of years with the goat project were partially focused on helping them make it sustainable. They gradually made changes so that every step from finding new villages to the contract they entered into with them, to how they would manage the profits was fair and intrinsically motivating. Our last year with them, things were going well, and it looked like the goat workers should be able to make a living at it with no more external funding or management. In addition, most of Dave's co-workers had become elders and leaders in their local fellowships. I wish I could stop there.

Unfortunately, no sooner had we left than a different project in another part of the province convinced APu, the goat project manager, to work for them for wages. By doing that, they pulled the human corner stone of the Salween project, sad to say. We haven't had the heart to follow up on what happened after that, since we can't do anything about if from here in Canada anyway, but we fear there won't be much left of the project when we go back.

So, was it worth it?

Well, isn't it always worth it to do our best, as unto the Lord? Dave did his best, and what happened after that is God's business. The Word says that on the last day, every man's work will be revealed by fire -- some will burn up like straw, and some will remain, as precious stones and gold remain. It's important to remember that God's ways of evaluating success are often very different from our own. His story goes down from age to age, generation to generation, and His plans will not fail. Palm Sunday looked like such a success, such a time of high hope, but Jesus wept over Jerusalem. The Friday he was crucified looked like such a defeat, such an ending of all that His followers were anticipating, but Jesus was actually taking the keys of Death and Hades, and leading captives in His wake. Sunday morning, the women and the disciples were sure insult had been added to injury by grave robbers, but He was actually risen from the dead!! It's just not the end of the story until that last day! "*Judge nothing before the appointed time,*" says Paul. "*Indeed, I do not even judge myself. My conscience is clear, but that does not make me innocent. It is the Lord who judges me. Judge nothing before the appointed time; wait till the Lord comes. He will bring to light what is hidden in darkness and will expose the motives of men's hearts. At that time each will receive his praise from God.*" 1 Corinthians 4:3-5.

It would have been nice to contentedly watch the goat project flourishing, bringing additional hope, truth and income to one impoverished village after another. That was the hope and the vision. As it is, there are thousands of Lisu farmers who have been trained to succeed in SALT farming. Many of them are continuing the practice even when they are no longer required to by contract. This is a good thing, and they can potentially pass it on farmer to farmer even without a "project" devoted to that. If those who have been trained persevere and succeed, there is hope for widespread acceptance of the new ways. Change is coming to the valley, with the government moving ahead with huge hydroelectric projects which are slated to necessitate the re-settling of at least 60 000 Lisu people from the flooded areas. Who knows where they will go, or what skills they will need to survive in their new lives? God. We need to trust (Philippians 1:6 "*He who began a good work in you will carry it on to completion until the day of Christ Jesus*"), and pray that God will accompany the "diaspora" of the Lisu people with an outpouring of His Spirit and truth, enabling them to escape from and resist the forces which are presently at work to destroy their way of life, faith and families.

"Scientific" Chicken Raising

Gloria

"MaMa! It's so good to see you! I've missed you so much! Aaa -a. Aaaa-a" (My kids know exactly how to make this sound that all the old ladies who want something from us make!)

It was Anni, her wrinkled face wreathed in a gap-toothed smile as she pulled me to her sagging bosom. She made a habit of dropping in whenever she went to market days to sell some produce or piglets, and never failed to press me to come for a visit up to her house as well. She had fairly advanced trachoma when we first met, but numerous vials of eye ointment had brought that under control. Now her main complaint was constipation, but I could not convince her that just drinking more water and eating more veggies would do her more good than "a little medicine".

Today, though, once the initial greeting was over, the worry lines took over. "Mama, I've just come from visiting my daughter, Gloria, who got married last year to a boy across the river. She's really sick; can't get out of bed and just coughs and coughs. She's even coughing up blood. I went over to help take care of her baby boy. Do you have a little medicine for her?"

"Could she come to see me here? I can't just give her medicine without even seeing her."

"I'll have to talk with her husband. If he's willing and can help her get here, then she can come."

"Okay. Try to get her here on Wednesday. There will be a doctor from America visiting. How's her baby? Is he coughing too?"

"Yes, he's been coughing as well."

"Okay, please bring them both, and we'll try to help them."

"A Ke Shamu, Mama, Shamu shi." [Thank you so much, teacher]

That Wednesday, we met Gloria. Her history was "red hot" for TB: night sweats, poor appetite, weight loss, cough lasting more than three months. The next step was obvious -- she should get a chest x-ray and then go to the government clinic for medication.

"Wait - you say she's pregnant? How far along?"

She was afraid to go to the hospital in case they forced her to abort her second child.[19] We didn't dare send her for an x-ray, because of the potential harm to her unborn child. The local hospital was pretty blasé about radiation; there were no notices up on the wall warning prospective mothers not to enter the area, or any lead aprons. We decided on a Mantoux skin test, which was often a very helpful diagnostic aid. It was negative.

"Well, that one lung sounds completely consolidated," noted Dr. Hudson, "let's treat her for pneumonia, see how she does and take it from there. I think this antibiotic is safe during pregnancy...let me just check."

Two weeks later, they told us that Gloria was "a little better". That sounded hopeful! However, a few weeks before the doctor came again, her mom made another visit, and came by to tell me that Gloria was still not doing well. In fact, she was emaciated, could barely hold herself up and coughed constantly, ineffectively, exhaustedly.

"Hmmm. I wonder if her immune system was too overwhelmed to mount a reaction to the skin test. Maybe she was a false negative for TB. She's over four months gestation now; I think we have to risk the x-ray. At this rate, I'm afraid she's not going to make it to term anyhow." Reluctantly, she went for her chest x-ray, and it came back full of TB cavities on one side, with spots on the other.

"Are TB drugs safe to take during pregnancy?"

---

19   Minority people are usually allowed to have two children before they are forced to have abortions or be sterilized, but they are required to wait four years between births. Gloria's boy was only a year old.

"I'm pretty sure they are...let me just double check here...yup - no adverse effects to the fetus noted."

"Okay, and since her little guy has some symptoms, and has certainly been exposed, we'd better treat both of them simultaneously. Can you help me figure out his dosage once we get a weight for him?"

The next step was to send her to the county infectious disease center where she was supposed to be eligible for free medications. Later that week, Anni trudged dis-spiritedly into the yard, sank onto a stool, took off the ever-present bright knitted kerchief all traditional Lisu women wore, and mopped her forehead with it. "They say they can't give her any medication unless she gives them a sputum sample."

"Well, can she do that?"

"I'll talk to her husband's family. Her husband left her a couple of months ago to go work outside the valley."

"Oh, no! She got pregnant after she had been sick in bed a few months, too, didn't she? And now he's left her on her own. Who will take care of her and little Apu?"

"His parents, but they say she's not a very good wife, since she's sick all the time."

A few days later, she trudged into the yard again. "The clinic says she has TB, but they don't have any more medication. They said they can't give it to Apu (Gloria's son) either, because he's too small."

"Oh, no. Seriously? Well, we can provide medicine,[20] but there's no one on that side of the river who can help us follow up on her and make sure she's taking it every day. She also needs good care and nutritious food. Could she come back and live with you just until she's better? Some of your neighbours have already completed TB treatment,

---

20   We would often provide a full course of TB medicine when patients had no money, which was often the case. After they were healthy and able to work again, they could pay us back so that we could continue to provide medicine for other patients. With no enforcement, we still had over 90% payback rate.

and could help us make sure she's taking her medication properly and getting better."

"She could live with us, and I'd be happy to take care of her, but she can only come if her husband's family agrees. If they don't, there's nothing we can do."

"But surely if you tell them it's a matter of life and death, they would agree?"

"If they agree, she can come, otherwise, not..."

"Okay, well, let me know."

A few days later, their family stopped in at our yard on their way up to their village. Gloria's older brother was carrying her on his back, seated on a sort of swing seat which was attached to a tumpline which went up around his forehead. I moved my rocking chair to where he could put her down in it. She coughed, spat on the porch, then weakly wiped the spittle off her mouth with her fingers and onto the arm of my rocking chair.

"Gloria - you can't do that! From now on, you must only spit into a tissue which you burn in the fire. Your illness has already passed from someone else to you, and now from you to your baby, and if you're not careful to wash your hands often, and burn up what you cough up, you may make the rest of your family sick as well. Also, you must use your own bowl and chopsticks; you mustn't chew up baby Apu's food for him, or feed him from your chopsticks anymore. No one but you can use your chopsticks, and you mustn't get food out of the common bowl with them any more. Do you understand?" Then came the big challenge of teaching Gloria how to take her medicine!   TB patients have to take about 18 pills per day.   Side effects range from nausea and headaches to blindness or liver and kidney damage. It took Gloria about two hours before she could confidently reach for the right number of each pill, and tell me which symptoms would need to be reported to me! After a little more teaching on which foods it was important to get enough of, I watched them start up the trail towards their village, and whispered a prayer for the young mother who was fighting an equally uphill battle for her life.

A few weeks later, Gloria's mother came hurrying into the yard to get the next month's medicine, and to tell me that Gloria had suffered a miscarriage, and a lung hemorrhage. She said she had coughed up a couple of bowls full of blood, but had survived and was starting to regain some strength. I made sure there was an iron supplement in with her multivitamins, and told them to keep feeding her as if she had given birth -- lots of nourishing chicken broth -- and to keep praying.

Little Apu, Gloria's son, gained ground rapidly; it wasn't long before he was chubby, active and no longer coughing. That was a great joy to all of us. Gloria was another story; it was a long battle, with many setbacks, including the total collapse of one lung, but eventually the day came when we could "graduate" her from TB treatment, and restore her to her husband. It was quite formal -- almost like getting married again -- so I guess I wasn't the only one who felt he'd neglected and mistreated her! Unfortunately, although Gloria was now beautiful and blooming, with an exceptionally sweet smile and disposition, her husband once again took to working away for extended periods, and gambling. Then, she heard that he'd taken a blood oath with another woman. She could only think of one secret so binding that it would be sealed like that: he'd taken a mistress. It wasn't long before Gloria was officially abandoned, so once again she returned to her parents' home, grieved and disgraced, stripped of her precious little son, who, as his father's heir, had to remain with his paternal relatives.

Thankfully that was not the end of her story. Perhaps a year later, she showed up in our yard, followed by a very handsome young man. Gone was the shy, naive "up-country" girl. Gloria was tastefully dressed and groomed, and introduced her new husband with joy and confidence. She had chosen this one carefully. He was a devout Christian, cared for her a lot, and lived in a village near her parents where she already had many friends. I was impressed by the protective way he sat near her, and the considerate, attentive way he participated in the conversation. They had a question. With her history, and collapsed lung - would it be all right for them to try to have a child? Just to be sure there was no lingering disease, we sent her out to Kunming for an expert opinion. The verdict was that she was well and truly cured, and they could see no reason she couldn't successfully have a child, as long as she took good care of herself. This, her husband promised to make sure she did, and they left, quite radiant with happiness.

A Farmer's Life

The phone rang after dark one spring evening after I had already anxiously been watching out for Dave's return for a few hours.

"Hello?"

"Hi, Hon." It was Dave on his cell phone. "I hate to have to tell you this, but I'm not going to be able to leave here tonight."

My heart sank.

"Oh. That's too bad. What happened?"

Just then Dave stepped through the door and gave me a hug from behind!

"Whaaa..? You said you wouldn't get home tonight!!"

"No, I said..." -

"...that you couldn't leave *here* tonight. (thumping him on the chest). Anyhow, I'm so glad you made it home! How did it go?"

"All right. Tired. I hope you were praying today. You wouldn't believe some of those trails! You know we started out at Three Peaks, which is a three hour hike up, and then climbed another 5 hours up from there! At one place, there was this big flat stone covering the path. The guy in front of me stepped up onto that with his uphill foot, and slipped. He shot right off the edge, and at that point there's a drop of, I dunno, at least 200 feet. Thankfully I hadn't stepped up yet, so I had a split second to react because I was a bit below him. I grabbed him by his jacket and managed to pull him back onto the path."

"Wow! So he was like, in free fall, when you managed to grab him?"

"Yeah. If I hadn't've been there, and below him, he'd have been a goner."

"Yikes! Good thing he had his jacket zipped up! What did he say?"

"A Ke Shamu! [Thanks a lot!] I told him, 'It's a good thing it's not me who slipped, because I'm so heavy none of you could have caught me.' "[21]

"That's true. But anyhow, what did you learn? What's it like up there?"

"Well...there's lots of kids, and they're really poor. Like, a lot of the younger kids don't have any pants on, and no one has shoes. They're really caught between a rock and a hard place: they don't want to have to have abortions, so they move up there, but then it's so high and remote that it's nearly impossible to really provide for their families."

"I know. I mean, if we were Lisu, that would be us."

"The other thing is they're so isolated up there, they hardly know what to do with guests."

"How do you mean?"

"Like, they don't know how to make small talk. It was kind of awkward because at first they all just sat around and stared at us. If you think about it, they know everything there is to know about each other; there's not actually that much need to *talk* about things. They almost never see someone they haven't known for their whole life."

"Huh. Did they feed you?"

"Did they ever! We got there, and our host disappeared for awhile, and next thing you know they're bringing in a goat they butchered. I felt really bad for a minute, and then I thought, 'Well, I don't have to eat very much of it, and the rest of them almost never get meat. It'll be good for them, especially the kids.' So that helped."

"We need to get a survey of all the people from that village for when the second-hand clothing shipment gets here. It sounds like they could use the clothes more than any of the villages lower down. Are you going to take them into the goat project?"

---

21   Dave weighs 85kg on a good day, but the average Lisu weighs about 60kg.

"I still need to discuss it with the goat workers, but they weren't really asking for that. Just that one guy who's been so pushy all along, but his dad actually already has goats from the project. I think he can get some young ones from his dad and start a herd that way."

Climbing to villages was an integral part of Dave's work. Thankfully, it was mostly local, so we still saw a lot of each other. Sometimes, though, he would be asked to assist in agricultural trainings in other parts of the province. On one such trip, he was travelling with a group of vets and agricultural experts, acting mainly as a translator, but planned to leave the tour a little early to go to Kunming and pick up my parents, who were coming for a visit.

Well, he left early all right, but not for that reason!

On the third night, he started having excruciating abdominal pain, which he assumed was gas. All night, he walked up and down the stairs and the halls in their guest house, trying to get some relief. The next day, he still accompanied the rest as they drove and walked around the sites, but did the translating from a miserable crouched position. That night, he phoned me, told me how he was feeling and said the pain had also moved down to his lower right side. I immediately said, 'Dave, it sounds to me like you could have appendicitis. You'd better call the doctor!" He did, and Dr. Hudson had him perform a diagnostic trick: you push in slowly and deeply just in from the right hip, where it's hurting. You wait until the pain subsides, and then release the pressure. If the pain on releasing is just as bad or worse than the pain when you were pushing, the odds are it's appendicitis. The test was positive, so Hudson asked him to get a blood test. If his white blood cell count was still relatively normal, he probably had time to get to a larger hospital. If it was high, he should check himself in where he was and have an emergency appendectomy. The blood test was still okay, so Dave excused himself from the group and bought a bus ticket for Kunming. Mercifully, his pain subsided for the five hour bus journey. When he got in that night, he was met at the hospital by a Singaporean doctor friend who taught at that hospital. He thought that since Dave's symptoms seemed to have settled down, they could probably wait until morning when he could have the procedure done by laparoscopy, rather than open surgery. So, this is what Dave told me.

When they checked him out by ultrasound, however, they felt that it would be very risky to wait until morning. There was a slight complication. Dave was supposed to be meeting my parents' plane that night at midnight, and now he was being prepped for surgery! Plan B -- if for some reason Dave wasn't waiting at the airport -- was for my parents to phone his cell phone and discuss alternate arrangements. That would have been one futile conversation, with Dave anesthetized!

My parents are bricks. They do spend a lot of time worrying about us, but when there's an actual crisis, they usually hold up amazing well. So, thankfully, our doctor friend knew a reliable driver who could meet my parents with a sign, and the doctor's phone number so they could receive an explanation of what was going on in English!

Also, by this time, the rest of the agricultural tour had also returned to Kunming, and Dave's trusty friend and co-delegate, APu, came straight to the hospital. He prayed for Dave during the surgery, and was there to wait on him hand and foot when he came out of it, too. Meanwhile, I had been busy as well. Originally, the kids and I were just supposed to wait for Dave and my parents to show up, but with him going in for surgery, I knew we all needed to go to Kunming instead. I phoned AJie, a van driver from our village, and asked him to please drive us to the bus station early the next morning, to get us onto the Dali bus. I also phoned our friends, the Nelsons, who live in Dali, to let them know what was going on. They offered to keep the kids at their house while I went on alone to Kunming to meet my parents and nurse my husband. That seemed like a good plan, so that's what we did.

While we were in AJie's van, just starting out, I got a text saying "Good morning, pyaari"[lovely] on my cell phone from Dave. Since I now knew he was awake, I phoned him back. I asked him how he was doing, and he said, "still aloive," in his best British accent, and then asked me if a low blood pressure reading could mean that he was bleeding. I said, "yes, but if you ruptured, the main symptom wouldn't be bleeding."

He said, "Oh, I've already had the surgery."

I said, "What!!? I thought they were going to wait until morning! You've already had the surgery?"

"Yup."

"All this time that I've been praying that you'd have peace and safety during the surgery, you've been post-op? What is your blood pressure?!"

"90/40, I think, but there might be a problem with her machine."

"Are you sure? That's really low! How are you feeling? Because if you're post-op, you *could* be bleeding!"

"I'm pretty sure her blood pressure cuff must have a low battery or something, because she's just gone off to get another one."

"So why didn't they wait until morning?"

"The doctor didn't think I could wait that long after they looked at the ultrasound, and he was probably right, because he said it was almost ruptured when they took it out."

"Well!"

"Oh, here's the nurse back again. Just a minute...okay, this time the numbers are 100/70. That's normal, isn't it?"

"Yeah. So you're okay? Hey! Where are Mom and Dad?! ...."

Well, we had some catching up to do!

When we got to Dali, Barry Nelson was waiting at the bus station. He gave me a hug, then handed me a lunch bag and a ticket for a bus leaving in five minutes, while his older kids gathered my kids and their luggage and ushered them to a waiting taxi for the ride to chez Nelson! Pretty slick, and very quick! Just like that I was divested of the six kids and on my way for the last leg of the journey to Dave. That express bus couldn't move fast enough for me. I inwardly fumed as the bus headed off the highway for the mandatory 45 minute rest just an hour and a half from my destination. It seemed like such a brutal waste of time, but then...a little miracle: a detour sign which convinced our driver to instead head back out onto the freeway!

Finally, I was rushing through the hospital doors, headed for Dave's room, when I bumped into him in the hall! He was already up, trying to walk off post-op gas and refusing pain medication. Another reason he was up may have been that his four-bed room was full of smokers and big bouquets of lilies, both of which he's allergic to! At least he had a room; many stretchers were out in the hall. Dave's getting up and mobile so quickly was a wonder to his room-mates, who were still scared to move even several days post-op, as was his little declaration of emancipation when he insisted that the nurses remove his IV (he had to sign a waiver) once he could drink. Anyhow, it wasn't long until we got him discharged, (after signing another waiver), found my mom and dad coming in from a noodle shop, and got the lot of us settled into a nice guest apartment which Dave had arranged.

Two more things stick out from that time. One was Dave's extreme pain when he had to leap out of the way of a motorcycle which ignored the pedestrian crossing, and the other was hearing that his surgeon had not waited for him to be completely "under" before starting to slice. Dave was fully conscious, but unable to move or protest for a good bit of his surgery. He says it gave him a new appreciation for the verse in Hebrews where it says, "Some were sawn in half," referring to the martyrs.

On that pleasant note...

A village up the mountain from us

The Crushed Thumb

"What are our neighbours doing, do you know?"
"Where?"
"Down beside the Teacher's house -- that tall pole with all the wires. They're not stealing electricity are they?"
"It's so out in the open, they must have some kind of an arrangement."
A few days later we heard for ourselves.
"Chuck-a-chuck-a-chuck-a-chuck-a..." -- our neighbours had set up a rock-crusher right across the road from us! From then on, as long as there was electricity, our lives would be accompanied by the sound of that machine.

One evening, a few weeks later, we ate a nice dinner in town with a team of doctors who came from Shanghai to do free surgeries and training in the county hospital.[22] One of our Singapore doctor friends arranged the outreach, and also asked us to encourage the team. They ended up encouraging us, though, because one of them broke down in tears and told us that there were many young people in Shanghai still praying for us. She said that they had read about our family in the newspapers, and thought, "Only Christians would do something like that," and started praying for us. Way back in 2002, some reporters scoping out something else came across Dave working out in the fields and wrote an article. For some reason, newspapers all over the country, and even in overseas Chinese communities like Boston and New York picked up the story. For several months there were reporters from places like Beijing, Shanghai and Guangzhou showing up in our yard at all

---

22 During the 10 years our team was in the valley, we hosted many medical outreaches. We will always be indebted to the wonderful surgical teams who so ably, humbly, and graciously relieved much suffering, and helped the local doctors to improve their skills and attitude. We really did see an improvement in the local medical system while we were here.

hours, along with impressionable young people who thought they wanted to join our "cause"! At the time it had felt so ridiculous, an intrusion and an embarrassment, so we were amazed to see how God had used it.

When we returned from our meal in town, our neighbour came up with his thumb wrapped tightly in a blood-soaked rag. He was a middle-aged man, short, swarthy, with wild eyebrows and kind eyes. He had a good, hard-working wife and five kids in school.

"I came earlier, MaMa, but you weren't here."

"I'm sorry, we were in town. What's happened to your hand?"

"I was using the rock crusher, and dropped a rock on it. A Ke Na [It really hurts] MaMa!"

"Can we take a look at it? Has the bleeding stopped?"

"Yeah, I think it'll be all right..." We carefully unwrapped it together, but the whole fleshy ball of his thumb flopped back like the lid of a step-can garbage container, while bloody cracks spread out from there in all directions like a smashed wind shield.

"Okay. Is the bone broken? No? Have you washed it at all? No? Well, the amount that's bled, it's probably fairly clean by now. Let's just put some antibiotic ointment on there before it gets bleeding any worse, and wrap it up again."

"When can I use it, Mama?"

"You're going to have to keep that clean and dry for a couple of weeks, I would think. I'll help you change the dressing every day, and if it gets wet or dirty."

"Okay. Thank you very much. Are you sure it'll take that long? I have to work and find the money to feed the kids and keep them in school."

"I know, but I honestly don't think it will heal any faster than that."

I had no sooner finished bandaging his thumb, than a senile grandma who sometimes visits us came by with a pair of size 10 or 11 men's shoes (huge by Lisu standards) that she'd picked out of the trash on market day. She saw them, and thought of Dave. He had to take his shoes off and show her that his feet STILL wouldn't fit even those, and then she headed for me and I had to take my shoes off, too...She left, and a crazy grandpa who dresses in army surplus clothes complete with hat and toy gun in a holster showed up with a bag of spoiled food and empty drink bottles, obviously also scrounged from the rubbish bins on market day. He cheerfully explained that they had plenty of produce to share at his house these days, and unloaded it at our front door, to the mingled amusement and concern of our neighbours who were on their way up to the chapel. He's actually a former pastor, but his son went over to Burma, and never came back. When his wife went over to look for their son, she died there as well and grief unhinged his mind. Dave handled the situation really well, and also did a great job of explaining to the kids why it was important to be kind to people with mental illness. We somehow got the kids put to bed while all this was going on, and it wasn't until I was in bed myself that I started to laugh. It had all seemed so normal!

Our neighbour came back for a dressing change on his thumb the next day, but the day after that he didn't show, so the next morning I went looking for him with gauze, scissors and bandage tape in hand.
He welcomed me in a with a sheepish grin and confessed, "I've been working." My eyes jumped to his wounded hand in alarm -- what had he done to himself using his hand so soon?
His thumb was unbandaged, with a barely discernible line where the flesh had been flopping off three days previously! Rough, calloused and stained from endless hard labour, his two hands looked identical!

I must have gaped, because they laughed and explained, "A relative came over from Burma, and they had a little native medicine made with HaMaGuZi with them."
"Made with what?"
"HaMaGuZi".
My total incomprehension made them laugh some more, and then one of them hesitantly came out with the Chinese word - "Da Xiang Pi"
"Elephant skin?! "
They had stuck his thumb back together with some kind of glue made from elephant skin, and he was able to use it within two days of his injury! Wouldn't Johnson & Johnson love to get their hands on *that* recipe!

Actually, I should have got some to send with Dave when he was working and just about lost all his fingers.

Most people visiting the valley for the first time try to cross a LiuSuo [zip-line] across the river for fun. Back when the only way into the valley was by mule train, the only ways to cross the river were by flimsy bamboo sampans during the dry season when the river slowed and shrank to a navigable width, or by terrifying rattan "bridges" which were really just two strands of the vine, one above the other -- one rope to sidle along, and one to hold onto -- linked by shorter pieces. Since the road had been put in, the government built numerous cable and concrete or cable and plank bridges over the river, but there were still long stretches where the only convenient way to land anywhere near your village was by zip-line. One of the villages the goat project took on was like this. In all our nine years in the valley, neither I nor the kids ever went over a zip-line. It felt like tempting providence to get our kicks in such a dangerous fashion, so we didn't. Dave never bought a motor bike or indulged his wish for a kayak for the same reasons. With seven dependents, we just didn't feel that expendable! But, in the line of duty, he did have to cross this zip-line, and it was exhilarating to say the least! That particular cable had sagged so that it dropped very steeply towards the jagged rocks on the near bank of the river, and then went up to the tower on the far side just as abruptly. The only way you'd have a hope of making it up the far side was to drop as fast as you could on the way down. The first couple of times, experienced villagers shared a pulley with Dave and directed the plunge, but the day soon came when he decided he'd prefer to be in control himself, rather than continue to stress-test those ropes and pulleys. The first time he did all right, but the next time, the gloved hand which he was using as a guide on the cable, snagged, and he just barely pulled it free in time to avoid having all his fingers removed by the pulley. After that, he copied the villagers and just used a handful of straw to keep his hand from getting ripped up by the cable as he shot down towards the river.[23] Another time, he forgot to do up the chin strap for his hat, and had to watch it go sailing off into the river. Since his face and neck were continually exposed to the strong sun, and because there were no locally made hats big enough for his head, that was a loss he mourned every time he had to tuck a handkerchief over his neck instead!

---

23   The river is so wide that there is always a sag in the middle of the zipline, so, unlike recreational ziplines, you can't just hang below the cable -- you need to have a hand on it to keep you from zipping back down to the middle of the sag if you don't go fast enough, or to slow you down at the end if you're going too fast, and to keep your body from rotating sideways, giving your face cable burns.

Switching Horses

Big Rock, Mountainview, Los Banos, Little Rock, Bridgeford -- our first decade in China went in a cycle: every two years we gained a baby, but lost a home! Our seven children were born in three different countries, and were usually the "first white baby" ever to be born in each Podunk county hospital. Dave was sold-out, and willing to go anywhere; God led and we followed, but it was getting hard on our family, especially on the older children, to keep uprooting. Then in 2003 He spoke through a friend these words from Isaiah 43:18-19 *"Forget the former things; do not dwell on the past. Behold, I am doing a new thing! Now it springs up; do you not perceive it?"*

The next decade God *did* do a new thing: we actually lived in one place, Valleyview, all that time! We had a beautiful view, but no indoor plumbing, and our fair share of cockroaches, rats, fleas and other "inconveniences". The path connecting the upper and lower parts of the village went through our front "yard", and since we didn't have a living room, we put benches out there, and it became the "clinic". I told the patients, "Praise God for giving us a clear day today; as you see, my living room ceiling would leak!" Back in 1999, God simply asked us, "Would you live in the village for me?" so we did. We believe He wanted us to share life with them: to be affected, available, accessible there. A witness and a participant in what life is like for them; to do what we could to be His eyes, His hands, His feet. By living with them, we were saved, at least some of the time, from offering pat answers. By experiencing some of their hardships, and by needing their help to get through them, we developed a love and respect for these tough, cheerful mountain people which I don't think would have come at a lesser price tag. They were not our "ministry", they were our neighbours, and they're pretty amazing.

The first five years in Valleyview, Dave was busy helping to get a tree-planting and goat raising project off the ground in about 23 different villages at a time, with the help of some Lisu co-workers whom he was training. In those days, he would typically arrive home at about 8 pm, muddy, hungry and exhausted after a day spent climbing up and down the challenging slopes of the Salween river gorge, helping farmers plant their steep slopes. Or, he was sick in bed. The good side of those sick times was that he was around, and able to spend a lot of time in the Word. He would also cuddle with the younger kids and read to them, or get the older kids caught up on their music lessons. Homeschool, and the home front, were basically my responsibility, and my nursing skills were mostly being used on my family.

By the time the goat project had matured to the point where Dave could act in more of a consulting role, however, I was getting absolutely swamped with requests from our village neighbours for medical help.

There was a small hospital in the nearby town of Riverbend, so why did people still line up at our house? It's difficult for village people to access health care. Most are uneducated and don't speak Chinese, so getting around a hospital or pharmacy on their own is really intimidating. Some of them live way up on the mountain peaks, have never been in a vehicle, and don't have the money for medicine.

Another, more frustrating, problem was the diagnostic and treatment limitations of the hospital. When my youngest was three days old, a neighbouring grandpa carried his pre-teen grand-daughter into the yard. She'd fallen from an upper storey, and injured her ankles. I did some first aid, gave them the money for transport and x-rays, and sent them to the hospital. Some hours later, they were back. I winced as I saw her dangling feet jarred by every weary step her grandfather took. The x-ray techs were attending a meeting. Some 'helpful' medical person had persuaded them to spend the x-ray money on an aerosol container of the Chinese equivalent of A535. Inwardly steaming, I did my best to make a splint and sent them home. In many cases, the hospital admitted patients until all their money was gone, then sent them home without ever establishing a diagnosis. Over the years, word leaked out, so many people who had exhausted their options ended up on our door step.

I remember another time, when we were deep, deep into making a huge batch of plum jam, someone came running to say a neighbour was having difficulty delivering her baby. Could I please come? "You've got to be kidding!?" But the kids and Dave shooed me out the door, and when I came back a few hours later, it was to see the kitchen cleaned up, jars all happily sealing in the pantry, and a hot supper on the table! I could also jubilantly tell them that their prayers for a safe delivery had been answered!

On other days -- beyond counting -- when I finally corralled all of my wriggling, reluctant students in from their play, everyone rummaged up a pencil and paper, and we managed to locate the read-aloud book, anxious faces would appear just outside the screen door, a beseeching voice would ask if I could just take a look .... and by the time I'd get back, my "class" would have scattered. How I have struggled with being so accessible, and so interrupted! But on the other hand, how could we fail to respond to these urgent and pathetic needs? On the one hand, by allowing ourselves to be interrupted, we were communicating to our children that school work was not so important, and they were quick to seize that attitude! On the other hand, if we told people to go away, what was that teaching our children? Trying to cope with all these conflicting demands gradually grew into a project: we had two paid local staff, and numerous donors and doctors who gave their resources and expertise to help me connect villagers with help. However, trying to keep up with it all was becoming an impossible task. Correspondence with doctors was taking up all my evenings, and I was becoming an insomniac. Something had to give, and I was afraid it was going to be me!

That was when a miracle of sorts occurred in our marriage. My parents had been visiting us, and Dave was going to escort them back out to the airport in the provincial capital. It meant getting some friends to take care of our kids for a week in order for me to go along, and four days on the bus there and back, but we succeeded in a three day getaway in a hotel with hot running water and central heating! No pets, no patients, no pests, no home school, no making kids do their chores ... Bliss! And during that time my husband read a little bit of my diary and realized that, for many months, all I had written about was how overwhelmed I was feeling. He said:

"I can teach the kids for you two or three days a week."

It was like someone pulled a plug, and so much stress just drained away. I felt reborn.

When my husband commits to do something, you can put it in the bank. I would never have asked him to take over "my job" like that, but he offered. My husband is a born leader and visionary. He doesn't naturally fall into a supporting role, but in terms of our marriage, this was one of the most affirming and important things he's ever done. We had been married 17 years, but this brought a new bloom on our relationship. I have never loved and appreciated him more. He was a fantastic example to our children, and they also benefited from interacting with his brain and experience for awhile!

Patients in our front yard

Bethany

Bethany was a beautiful little girl with huge, almond shaped dark eyes. She came from a family of six attractive children, and she was the loveliest, and the saddest. Up until she was nine or ten years old, she ran and played and went to school with the others, but then a terrible illness struck her, and she spent three years in bed. She was feverish and in so much pain that her parents hardly dared move her. Because of their many children, which put them in conflict with the one child policy, they lived warily, very much like illegal immigrants. They were from a generation and a faith community which had as little as possible to do with the Han-ruled government infrastructure, so her parents never took her to the hospital. Finally the agony subsided, and she could sit up and eat and focus on something more than enduring, but the damage was done. Her knees, her hips and her elbows were locked into the fetal position she'd maintained for so long.

One day her parents heard that there was a "white doctor" who was helping people in the village of Valleyview, so her father picked her up under the arms and carried her, all curled up like a kitten held by it's scruff, down the precipitous path from their home to the road. From there they caught a ride, and Bethany endured the bumps until she could be carried up to our house. Thankfully there really was a doctor visiting us that day, not just me, and she was immediately diagnosed with Juvenile Rheumatoid Arthritis. At first we hoped that with aggressive physiotherapy she could regain some mobility, but x-rays showed complete destruction of her affected joints.

What to do?

The doctor felt that, with appropriate medical treatment, her disease could be mitigated, but did not dare initiate such treatment while she was still in such a primitive health care setting. He said that if her family was willing to bring her to Kunming, he would be happy to get her stabilized on a drug regimen, and do what they could with physio and occupational therapy to help her regain her life. You see, for five years, Bethany had hardly seen anything but the back of her eyelids or the soot-blackened walls of the family kitchen and living room. She was extremely withdrawn and passive, which was how she had coped with the prolonged torture of her illness.

Taking Bethany to Kunming was not a simple proposition. None of her family could speak any Chinese, so she would need a translator. One of her parents would have to carry her to the bathroom, carry her meals to her and otherwise help her with all her daily activities. The parent who was left behind would be alone to do the spring planting and care for the rest of the family. To their credit, they decided to go for it. At first she and her father were very homesick, but within a couple of weeks we were hearing more cheerful reports. The doctor couple who had taken an interest in her really took her under their wing. Their daughter was about the same age and had a lot of fun sharing favourite treats and activities with her. She showed her how to colour and it wasn't long before Bethany was quite adept at a lot of handiwork. Even more wonderful, she started to smile and laugh again. Her wan cheeks plumped out, and her beautiful eyes started to sparkle with a renewed sense of life and fun. We hardly recognized her when they got off the bus a couple of months later! We sent her back home in a new wheelchair, with her bags of medicine and supplements. We gave thanks and hoped that a better life was now beginning.

All went well for a long time, but then her father came by to say that she was "sick" again. Actually, she had run out of a number of her medications, and he had not notified me or tried to replace them, as he had been instructed to do. This became an ongoing issue, not just with her, but with virtually all of our patients with chronic illness needing sustained treatment.   The Lisu consider that once someone is "better" they should no longer need medication. The idea of controlling a disease as opposed to curing it was a really foreign one.

My parents had been praying for Bethany for several years by this time, so when they came to visit us for a few weeks, we took a hike up to Bethany's house. In the same way, whenever a physician who knew her, or a physiotherapist came into our area, we would arrange a trip up to Bethany's. I asked my medical helpers to keep track of how she was doing as well.

For a couple of years, Bethany's arthritis seemed to be in remission, and at the same time an American doctor, Dr. Hudson, took an interest in her situation. He had just helped a young woman, with a very similar history, to have bilateral hip and knee replacements done at a hospital in Thailand. She had gone there all contracted up and crippled, and come back walking. When I talked to her on the phone, she said that the surgical pain and long period of rehabilitation had been totally worth it - her life was so much better now. At the same time, we received a substantial, unsolicited gift to be used for our medical work.   We decided to ask Bethany's family what they thought of the idea of Bethany and her father going to Thailand to see if joint replacements were possible for her as well.   This was a big departure from our usual low-budget, low-key approach to assistance, but the thought of Bethany being released to enjoy at least the next twenty years of her life was irresistible. Her parents agreed, although it would mean the mother had to once again cope with the prolonged absence of her husband. Thankfully by this time, her oldest son was big enough to help with the plowing and heavy work.

So, our friend Ed helped them get passports and visas while we contacted friends who were living in Thailand and asked them to help as they were able. Those friends arranged for them to spend any time they weren't actually at the hospital with a Thai Lisu community at a nearby seminary.[24] They also arranged for a Christian Thai/Lisu translator to accompany Bethany through treatment. Then we prayed.

What we didn't know was that the American doctor who had provided oversight for Dr. Hudson's previous patient was now back in the States. Her Thai staff, though sweet and willing, lacked the experience and expertise to guide Bethany's tests and treatment. She had used up most of her three month visa, spent huge sums on tests and travel expenses and received increasingly contradictory reports on the feasibility and cost of surgery before we learned the reason for the hold-up. When Dr. Hudson, who was also in the States, finally talked directly with the specialist we had mistakenly assumed was aware of and overseeing Bethany's case, she contacted her staff and arranged for a conclusive test. The conclusion was "No."

Although she was 18, Bethany was still as slight and undeveloped as an eleven year old. Because she had not done any weight-bearing for so many years, the long bones of her legs were thin and weak, and the surgeons were afraid they would just splinter when the prosthetic joints were introduced. Thankfully, Dr. Hudson graciously arranged to pay our medical fund back for all the money which had gone down the drain, but we all felt so badly for Bethany. Our friends in Thailand did what they could to compensate by arranging for her and her

---

24   Since her father was a deacon at their church, we hoped this would be an eye-opening, life-changing experience for him. Chinese Lisu have been very isolated from the worldwide Church, and tend to be very ingrown and legalistic compared to Lisu communities in other Asian countries.

father to go elephant-riding but at the end of the day, they had to come home.

Sadly, the first thing we heard when they got back was a semi-hysterical phone call from the young woman who was their China-side translator and advocate. She had gone to the airport to meet them, but then an ex-pat doctor on the same flight offered them all a free ride home to the rehab center. The translator then asked Bethany's father if she could have the funds back which he had been given for their taxi ride from the airport. He hadn't used the money, and she had run short of ready funds for several other patients who were in Kunming under her care. He flew into an absolute rage, verbally abusing her and accusing her of wanting to steal the money! I guess those of us who have never lived hand-to-mouth can never really understand just how much it means to have some cash in hand, but we were really sad and shocked that a man who had just been given so much could turn around and be so selfish. He actually also had several hundred yuan which the believers at the seminary had collected as an offering for them. When they returned back to the valley, I had a debriefing time with Bethany's father. We talked about the incident with our translator, and I also learned that he had come down with what must have been Dengue fever while they were living at the seminary! There was no question that it had been a stressful time, though very enriching and broadening in other ways.

Once her dad was home, her family built an addition onto their house. It was a nice, clean new room which would be Bethany's "apartment"! We rejoiced that they did this for her, and brought up some pictures for her walls.

One day, my medical helper told me that she had bumped into Bethany's father, and he mentioned that, for a couple of months, she had been in severe pain, huddled upright on a piece of sectional couch and hardly eating. I was afraid that her arthritis drug might have started killing off her bone marrow. Could they please take her to the hospital for tests? They were reluctant, because of the excruciating pain it caused her to move, but they finally took her for the blood test. When I saw the results, I could have screamed with frustration; true to form, the hospital had done the wrong test! I pleaded with her dad to try once more, and promised to meet them at the hospital and make sure we got what the doctors needed to figure out what was going on. The results showed that she had not developed the life-threatening complication I feared, or calcium deficiency[25], but her disease, which we hoped had "burnt itself out" had flared up and come back with a vengeance for all her previously unaffected joints. Now her neck, spine, toes, and fingers were in agony. I began to wonder if her parents had just given up on her, and asked my medical helper to get to the bottom of why they had let her suffer so long without contacting me. The answer was basically, yes. They had lost hope that she would ever recover medically from this awful disease, and were waiting on God for either death or healing.

When my helper went to visit her a few weeks later, it seemed that death could not be far off. We grieved that her life had been so suffused with pain, and could understand how they were all ready to release her to a better place. I tried not to judge, and to remember how much her illness cost them as a family. They had sat up with her and helped her change her position through all the endless nights. They had carried her, washed her, and done all they could in their limited context to take care of her. Her father had spent months with her in hospital and away from home. And now she was as sick as she'd been in the beginning.

Useless to wish they'd sought help earlier, or followed instructions more conscientiously. Useless to try and coerce them into doing what we would do. We

---

25   Once again, her father had let her supply of supplements lapse.

prayed for a quick and merciful release, and gave thanks that she had put her trust in Jesus, and could look forward to being with Him.

A few months later, I ran into her dad in town. Bethany had not died, but gradually gotten better! He said that they'd stopped all her medications except a little bit of locally available Ibuprofen, and that she was basically doing all right with that. The last time I saw them together, Bethany was nestled trustingly in her father's arms. There was such a great tenderness between them, and a total closeness and intimacy which needed no words. She appeared utterly content and at peace, and he helped and handled her with such practiced kindness. Watching them, and the total adjustment they'd made to her handicaps, I could finally "fang xin" [lay my heart down] and acknowledge that they had attained something as rare and wonderful as a complete recovery. Watching them together brought a mental picture of Jesus, the Great Shepherd, carrying a lamb. I now view some of what we tried to do for them as sheer interference, though hopefully knowing we cared and were trying to help also gave them some encouragement. It was encouraging to me, at least, to see how beautiful "failure" had turned out to be.

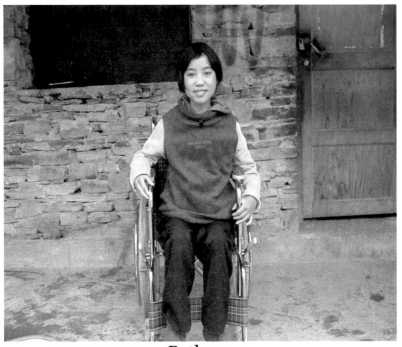

Bethany

Setting Boundaries

When you look at the roots of holiday [holy day], or recreation [re creation] it seems clear that there needs to be a focus on doing things which restore our inner person and move us toward deeper communion with our Maker. Our holidays always seemed to restore our perspective, too, and leave us eager to get back to our home and life. On one holiday, though, we were actually *dreading* the thought of going back home -- a sure sign that we were not coping well. This was after our first couple of years in Riverbend county. We had two babies in our first two years there, and were trying to combine a lot of outreach to our neighbours with our first couple of years trying to home school while learning a new language. It was a heavy load! During our retreat time, we saw the need and wisdom of setting some boundaries around our family time, and decided what those would be.

The first boundary we agreed on was that we would not interrupt our Bible time for anything less than a major crisis; we sometimes invited people to join the breakfast table and read along in their own language, but we really tried not to be led off track.

Another sacred time was family meals. We occasionally made exceptions, but we tried to make it a priority to eat together. We reasoned that no matter where people go to access medical help, odds are they'll have to wait a bit. It was really rare that the issue could not wait 15 minutes for us to finish our meal.

The third time we protected was our sabbath. Since we lived in a context where we were exceedingly accessible, and almost always feeling "over our heads", we decided that it was really important to do what we could to refresh one another. Having both of us "on duty" 24/7 with a large family was wearing us both down to a nub. I think this was particularly true because both of us are introverts, and living with a crowd all the time prevented us from ever having some "alone time" to recharge. On Saturday mornings, Dave would take his guitar and his Bible, and take off. We would see him again for team meeting (what we called our fellowship), in the afternoon. On Sunday, I would go somewhere else, preferably clean and quiet, where I could enjoy an extended time of prayer or journaling away from all the usual demands. This was the only way to get away from incessant medical requests as well. It was amazing how a few hours away from the fray, in uninterrupted times of fellowship with the Lord, would decrease stress, unclog prayer channels and release a burst of creativity. Most of my thorny problems with the kids, school and patients were solved during those hours of rest and reflection as I sought the mind of the Lord.

A final thing we tried to cordon off were school hours from 9-12. We were not as rigid about this because we certainly felt that an important part of our children's education was to learn to respond compassionately to other people's needs. Once, I was trying to dress the badly burned foot of a feisty toddler, who was throwing a major tantrum, thrashing about and banging the wounded foot into the dirt. She needed to be restrained, and her mother and brother seemed completely helpless to do it. At that point my eldest daughter came over, said, "I can hold her Mommy," picked her up and gently but firmly held her on her lap. The amazing thing was that within three minutes, while I was still cleansing her wound, she had fallen asleep, perfectly content in my daughter's arms! What would I have done without her help?

On the other hand, if we allowed ourselves to be interrupted all the time, that communicated that education was not very important. If Mom and Dad would just slip "off task" every time someone came into the yard, the kids were quick to feel that they were justified in doing the same! So, if near neighbours dropped in because they were going by and remembered that they had a small medical problem they'd been meaning to ask me about, we would ask them to either wait with a cup of tea, or to come back in the afternoon. If, on the other hand, a group of people from a distant village arrived carrying a patient, I would ask the kids to do their "self-study" subjects and try to take care of them immediately.

Eventually, we acceded to the suggestion that we set up a "clinic day", rather than handling patients every day. I resisted this for a long time. For one, I did not feel qualified, and wondered if people would expect more of me than I could really deliver if I made it so formal. I also wanted it to be clear that it was a "labour of love" because I felt constrained as a Christian neighbour to respond to their needs, rather than my "business" in the village. For another, it felt inhospitable to ask people to come back another time.

However, it was proving to be impossible to maintain translator support on an "on call" basis. My wonderful translator/medical helper was also a woman with a family and other responsibilities, and she needed regular hours and regular pay. It also gave visiting doctors a day to "aim for" when they were planning their trip, and assured patients who were trying to arrange carriers or transportation for an ill family member that they would catch us at home and at a good time.

Dave made sure he was there to take care of the children, the schooling and the meals on clinic day, freeing me up to take care of others. He was very committed about that, and basically never "left me in the lurch" if it could possibly be arranged otherwise. For me, being set free to do one thing well rather than several simultaneous tasks poorly was as good as a holiday! Before he started helping with the home schooling, I was forever mislaying lab reports because they'd been handed to me as I was running up the stairs with a load of laundry; or I was waking up with a jerk in the middle of the night, wondering if I'd remembered to email critical lab results to the doctor. By enabling me to be assured that both the home schooling and the health of our neighbours were being properly cared for, Dave relieved me of a constant sense of guilt and distress.

Perhaps more important than setting these time boundaries was the need for some heart boundaries on my expectations of myself. Why did I feel it was my responsibility to get everybody "better"? What if, in fact, their illness was God's work in their life, or a consequence to get their attention? Perhaps I should be asking them, "What do you think God is saying to you through this illness?"

"What do you think He may be trying to accomplish in your life by allowing this?

"Do you love God? Then 'all things work together for good to those who love God.' If not, then perhaps He wants you to remember that you are dust and will return to it, and to 'number your days aright'. He cares for your eternal spirit even more than your body, which will perish, and in His love will do all He can to help you repent and receive His salvation before it's too late."

Finally, I could pray, "Thank you, Lord, for how you have delivered me from anxiety over my patients. We can trust You to work everything together for their good. Be my passion, Dear Lord. Help me to study Your word, and to retain it for the encouragement of others. Thank you so much that through Dave's help and the support of many ex-pat doctors, and most of all through the help of your Holy Spirit enabling me to trust You with the patients, I am at peace -- not taking so much on myself. You really can heal if You want to, and You really can use illness to bring to repentance, or salvation, too. And You can enable me to show mercy cheerfully." (Romans 12:8) And I laid hold of these words: *"Never be lacking in zeal, but keep your spiritual fervour, serving the Lord. Be joyful in hope, patient in affliction, faithful in prayer."* (Romans 12:11,12)   *"The Sovereign Lord has given me an instructed tongue, to know the word that sustains the weary. He wakens me morning by morning, wakens my ear to listen like one being taught. The Sovereign Lord has opened my ears, and I have not been rebellious, I have not drawn back."* (Isaiah 50:4-5)

     "What do you want me to do for you?" Jesus once asked. Instead of praying *for* people, as they were always requesting, we started getting them to approach God for themselves in Jesus name, laying their petitions before Him while we said "Amen!" And we gradually stopped assuming we knew what people needed and wanted, and took the time to get their perception on their needs before organizing a treatment plan. True medical emergencies were actually quite rare; there was almost always time to pray and discuss and seek information from the family and the community before rushing into the decision to send someone out to Kunming or in for surgery. The times we neglected to do this, we were often sorry.

Retreat

AKe MaPa

I came flying out of the kitchen into our yard one day, and there was a tall, fine-looking older man standing there, waiting humbly with his hat in his hands. He had no hair, and the end of each sentence slid into a diffident mumble. That day he was there on behalf of the young girl standing by his side. He said that she was an orphan with a bad cough; could we perhaps help her get some treatment?

This man, AKe MaPa [pastor AKe], had been in the Chinese army for a few years, traveling around with them and learning Chinese. When he retired from that, he was due to receive a bit of a pension, but only if he gave up his idea of working as a pastor, since government employees must be official atheists. "Then I guess I won't get a pension," he decided. He and his wife lived in a simple bamboo hut, raised their five children and shared life with the rest of the "AGa" [Up there] folks. He and the rest of the upper villages on that "bench" of the mountains would go through our yard on the way to town. One time he asked if he could please leave his beiluo [back basket] of Tung nuts there until the next day. He had already carried it the 12 km to town and back, but had been unable to sell them. The ride into town cost only two yuan each way at that time, but they couldn't afford it. Since he'd been unable to convert the nuts into money, he had also come without any of the necessary items, like salt, which he'd been hoping to buy.

And he still had the two hour uphill hike to get home. [26] Hard.

Whenever we were due to have a doctor come in to help see patients, I would be sure to let AKe know, because he would faithfully organize a little entourage of the chronically ill, lead them down the hill on the appointed day, and give me a bit of a patient history. All that was missing was the shepherd's crook.

When we'd get a case of vitamins, AKe helped distribute many bottles to women in his pastorate who were worn out from much child-bearing on a very meager diet. It was so exactly what their bodies needed that the results seemed miraculous to them! His health wasn't good, either, so I gave him a bottle. He gave that away, too. The next time he came, he asked for permission to use just a few of the vitamins to help his little grandson, who he finally revealed had been really ill for several months. That, too, was typical of him. He never presumed on his relationship with us, or his role as mediator, to derive benefit for himself or his family. He was amazingly, incredibly non-partisan for an Asian, and could be trusted to put the neediest and sickest first, even if they were from other villages and no relation of his!

One time some friends of ours in the city were given all the remaining stock when a stationery store closed down. So they brought it out to us. "Umm, thanks." {*Where are we going to PUT a 50 year supply of pencils and notebooks??!*} But then, as we prayed

---

26   Many times, women from the upper villages would also leave us their unsold produce, rather than lugging it all the way home to feed to their pigs. We accepted it with thanks, gave them a cup of cold water, and did not offer to pay. Most of them had received help of some sort from us, and it made them happy to be able to reciprocate in this fashion. And there was often a good reason that their produce hadn't sold -- either because there was a glut of it on the market, or because it was over ripe, buggy and wilting -- so what we couldn't eat, we fed to the goats and rabbits. We had no wish to become responsible for buying all our produce from what other people were needing to dump.

about it, I got an idea. For a couple of years already, we had been talking with AKe about how to help his people become bilingual. Most were content with only speaking their tribal language, and being illiterate, but -- as one of the few people from 'up there' who had ever been out of the valley -- he knew, as they did not, how necessary Chinese, and a basic education, was going to be to their future, especially the children's. We asked him if there was anyone up there who could write Lisu and would be willing to teach the children and any other illiterate people. He thought yes, and understood that literacy in the mother language was the most important first step to becoming literate in a second language. A few days later, he came back down with the prospective teacher in tow. We explained that we could provide all the stationery supplies if they could use the church as a school house and come up with the money for a black board. They were pretty excited about it!

A couple of weeks later, I met AKe in town. His arm was out of it's sleeve, and he rather sheepishly told me that he was trying to buy some gauze.
"Why?"
He gingerly lifted his arm and exposed a number of deep burn holes. Trying to rig up a home-made hydro-electric generator so that their new "school" could have lights for the adult evening class, he had electrocuted himself! It took him a long time to regain consciousness, and his horrified congregation had buried him up to his face in a trench, hoping that the earth would somehow draw the extra electricity out of him! We so nearly lost him just like that! Praise God that he recovered!
"Why on earth didn't you just stop by our house? We have lots of bandaging materials which visiting surgical teams have left behind." When he heard that, he gladly came back with me so that his wounds could be properly treated.

AKe was such an able Shepherd and village leader. Once everyone in his village had graduated from the Lisu class, we started looking for a Chinese teacher. I was worried this could be a nearly impossible task, so we prayed about it. Where could we find an educated person who would be willing to live in such a remote and impoverished situation? When we brought it up to AKe, he said that there was actually a former teacher already living up there. Maybe he would be willing to take on the task of educating the rest of the village! We suggested that we could start off paying the teacher's salary if the village would come up with a plan to gradually take on the responsibility over five years. What ended up happening instead was that when the local government saw what they were doing, they paid the teacher's salary, but they actually allowed them to keep using the Bible based literacy program a friend of ours had made available! They had over 200 students, and really persevered with it, only taking a short break over Christmas and Easter.

One time, when Dave and I were feeling quite snowed under with our regular responsibilities, we received news that a friend had arranged for a high school class in Hong Kong to come spend five days in the valley with us. Could we please find them something to do? Of course our first response was, "Couldn't somebody have first *asked* us if this was a good time and a good idea?" And then I flippantly said, "Well, we've been talking about teaching the villagers how to build composting toilets; the students *could* dig toilets!" So we asked AKe if this bus full of kids could come up to his village and help them build toilets. He very graciously agreed to the scheme, and they laid themselves out for these guests from afar. A lot of the kids had never been in such steep terrain, so the villagers ended up carrying most of their backpacks and assisting a couple of the kids to make it up as well! Then, according to the kids' report, they slaughtered animals constantly and fed them about five times a day. They would come out from eating and find that the men of the village had finished digging their hole for them! Anyhow, the supreme hospitality touched the HK kids deeply. When it was time to go back down, they were accompanied by virtually all the young people of the village. They all clung to each other, weeping and hugging and holding hands! It was an amazing thing.

When I saw AKe after he'd done shepherding all the kids back down, though, I was shocked. He was gaunt and his eyes glittered with fever. It turned out he'd been very ill with a kidney infection the whole time, but had not let it slow him down. We felt pretty guilty, then, for the heavy burden we'd laid on him, and decided we'd never do that again. The school was hoping to send a group of students another year, but public bus bombings in Kunming, the capital city they'd have to come through, discouraged them from coming.

AKe also struggled with chronic prostatitis, and we actually took him and another villager out to Dali one time to see a Christian doctor friend there. Our friend gave AKe an excellent overhaul, and put him on a regimen which cured the problem. I had been wondering the whole time we were on the bus to Dali what our village friends' impressions would be. Personally, the contrast always hit me, driving out of mountainous Lisuland into the fertile plains which marked the ancient Bai Kingdom. Lisuland consisted of little hamlets scraping out a living from their near-vertical, rugged corn patches. The Bai lived in prosperous two-storey, tiled houses with intricate patterns painted on them, and went out to plow with water buffaloes or tractors. Their land was just so rich! AKe and his friend never stopped marveling the whole time they were there. They had never seen anything like ErHai (a 40 km long lake) or the flat, fertile fields filled with lush crops of garlic, broad beans and flowers! They would go up on the roof and watch the sunset over the lake for hours. They slept between clean, white sheets in a beautiful little guest house, and got to eat pizza and cheesecake and all kinds of western "treats" for a week. Then, when we got home, after a nine hour bus ride, I invited them to rest and eat at my house before climbing back up to their village. They declined, which didn't really surprise me, because AKe had never taken us up on an invitation to eat before. However, when Dave pointed out that there was a pot of left over "Ohshwa pala" -- their staple corn gruel -- they weakened and stayed for a meal! They just couldn't resist a taste of the food they'd eaten almost every day of their lives up until that week. Contentment. That was one thing they owned in abundance.

AKe truly loved his people and always rejoiced and gave thanks to God when there was any kind of opportunity for them medically, educationally or spiritually, even though this invariably meant more work for him. One time a young Australian doctor came with a friend of his who knew Mandarin. They, too, just loved the Lord and were happy to serve in any capacity. They helped me do a one week "maternal and child health" training for village women. They not only prepared the trainings, they carried my shopping, helped prepare lunch for all those ladies, and were often caught doing the dishes as well! There were 16 ladies .... and AKe MaPa! He refused to be embarrassed or intimidated by the fact that this was a ladies training about things like safe childbirth. He loved to learn, and felt that this was life-saving information which he should be responsible for as the village leader. Although I had not originally planned it this way, it was wonderful to have him there, because it was culturally and politically appropriate for him to do the scripture reading and opening prayer. It also validated to the ladies the worth of the material they were learning.

AKe and his wife really loved their children, and he was very attached to their youngest daughter in particular. One day she disappeared. Neither he nor his wife could eat or sleep, but prayed and searched and tried to galvanize the police into action. Finally they learned that a distant relative, recently returned from work in the city, had convinced her and her cousin to run away to the factory. AKe was such a gentle and long-suffering man, but he left the woman in no doubt that she would be very, very sorry if she did not at once assist him in getting them back. He had gotten in the habit of stopping in our yard as he came and went in his ceaseless quest, so we knew what was happening, and were praying fervently. He told us he'd found them, but they were being kept as virtual prisoners in a province far to the north east. It would take almost a week of travel and a couple thousand yuan, which he didn't have, to go fetch them. I mentioned this to my parents, and a friend of theirs, who had unexpectedly come into a sum of money, felt constrained to finance the rescue. When AKe came back with the girls and got off the bus near our place, we were shocked by their appearance. They had been telling him that they were not being paid, and that, to escape, they needed to outwit the people who were keeping them there. However, when they got off the bus, they had obviously been spending a good deal of money on make-up, hair dressers and clothes! Our hearts sank as we realized that AKe's daughter had deceived him, and caused her father and mother so much needless exhaustion and distress. They may have eventually become homesick and regretted their decision, but there was no doubt that they had been willing enough to go, and had made the most of their time in the city!

A couple of months later, they disappeared again. In grimness and grief, AKe and his wife accepted that she was lost to them for the time being. Like so many other Christian parents of wayward children, they pray.

I remember Jill Briscoe telling a story one time of her ministry to street kids. She and some friends would go down to the park or the pubs, where the kids would hang out, to talk with them and offer them a clean, safe place to sleep for the night. One time a teen-aged girl agreed to go with her, and got into the car. As they talked some more, Jill learned that she was from a Christian family. She casually reached over and locked the car door. In answer to the girl's nervous, "Who are you?", she said "I'm the answer to your mother's prayers." The girl rededicated her life to God that night, and was reunited with her parents. Prayer is a force to be reckoned with, and as James says, "The prayer of a righteous man is powerful and effective."

Since writing this, we were devastated to hear that AKe has fallen into adultery. He has repented of it, and has resigned his position as pastor. He hangs his head now, and says little. It's a sober reminder that we have an enemy, and we're always in his sights. We still hope and pray that God will somehow work good out of this situation, and continue to use this brother to bring a blessing in his village and beyond.

Planting Steep Slopes with Dave

"Dave: "Okay, just use the seeds in this bowl to plant a new row under the Pigeon Pea and those in the black tin for skips. Karen can help you."

Christie: "Okay."

Karen: "Don't hoe that, Mommy, that is definitely not a weed -- look!"

Christie: "Oops. Uh, Dave? Have the kids already re-planted here in the not-so-distant past? There seem to be some baby trees here where you told me to plant."

Dave: "Yeah, but don't plant where they are -- just plant where they aren't."

Christie: "Well, maybe it's obvious to you, but I can't tell the difference between weed cotyledons and tree cotyledons. Maybe I'd better plant beside you...either that or give me something REALLY obvious to do!"

Dave: "Alright -- uh, you haven't been hoeing up these Mulberry shoots have you? Or these wild figs?"

Christie: "Um, right, Mulberry and wild figs...what do they look like?"

Dave: "Look out for the corn shoots..."

Christie: "Where?"

Dave: "The ones going 'crunch' under your feet."

Christie: "Oh, no! Sorry little corns. Aaaaa!!! {Wildly grasping at the air as her feet go out from under her} Where's Kent (our children's volunteer tutor that year)?"

Dave: "Getting more goat poop."

Christie: "Oh."

Kent: {Scrambling up the hill, trying to balance two heavy buckets of manure while stepping only between corn hills on a rain-slick slope, slippery as a buttered pan}...."Waaaah!!"

Christie: "Kent!! Are you all right?! That was hilarious!"

Kent: " Don't laugh -- it could happen to you! Uh -- you're standing on the pumpkin patch."

Christie: "I am? How do you know?"

Kent: "I almost hoed there, and Dave told me."

Christie: "Aha." {Moving offending feet and continuing hoeing} "AAH! LOOK OUT!! I'm so sorry -- all I did was turn around and that rock rolled right off the edge! Nathan, get out from under where I'm working here!!

Uh, Dave -- this is definitely not vetch -- don't tell me there are more baby trees you didn't tell me about..."

Dave: "Yeah, that's not vetch -- don't hoe that."

Christie: "I already did. Stop laughing Kent, it could happen to you!"

Karen: "Mommy, you haven't been planting there have you? I already *did* that!"

Christie: "You did? Well, it's well planted now! Well, I'll say this for planting on a steep slope: it's easier on your back -- you don't even have to bend over! All the same, maybe I'd be more help if I went and made some lunch..."

Lisu are amazing. They go absolutely everywhere in flip-flops. We stagger and slip on the same trails in our good hiking shoes. They move up and down their "fields" in an orderly and apparently effortless fashion, while we spend a lot of time teetering, slipping and inching down on our behinds. They've got to be wondering, "What do you suppose all those white people are REALLY doing? How come they can't even stand up?"

And for the record, our corn fields were much more complicated to manage than the villagers' Dave was training, because our land was the "control plot" for many experimental species which had not been introduced to the farmers yet.

Ah, Life!

A neighbour asked me what could be done for a child with rabies who was having seizures in the hospital. Aghast, I said, "Nothing! Oh, it's so terrible they didn't get the shots rights away!"

Dave asked how they knew for sure that it was rabies:

"Oh, because a dog bit him, and then he got sick."

"And the dog died shortly after, frothing at the mouth, right?"

"No, the dog is fine."

"Really? And how long ago was he bitten?"

"Nine months ago."

The animal would normally die within five days. Could it be possible that it was NOT rabies? I asked for him to be brought to my house so that I could observe him. That was such a disturbing morning, because he was in severe pain part of the time, and during his fits, would growl like a beast, and try to bite his parents and himself. The horrible, raging, agonized sounds scattered the other patients to the far ends of the yard, and brought my kids out on the upstairs balcony, all wide-eyed and concerned. I emailed a doctor friend to ask what else it could possibly be. Would you believe a neglected strep infection? Praise the Lord, this little boy responded amazingly to some basic antibiotics and a bit of seizure medication! He is completely well!

When I think of our time in the Salween valley, certain experiences stick out like peaks through the clouds. The sharp lessons, the traumas, the miracles. It's easy to write about them; a lot harder to do justice to the bulk of the days and weeks and months and years of daily response to situations which became our "common place", our normal. Those tend to blur together. Dave brought agricultural and Biblical knowledge and support to thousands of villagers; I saw hundreds of patients. Our 'normal' certainly seemed challenging enough to friends flying in from developed countries or cities, and romantic and adventurous enough that tourists liked to stop off and check us out. When it was all said and done, though, the "villagers" and "patients" were our neighbours, and most of them had life stories full of such pathos and courage, such resilience in the face of adversity, that we spent a lot of our time feeling like we had no right to complain about anything, and were unworthy to tie their bootlaces, assuming they had boots!

There was this one tall, craggy old man who came to visit whenever he went to town. Unlike a lot of people, he really had a fatherly regard for Dave himself, and frequently showed the goat workers hospitality when they passed through his village. He and his wife were from a high village and had somehow raised all ten of their children to God-fearing, hard-working adulthood -- a feat not many were able to accomplish, where infant mortality is so high, and where they had to eke a living off of incredibly steep mountain slopes. He would get into deep theological discussions with Dave, and obviously enjoy every minute of it. "A ke Pfu. A ke Pfu," he would say with a satisfied sigh as he prepared to go. ["It's been rich. It's been very rich." Of course, if you say those same sounds with a slightly different tone, it becomes "Open the door, open the door," but anyhow...]

One time he dropped by on a day when we were running low on groceries, so were just eating a quick meal of hash browns for lunch. He gave the spuds a disapproving look and declined to eat any of them. Later, as he prepared to leave, he pressed a 100 yuan bill into my hand! This represented at least a month's income for him. "For the children. Buy them some meat," he said. In vain we remonstrated and told him we *liked* potatoes, that they were one of our favourite foods where we came from, and that he should keep the money because we didn't really need it. He was adamant. Potatoes were a

poor substitute for corn and rice, and should really only
be eaten during the lean months before the new corn was
ripe.   According to the hospitality code in the high
villages, where guests are a rare and celebrated occasion,
company would always warrant slaughtering at least a
chicken, if not a suckling pig or goat. We didn't have any
chickens, so had not done that for him; clear evidence
that we were really scraping the barrel. The Lisu down in
the valley, along the road, took visitors much more in
stride and would not usually prepare a meal either.
Generally speaking, I took my cue from them, as guests
and patients were pretty much a daily occurrence, and
trying to feed them all would have been impossible.
Some time later, when Dave was travelling, I received
word that this man was sick. When Dave got back, there
was a message, delivered by one of his sons. "Please tell
my brother that I can't wait for him, but I will see him in
Heaven."

Of course, some Lisu were wrecked by their
hardships; became selfish, callous, insane, addicted,
dishonest, divorced. The challenge was to discern where
people were at, and what part God wanted us to play in
their lives.   To put ourselves at God's disposal and
respond to who He brought to our door step -- even when
we were "behind" in home school, or sick ourselves, or
dealing with the yearly mold and insect invasion, or on
the verge of departure.   His grace was *always* sufficient,
but we didn't always avail ourselves of it.

One day, a young mother walked into our yard,
untied the straps of her "bei dai" [baby carrier], sat down
and slid the infant onto her lap. It was a tiny baby girl.
The bones of her face and head were deformed. The top
of her head was covered in a thick, dark scum of cradle
cap. There was pus running out of her ears. "I've come to
beg a little medicine," the young mother stated.

Something exploded inside me.[27] With an exasperated little laugh, I said, "You've come to beg a little medicine? Have you been to the doctor? Have you ever taken her to the hospital? No? You think I have 'a little medicine' which will fix all these problems? Why didn't you ever take her to the doctor? How am I supposed to magically reverse all this neglect?" I don't think I actually said all of that out loud, but it's what I was thinking! I was so tired of people trying to dump all the responsibility for their health issues on me! I was so tired of being called into situations which might originally have been fairly simple to treat, but had become almost hopeless thanks to the long period of neglect: ruined ears, ruined eyes, pneumonia and TB which had been let go until bones and lungs were destroyed and life itself was at risk.

Feeling a little repentant for having vented at the young mother, I went inside to get my stethoscope. When I came back out, she'd gone. Now I really felt guilty. After all, she *had* finally tried to get some help for her poor baby, and I had crapped all over her head. Jesus would not have done that. Our frame of reference was completely different, and she could not possibly know what she should have done, or be held responsible for it in the same way that I, or another well-educated western mom or medical professional, should be. Now what could I do? I prayed that somehow I would be able to find her again, and treat her and her child with the compassion and respect she deserved, regardless of whether anything could be done medically.

---

27   One time on the playground, a little girl came up to me and asked shyly, "Do you have a band aid?" When we followed her back to the sister with the "owie", it was to find her with her bare foot laid wide open from broken glass. She was more in danger of bleeding to death, and needed a pressure compress and stitches, not a band aid! This was like that.

Thankfully, a few days later, she came back with a blood test in hand; she had actually gone to the doctor after all, and humbly returned. I was so happy to see her I could have kissed her! The following week, I arranged for her to be one of the patients to see Dr. Hudson when he came to visit, and at least the infant's ear and skin infections could be dealt with. The pediatrician we contacted said the deformities did not answer to any of the treatable conditions he had ever heard of, and guessed it was a rare syndrome for which there was probably no treatment. That young mom was touchingly grateful to receive just "a little medicine" for her baby's ears after all, because it was lovingly administered.

Time and again I was humbled and devastated by the parents or grandparents of babies with neglected hydrocephalus, or infections, or cancer, or other awful conditions. Devastated because so often there was little we could do to alter the outcome. Humbled by the gentleness, devotion, patience and awe-inspiring long-suffering of their caregivers. Although most of them had not camped out at the hospital until they got some answers, as we would do, there could be no doubt that they loved their children. Their life-experience had not given them much knowledge or expectation of the powers of medicine, and the local hospital at that time failed people so consistently and abysmally, it wasn't really surprising that they didn't put much faith in it. But as they carried, and nursed and did their best to address the needs of their pathetic children, patiently bearing the extra work and hardship of running sores, or sleepless nights due to constant, fretful whining and crying, there could be no doubt that it was love that sustained them in it.

I vowed at that time to just not judge. To some-how get a little of God's grace, and let Him instruct my tongue and my help. To support people who had gone to the trouble of bringing me a patient, and forget about what they "should" have done before that.

I had never walked in their shoes: the shoes of poverty, illiteracy, racial prejudice, ignorance, superstition ... and stubborn hope.

I think He always enabled us to *forgive* neighbours for coming into our kitchen, seating themselves and joining the meal as if they had missed us so much and just *had* to see us, only to find out after they had tied us up for half the morning that their real reason for coming was to jump the queue for medical advice, or to ask for OTC medicine which they could have picked up for themselves in town. I'm afraid that at that point, my warmth and hospitality often suddenly flaked off like cheap nail polish. When it didn't, it was a direct result of one of two things: for once I was not feeling frightfully behind on everything, or God Himself helped me to treat that person as if they *were* Him. Those moments were worship, though they didn't feel like it. "I will not offer the Lord anything which costs me nothing". Sometimes it was intrinsically satisfying to serve, because they were so nice and thankful, or because the "case" was interesting and responded so well to treatment -- "I tell you the truth, they have received their reward in full." If only Mother Theresa's words had framed everything we did: "We can not do great things. We can only do small things with great love." Like 1 Corinthians 13:4-8 ...

> *Love is patient, love is kind.*
> *It does not envy, it does not boast, it is not proud.*
> *It is not rude, it is not self-seeking,*
> *It is not easily angered, it keeps no record of wrongs.*
> *Love does not delight in evil but rejoices with the truth.*
> *It always protects, always trusts,*
> *Always hopes, always perseveres.*
> *Love never fails.*

Some people in this world do have the ability, the calling, and the privilege of doing great things. So far that has not been us! We have bumbled through! Having to multi-task almost all the time, when neither of us can really do that, has led to some hilarious moments. Like the times in the middle of a "clinic" when I was working in English with the visiting doctor, Chinese with my translator and Lisu with the patients when I would suddenly realize I was asking the doctor questions in Lisu, speaking English to my translator, and Chinese to the patients! Or the times when my helper and I were trying to take a patient's history and would realize that we needed the scale, or the thermometer or the blood pressure cuff, and could only look at each other and chuckle. Neither of us could jump up and get it, because we were both nursing our babies!

A Village House

There were a lot of nights in our village house where the moths would keep us up until all hours, waiting until the light was turned out to start caroming onto our faces or up against our ears. In the summer, Dave's night time routine involved a wild ballet around the bedroom with the fly swatter, trying to kill more than were being attracted in by the light. One night I kept seeing the white belly fur of one of our resident rats up against the screen which filled in the gap between the top of our wall and the roof. It was rearing up against the screen, catching one moth after another. The spiders took their share, too, and most days I could count on sweeping up at least a dust pan full of moth wings from where they'd fluttered down from the spiders' webs. When it wasn't the moths, it was the rats, squeaking and scuffling and knocking things over. Or the cat trying to catch the rats. Or the neighbours' dogs and roosters. Or the baby. Suffice to say that we rarely woke up feeling rested. Often we dragged ourselves out of bed long after we "should" have been up, and faced the day feeling foggy, and out of sorts, and behind before we started. So, we were thankful for strong chai or coffee, and a community which still operated by the "sun up to sun down" principle! During the short days of winter, hardly anyone got up to brave the nighttime chill -- we'd all stay right in our cozy beds until the sun came creeping down the mountain sides to thaw things out a little! Often, it was the coughing of our patients outside -- sometimes discreet, sometimes paroxysmal -- which woke us up in the morning. During the winter, we would all wear three or four layers, (including my fuzzy yak wool long underwear) and we would just strip the dirty outside layer off the kids before tucking them in. Stripping them down to the skin to put on and take off pyjamas was just too traumatic for them!

When it rained, our roof leaked. The first step was to get up and try to remove sensitive things like computers, keyboards and lab reports from under the drips. The next step was to move the pee buckets or the garbage cans under the drips to prevent puddles on the top floor leaking through into the "library" and storage room down stairs. At other times, the downstairs was protected by the tough spider webs on the ceiling down there, which caught and held literally pounds of sand and dust which sifted through cracks in the floor!

Our spiders were so industrious, we basically let them be. Once in a while when we were expecting visitors, we would get busy with the broom to give the illusion that we were on top of the cobwebs, but by the next night the spiders would have spun them all back, with interest!

We rarely showered alone. Two or three spiders the size of our children's hands lived in the cracks of the cinder block shower room wall. It got to the point where only actually touching them when reaching for the light switch would cause either them or us to jump. In summer, several unnerving things were prone to happen. Preying mantises and katydids joined the moths near the bathroom light, and they usually waited until you were stripped down to suddenly launch themselves onto your bare back or shoulder. Since they are large, crunchily armoured, and able to either nip with their mandibles or rasp with their thorny front legs, we felt quite justified in dreading their assault! Then there were the toads who staked out prime territory on the damp bathroom floor, where they could gorge on all the bugs attracted to the light. That was fine, but it did take some self-control not to yelp and launch them into the brick wall when they plopped their clammy bellies on your bare feet! Earthworms are a wonderful thing for the garden. We were thrilled when huge clumps of "red wrigglers" started to colonize the dirt under the goat pen. It was not quite so fun when they started to congregate under the soap dish, in the folds of all the face cloths, in the inlet to the washing machine and the outlet to the shower! Clots of soggy earthworms coming out with the shower water, having to be shaken out of the clean laundry…

In the winter, we had a more endearing audience. The Muscovy ducks lived under the goat barn, and when the ducklings heard the shower running, they would come traipsing up through the hole in the brickwork which served as a drain, and join the bath! If we were scrubbing away and suddenly got the uncomfortable feeling that we were being watched, we learned to look up. There on top of the hot water heater, toasting their little toes, would be a row of kittens staring down at our wet ablutions with wonderment!

Our wonderful cat, Ebony, kept us regularly supplied with kittens -- usually three litters a year. She was a beautiful, glossy black cat, fine-boned and dainty. She had a sweet mew and the endearing habit of being cuddly without being demanding. She was gentle, cooperative, and an amazing ratter. And she lived for seven years! That was the amazing thing, because the year before she came, we lost nine cats to disease, rat poison and vehicles on the road! The kids were truly becoming afraid to give their hearts to anything or anybody, and I felt that losing one pet after another like that was an assault on their hearts by the one who comes to "steal, kill and destroy". On top of which, the rats were taking over and we were desperate for some help! Ebony's longevity and graces were surely an answer to my earnest prayer for God to give us a good cat, and watch over her life. She was run over by a car shortly after we moved to Canada, but the countryside is well-populated with her wise, talented off-spring.

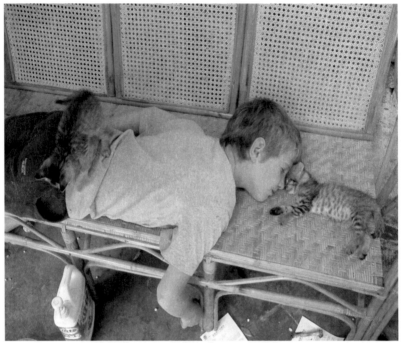

Naptime with Ebony's kittens

A much more significant "animal legacy" we left behind were our pack goats. One of the first things we did after we got our house finished was to hire a carpenter to build a goat barn. We had picked up a little book called "The Pack Goat" in Walter's apartment in town, and determined to try it. It seemed to us that Lisuland, with it's precipitous paths, was the perfect place to get the people hooked on using goats as beasts of burden. They can forage for themselves when on the trail, can carry at least a 50 LB pack anywhere that a human being can walk, can be trained to come along without even a lead, much like a well-trained dog, and are much cheaper, safer and easier to handle than mules. The only hitch was where to get the right kind of goats? Walter's Nubians are well-adapted to the heat, and are a large, strong goat, but are also totally adapted to the sedentary life. They are all about conserving energy and will not take to hiking! We needed one of the European breeds, like Saanen. Well, when we started asking around, we discovered that the government had actually brought pure-bred Saanen goats in to the valley several years before, and we finally tracked down the remnants of that herd, just as they were about to be sold for meat! We praised God for His timing in letting us find out about them before that happened. It would have been very expensive and troublesome to import them ourselves! Saanen are milk goats, but are also tall and athletic, as well as affectionate. They bond easily to humans and can be developed into great pack goats.

The arrival of the goats added a lot to our lives! First, they added a lot of work! We had nowhere to graze them, so all the goat fodder had to be located by Miriam and Karen, cut by hand and carried back in their back baskets, six days a week, rain or shine. To cut fodder on the Sabbath would have put us outside the pale of the community of Christians in Lisuland, so they had to gather twice as much on Saturday. The goats also contributed fertilizer, and we were full of high hopes as we started hauling buckets of manure out to our pathetic garden. That land had been heavily used for corn, with nothing put back in, so was very hard and depleted. It worked, of course. After four years of SALT planting, with leguminous hedgerows and goat manure, the land was soft, black and rich. The corn went from being about the size of a man's thumb to ears as long and full as my forearm! And then there were the kids! By God's grace our goats were very prolific and always had two if not three kids each. Lietz kids and Liu kids competed to choose the most ridiculous kid names! There were Hazel, Star Lily, Kabul and Tortuga (now great-great grandparents of large, healthy herds), Vanilla and Icecream, Babushka Isabella Laquonkwa III, Frederic D' Maximillian le Francais, Chaco, Lickety Split and Skittle...

The milk these little clowns didn't drink, we turned into kefir and cheese. Miriam would always bottle feed the babies part time so they would become very attached to her. When they were bigger, she would let them out and tempt them on walks with a pocket full of corn or other treats. Once they were in the habit of going wherever she went, she would strap empty packs onto them, gradually adding weight as they got bigger and stronger, until they would be carrying everything the group needed when they went up to the high villages. Hiking when you didn't have to carry water and your lunch and your coat was so enjoyable! Once, when Miriam was about eleven, they were on a hike up the mountain. They stopped for a bit of a rest along a stretch of trail which formed the rim of a bowl-shaped, terraced valley. You could often see hawks playing in the thermals down below there. Miriam's half-grown pack goat decided to kneel down on the edge and stretch for a tempting mouthful of shrub which was just out of reach. Unfortunately, she mistook a clump of grass for solid ground, and knelt on thin air! Over she went, pack and all, and would have been a goner if it was not for Miriam's lightning quick reflexes and pure strength! What Miriam did threw us into conniptions, because we were expecting her to be jerked over the edge as well, but she actually caught her goat by the pack and hauled it back up!

One day Dave, APu, Miriam and Karen hiked up to a village to see a TB patient. They took the pack goats with them to carry the coats, water and some things for the patient. Okay, the main reason was to give them some exercise and training! Anyhow, the village official was doing some paperwork at a desk under a tree. He, along with the rest of the village, was pretty amused and delighted to see goats being used in such a novel way! He went on and on about how clever and obedient Hazel (Miriam's goat) was until he turned his back on her for a moment and she sidled over to the desk, grabbed, with her teeth, the *bottom* report from a tall stack, and jerked. The whole pile of papers flew into the air! Let's just say that particular official's opinion of goats underwent another major transformation, and his colourful imprecations kept people chuckling for a good while afterwards!

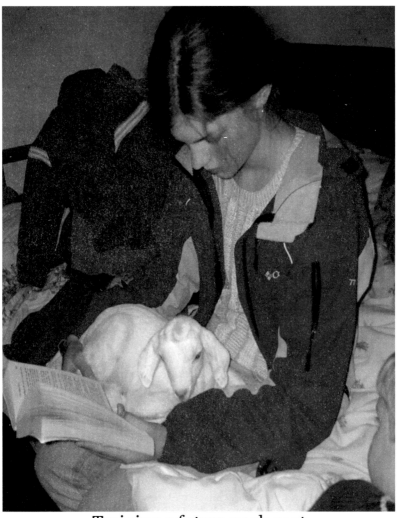

Training a future pack goat

AKe

One day while walking along the road to the Liu's house, I came upon a pool of blood on the concrete. A quick check of the ditches didn't reveal a dead dog or anything, so I looked around for someone to ask about it. The only person around was a handsome young man who walked with a staff because his lower body was crippled. I gestured at the blood and asked in my pidgin Lisu what it was from. He did not speak any Chinese, but managed to make me understand that they had bled a sick horse there. "Interesting, I didn't know they did that," and I walked on. However, the encounter had built an odd little bond between that young man, named "AKe", and me, so every time I went by, we smiled at and greeted each other.

Some time later, I came across a group of men from our village digging a grave. I asked who's it was, and they explained that it was AKe's older brother. They said he died of TB, and had been dead a couple of days before his body had been discovered. Their faces were really sombre, and it was clear that they felt regret not only that this young man had died alone, but also that he'd wasted his life. They told me that the brothers had been fatherless, and had become the "bad boys" of the village. They ran a pool hall and gambling den, and were frequently implicated in petty theft in the neighbourhood.

Another time, Dave caught a ride home in the same vehicle as a raddled older woman who said she was bringing a case of cheap whiskey home "for her son." She got off at AKe's house, by the creek. Neighbours told us they were both alcoholics. I started praying for AKe every time I walked by his house, and one time I decided that I would boldly ask him to tell me his story. I was walking Meimei home after a clinic day, so I asked her if she would help me with the conversation, as I was pretty sure to be out of my depth linguistically. AKe and another AKe - a little boy who was blind in one eye, not loved by his step-mom and also notoriously naughty, were sitting on a board outside his house with their arms around each other, basking in the sun and just exuding camaraderie and contentment. I hated to break in on that, but strengthened my resolve and asked if I could talk to him for a minute. He sent the younger AKe scampering off with a swat to his rear and looked at me. I said, "Would you tell me your story?" He looked at me in shock, then looked away and said, "No. It's too shameful." Meimei tried to reassure him and encourage him, but he wouldn't say another word! So, I went home telling the Lord, "You see how it goes? You see what a great evangelist I am? What can I possibly say as an opener next time? If I am the best that You've got to send out here, and this is how you answer my prayers, then I feel really sorry for these people!"

The next week, though, AKe showed up on my door step! He explained that he'd been to the Communicable Disease Clinic and had tested positive for TB. He showed me the medication he'd been given, and wanted to make sure he was doing everything right. I was secretly elated! I thought, "Ha! Now, for a whole year, you are going to be involved in a group where we not only carefully monitor people's medications and progress, but pray together for each one's healing, and hear people's testimonies. Thank you, Lord!"

I explained to him that because alcohol is hard on the liver, and TB medications are also destructive to the liver, they cannot, repeat CANNOT be used together. If he wanted us to help him get over TB, we were happy to do that, but he was going to have to quit drinking for the duration of treatment. He said he understood that; they'd told him the same thing at the clinic. He lasted two months, and then I saw him drunk. I took an American doctor friend and Meimei. We went to his house, sat down by his fire, and poured our hearts out for him. Our doctor friend prayed while Meimei not only translated everything I said, but with tears, shared her own testimony of hardship and God's redemptive power. AKe nearly broke down himself, and said that his father had been killed by police in a dispute over the "one child policy".   He said his mother had no choice but to remarry,[28] leaving her five boys to fend for themselves. They lived like rats, eating what they could find in the garbage in town, with no chance to go to school or make anything of themselves. Because he was crippled, it was particularly hard for him.   He said that he couldn't remember feeling happy for even one day and would sometimes hobble down to the river and consider throwing himself in. I pointed out that alcoholism is a form of slow suicide, and that of the two deaths -- death by pulmonary TB or death by cirrhosis of the liver -- TB was the easier. We told him how precious he was in God's sight, and how much God longed to forgive him and receive him as a son, giving him a hope and a future. I told him that there was no way to explain the depth of love I had in my own heart towards him except to say that God put it there. "God has watched over you your whole life, and has seen your hardship. He cares so much that he died in your place and will give you a new heart and a new beginning. He is also able to deliver you from your addiction and heal your disease, but you must choose ."

He was almost persuaded for a moment, but then turned away. I explained to him that if he did any more drinking, we could no longer supply him with medication, because we would just be helping him poison himself, and we left.

A few weeks later, I saw him raging drunk, attacking another man with his staff, and then he showed up at our house, hangdog and maudlin with his hands all

---

28   She has been married and divorced many times since then.

gouged up and bloody. He confessed that he had gotten drunk and also attacked his mother, which was why his hands were such a mess. "Oh, AKe." I got a basin of soapy warm water and washed his hands. I had so hoped that God would make a "trophy" of AKe. There was such a chasm culturally between the "good people of the church" and the "sinners". I so badly wanted AKe to be soundly converted and turn his "den of iniquity" by the creek into a place where others like him could hear the good news of the "Friend of sinners", not just a recitation of all the sins and vices they'd have to give up if they were to be considered for admission into the "company of the upright". When I told him that we were going to have to let him go from the TB program, he said "MaChi, MaChi." ["It's ok", or "that doesn't matter."] I felt like shouting at him, "It does so matter! You matter!" That night I agonized over what to do. I was so upset that he was choosing to self-destruct. I even fantasized about things like gouging my own wrists in front of him and saying, "MaChi, MaChi", when he told me to stop it or got upset with me!

"Oh, Dave, what do I do?"

He rolled over and looked at me. He said, "I think you need to let him go. You've already bent over backwards, and he is starting to manipulate you. He's been warned and forgiven, and it's time to let him experience the consequences. If you don't, he will lose all respect for you and you won't be able to do anything with or for him." He rolled back. I sighed, "Okay."

The amazing thing is that AKe is the only person I have ever known or heard of who was cured after just three months of TB meds! After that,he also told anyone who would listen that I had washed his hands, and that I was his friend and would shake hands with him. The Lord has not yet come back, and AKe is not yet dead, so it's not yet the end of the story either.

Crystal's Tales

For years we prayed that God would bring spiritual awakening to our village, and open a way to reach the children for Jesus. We were also praying for a Chinese tutor for our own kids, since our neighbours only spoke Lisu. It just seemed too sad and ironic that our children were growing up in China, but had no fluency and were illiterate in Chinese! Little did we know that God was about to answer all those prayers in one small person! Our landlord's little brother got married in Burma and brought his wife and baby girl back to live in his village. Her name was Crystal, and my heart went out to her as she tried to set up house and fit into a community where she couldn't speak with anyone -- not even her in-laws. Crystal had sparkling brown eyes, a big smile, a strong voice, a lot of energy and the thickest braid of shiny black hair you ever saw. She gladly agreed to teach our children Chinese, and started off with a seemingly inexhaustible supply of gospel songs. Next, she delved into the shelves of picture books we'd supplied her with, and when those stories were exhausted, she started sharing far more interesting ones of her own. They had a personal Scheherazade!

She grew up an orphan, in a jewel-mining area of Burma, and learned how to polish gems even as a young girl. Of course, the common people rarely got to keep the gemstones they found, as the government had a habit of collecting them all for the "royal interests", and foreigners weren't allowed into the area at all. Crystal talked about how the princess of the ruling junta decked herself out in so many jewels for the royal wedding that her fat person could hardly be seen.

Crystal's brother worked in a mine for awhile. The owner who had developed the mine worked it for years without finding much of anything. When he ran out of capital, he sold it for peanuts. Wouldn't you know, the new owner had not been in operation more than a few months when he hit a rich vein and started bringing in money hand over fist. The original owner came back and asked for a share, but the new owner laughed in his face. That night, when Crystal's brother came back to the mine workers' dormitory, there weren't enough bunks for everyone, so he offered to take a spot on the floor right next to the furnace. No one else wanted to sleep there because it was too hot. In the middle of the night, there was a terrible explosion and the roof collapsed; he staggered out with his ears ringing and plunged into a nearby pool of water because everything was going up in flames. On the bank, he noticed a couple of other men trying to crawl to the water and he started to get out to help them. "BAM!" a second explosion blew him back into the pool. When he got up for the second time, he was the only thing still moving. He was the sole survivor of the original mine owner's revenge. His jealousy drove him to set off bombs which slaughtered the entire work force. Crystal's brother only survived because he did the unselfish thing and laid down right next to the cast iron stove, which sheltered him from the main force of the blast and the weight of the falling roof.

Her husband, AKe [yes, another AKe], also worked in a mine for awhile. One day there was a collapse which buried many men, including him and his older brother. AKe was nearer to the entrance, so they managed to dig him out before he suffocated, but his brother didn't make it.

In Burma, Crystal was a teacher in a large orphanage attached to a seminary. It was clean and well-run, but chronically short of everything but love. They never had quite enough to eat, or quite enough covers to keep warm in the rainy season. So, they would all get up early and do exercises together to shake off the chill. The young people were sometimes organized into teams to tell people about Jesus in the surrounding villages. They experienced hardship and opposition in this work, but found such joy in it as well. She says they were absolutely of one spirit, and did not consider the deprivations and tiredness of any account.

One time, as they were preparing for a conference, a demon-possessed woman showed up at the gate. She would nod her head and look around with a crafty smile, but when the demons manifested, she was truly fearsome. Crystal said she would roar with an unbelievably loud voice, and be filled with such fury that it took many men to subdue her, and -- just like the demoniac in the Bible -- she could break ropes and chains. It was their duty as Bible school students to take their turn praying for her and trying to exorcise her. Crystal said that she had always been too shy to pray out loud, but when she and another girl had to take their turn, their knees were knocking, and she was so frightened that when the demon possessed woman started to roar, she began praying and singing praises at the top of her voice! Just like that, she learned to pray, and that woman was eventually delivered and became the most devoted and sincere servant of God. For many years now, she has lived near the gates and gladly swept the floor or weeded the garden or whatever other humble tasks needed to be done. She is still so full of joy and grateful to God, and sings all the time.

The seminary is next to a temple, and the priests, visitors, and devotees alike made a habit of drifting over to the seminary whenever there was a celebration or feast day of some sort. Sometimes there would be so many uninvited and unexpected guests that the number of diners would be about double what they had prepared for! Now, for many years, the priests at the temple had kept a sacred snake. This was not just any snake, but a huge python which was capable of eating a whole pig at once. One day it escaped and showed up at the seminary.... and let's just say that the students made up for some of the eating that the priests had done over the years!!

The longer Crystal was in our community, the more burdened she grew for the children. She saw that very few parents or grandparents were teaching their children about God, and that the church had no children's program. Most of the children roamed about in little packs, doing whatever they felt like, except for the three hours a day they had to be in the village school. Sadly, burns and drowning were very common because of this. In recent years, all the children age six and up are required to live in boarding schools, and the village schools have been closed. They get to see their families 3 days a month. We feel so sad for them, knowing that many are crying themselves to sleep, with no one to care or comfort. They are also losing so many things: a sense of family, a sense of community, a sense of cultural identity, the freedom to use their mother tongue, ability to attend fellowship with their families on Sundays, indigenous knowledge and willingness to do their traditional field work, and the list goes on. A better education in bigger schools would be a great addition to these, but is a lousy substitute.

Both Crystal and I were consumed with the desire to do something to celebrate the children and express a little of the lavishness of God's love to them. We decided to collaborate on a children's library, and on special children's programs during their holidays from school. Our family contributed the funds to buy meat, vegetables, fruit, treats and prizes, and Crystal and a couple of friends cooked up a delicious meal for the children each day of the program. She also led from between 60 to 80 children in rousing choruses, told them stories, and helped them do a lot of memorization. She begged the help of our older children and some of the young people involved in an orphan care project to lead active games outside. It was such a joy to watch these kids expanding before our eyes. None of them had ever had a birthday party; very few had ever received a gift or had anything organized for their enjoyment. Most of them had never heard that Jesus loved them or why He'd died either. Almost all of them indicated that they wanted to put their trust in Him.

As we contemplate the the spiritual, emotional and cultural wasteland that residential schooling has made of children's lives all over the world, we pray that the childlike faith of our neighbours' children would somehow save them, that they would discover for themselves that Christ is a friend who sticks closer than a brother, and that their Heavenly Father's love would provide their love and attachment needs until such time as this ruinous policy is reversed and they can be restored to their families.

Children's program

Mingram

"Hurry up and get breakfast on the table, Karen. Today's clinic day and Dr. Hudson's coming! "

"Did he bring anyone with him?"

"Yeah, actually, a couple of people from the clinic in Kunming. I don't know whether they drink coffee or tea or what. Dave, can you...Great, you're already making the coffee!"

"Mom, there's already like twenty people outside. Shouldn't you be getting started?"

"Meimei - Hwa Hwa! Zazaleh!" [Hi Meimei! Come and eat!]

"Hi Hudson! How are you? How was the night bus?"

"Hi, Christie, Dave. Not too bad, this is Bess..."

"Hi, Bess. I remember, we actually met at the spring retreat!"

"That's right! Hi, Christie, how are you? So this is your house, and those are your patients!"

"Yup."

"And this is my colleague from the Kunming clinic..."

"Hi! Come on in and grab a seat. Do you want coffee or tea or...?"

And so a very long, challenging but satisfying day would begin.

We'd first ask anyone who had not previously been to the hospital to go and see what the local doctors could do for them. Often they would be back in a few hours with some preliminary lab work, which was sometimes also helpful. Then we would get out the sheaf of patient histories and start calling forward the people who we already knew needed to see the doctor. Some of them were people he'd seen two or three months before, and needed to follow up on. Some were complex cases we'd already discussed through email, but who really needed a thorough examination by a physician before we could make any more head way. Sometimes, though, we'd get people just showing up who needed expert help in a terrible way, in answer to our prayers that God would bring the people only He knew about.

Mingram was one of those. Halfway through the morning, we noticed a commotion with the bushes overhanging our path. Someone was hacking or breaking some of the branches, and then a group of people carrying a young man on a chair emerged and set him down in front of Hudson. His story was arresting. He was a young tribal man from a high and remote village in Burma who was in his fourth year at a seminary. Four months previously, he had suddenly lost the use of his legs. Finally, some of the teachers and pastors decided they had to do something, and it was actually closer for them to come into China for medical help than to make their way to a bigger center in Burma! At this section of the China/Burma border, the Chinese side is comparatively densely populated and developed. Once you cross the mountains into Burma, there is nothing but jungle for a seven day's journey. Burmese often come over seeking such simple necessities as salt, pots, shoes and medicine. Anyhow, they got on a bus, went to a hospital, and from there heard about the free clinic at the foreigners' house! Dr. Hudson gave him a careful examination, and then shook his head. "It's almost certainly Pott's disease [TB of the spine]. And look, the x-ray report from the hospital confirms that. These bones here in the thoracic region have just been eaten away and crumbled so that the spinal cord is pinched. He's got basically no function left in his legs."

"If we put him on medication, is there any possibility that he could get some of it back?"

"No. I can't see that there's much hope of that. His cord has just been pinched for so long...but he should still go on the TB meds, to knock out the disease."

"And we need to pray for a miracle, too. How is he going to live and get around to preach the gospel in those mountains if he can't walk?"

Like the warm, brown eyes of a faithful dog, the eyes of the young man had moved searchingly from the face of one speaker to the next throughout the discussion. Finally he looked pleadingly at me. I spoke in Chinese to Meimei, who spoke in Lisu to the Lisu member of the delegation, who translated the answer into Burmese for the young man. He nodded, then asked a question which was finally fielded to me. "I don't have any money for medication. What can I do?"

Well, putting him on 18 months of TB treatment was certainly an issue. There was no way we could do that if he returned to Burma, but if he could find a way to stay in our neighbourhood for that length of time, we told him that we would cover the cost of his treatment. Did he have any relatives here? No. Did he know anyone here? No. Who could stay with him and take care of him? His brother, Kinram.

Now who did *we* know who might be willing and able to take a non-Lisu speaking, TB positive, paraplegic man and his brother in for a year and a half? Our house would not work; there was simply nowhere to put them, and the path up to our house was steep and difficult to carry someone up to. Together, we prayed that God would touch the heart of someone to do this generous thing. Our first thought was another young man, the brother of a widow in our neighbourhood, who had also lost the use of his legs due to TB, and made a complete recovery. He still owed us for the medication, and we figured that he would understand how this young Burmese man was feeling, and be eager to encourage him.

When we contacted our former patient, he said he would be happy to take them in. He and his pregnant wife were actually moving closer to his work, so their house would be empty and available. He invited us up to take a look. After a stiff hike, we finally arrived at a village ... and then continued right through it and up to a sun-bathed but isolated bluff. I tried to imagine what it would be like to live there alone for 18 months and asked the pastor who had come with me, "Don't you think they'd be lonely?" He looked around and said simply, "Yes." The return trip clinched it. My former patient led us down a steep path through a Tung nut forest, where we were literally ricocheting off trees as we grasped at this one and that one to slow our slithering descent a little. Once we got out of the forest, we had to pick our way through the blasted rock of a quarry and along the banks of a stream. "This is how my brothers got me down to your house when I was taking TB meds," our guide casually informed me. And I had been annoyed with him on the days he didn't show up! "I am so sorry. I had no idea what was involved. If I had known, I would not have been upset when your sister got your medication for you!" "Ma Chi, Mama! [Never mind, teacher] I'm better now. I can walk down here myself, and work, and we're going to have another baby soon. I can never thank you, or God, enough."

"BaBa deh shamu [Praise the Lord]. But I think that if we can find somewhere closer to the road for our Burmese friend, that would be better."

"Okay, but he's welcome to stay at my house otherwise."

When we got home, Crystal, the children's Chinese teacher, was there. Right away she said, "Oh, I wish that we had room at our house for them. He's very appealing, isn't he? I heard he's a Bible school student? Oh, I wish that someone would help them. We have to pray about this." For a few days, we all thought and prayed, but nothing seemed to be opening up. Crystal and her husband AKe brought the matter up to the elders of our village, and we made some phone calls, but nothing. Then, one morning Crystal came running up to our house, with her eyes alight and said, "We had our family prayer time yesterday, with all of AKe's brothers, and our GeGe [older brother] said, 'Why didn't you tell me about this? He can stay in our downstairs room where I keep my carpentry stuff.' He wasn't there the first time I brought it up. He said they have a bed and a rice cooker that they can use, and they don't have to worry about buying rice. He has enough to share."

"Well, that's great! Thank the Lord!"

So, we went and had a look at the room which had been provided. It certainly wasn't fancy, but it had a window facing the river, and was along the road right next to the school and the basketball court, so they wouldn't lack for company. Also, although their tribal language was unknown to Crystal, they could also speak a little Burmese, so she was the best one to communicate with them until they learned some Lisu -- and she was right next door. AKe's older brother was actually the village head, and we had sent him out to have a non-malignant tumour removed from his thigh bone the previous year. It was heartening to see how our kindness to him was now being passed on in kindness to a complete stranger.

We had fun with the next bit. Shopping! Mingram and Kinram, his brother, had come dressed for a hot climate, and winter was coming on. We found them quilts, and bought some warm clothes. Our first stop was at the "quilt family's". They were a Buddhist family from another part of China who sold quilts, clothes, bikes and musical instruments. The first time we went in to place an order for 80 quilts, they wondered what on earth we were up to. When we explained that we had learned of a bunch of households which were so poor they did not have winter bedding, and were buying them some, they were very touched. They sold the quilts to us at cost, and threw in some big gunny sacks full of clothes which had not sold and were now out of season. Over the years, a friendship grew up. They never failed to invite us in and offer us tea and fruit if we were in town, always contributed to our quilt or clothing drives, always gave us an amazing price on items we were wanting to buy, and biked out to our house for Christmas. They listened carefully when we explained the Gospel, and watched the Jesus film. The wife and son in particular seemed very touched, and asked lots of good questions, but they did not cross the line then. When I went in to ask about clothes for our paraplegic friend, they regretfully informed me that they had already sent in all their unsold items for that year, but then remembered some serviceable clothes that her husband no longer needed, and searched those out for us.

The next time our family went to Dali, Dave and I went on a date to find a good wheel chair for Mingram. Experience had taught us that the more inexpensive Chinese ones had a working life of about 6 months, especially if the patient was an active young man, so we found a place which sold made-for-export to Japan models and got a solid one there. Getting it home was fun -- my feet were hurting, so Dave put me in the chair and wheeled me at high speed down main-street! We decided it handled really well, and got a little kick out of the looks people gave us when I jumped out of the chair at curbs!

Crystal's "GeGe" was truly very kind to Mingram and Kinram. He lent them a guitar, and welcomed them to come into the family room and watch TV or visit with them in the evenings. Kinram was also a gem. His dedication stunned and humbled me. He was also a church elder in their remote mountain home, and had a wife and four kids, with another one on the way. It was no small sacrifice to stay with his little brother to nurse him and carry him around. I worried about his wife, and prayed that others in their area would help her with the crops, with the birth and with any other needs which came up. He also very quickly made himself available to do what he could to repay their hosts. Many days, I would see him helping them mix or haul concrete, bringing in driftwood for the fire, or planting and harvesting with the rest of the family. Because Mingram was so helpless without him, though, we told him not to get a job which would take him away for hours or days at a time. We covered their grocery bill until someone else stepped in with a gift for that purpose. It was beautiful to see how the community took the brothers to their hearts. And we were all praying for his healing.

One day, Crystal came up to our house all out of breath, and with shining eyes said, "He can move his feet!" I rushed down to see for myself. I couldn't believe it! I thought maybe she meant he could twitch his feet a little or something, but he could bend his knees and draw both legs up fully! "That's wonderful! Does it hurt when you do that?" "A little."
"Please be careful. Your back bone is still broken, and a fall at this point could cause you to lose what you've gained. Exercising in bed like you're doing right now is perfect."
"Okay."

Dr. Hudson was due for a visit not long from then, so we took him down to see Mingram's progress. By then, Mingram could shuffle around the room if someone held his arm to help with balance and prevent spills. The doctor was excited, and wanted to take him out to Kunming to see a specialist and see if surgery was in order to remove the pus and bone fragments, and to fuse the site of the break so that he could move without doing further damage to the cord. "What about the cost?" "I think I can cover it. Let's see what the surgeon says."

There were still a couple of hurdles. Mingram and Kinram were in the country unofficially, or illegally, but if they were going out to Kunming, they'd have to go through an army check point where their documents would be checked, and of course, they couldn't be admitted to hospital without them either. Thankfully, both the local police and the prefectural visa office were kind and informative. They told us exactly what to do, and then granted the permission. The second hurdle was to get Mingram to Kunming on the bus without hurting his back further, but, again, the driver of the night bus was considerate and helpful, and made sure that Mingram had a bunk right at the front, where it would be easiest to get him on and off, and where the bumps were felt the least. Mingram had surgery, then went to the rehabilitation department of Bless China International, an organization we worked closely with. He came home a couple of months later with a cast under his shirt, but walking!

"Oh, Mingram! You can go home now! Your family will be so excited! And Kinram can get back to see his new baby!" That's when they broke the news that actually, they couldn't. Not until spring. The snow had sealed the high pass they would have to go through.

"Oh. Well, that's hard. But on the other hand, it will give your back a chance to heal completely, and, so long as you're on the TB medication, you really should be somewhere where we can check how your liver is doing."

"Yes, and actually I could never make it all the way up the path to our village yet. I need to regain my strength."

It was so special to meet their family the next spring when travel was possible for them! First, a younger sister came with some gifts from Mingram's mother. She gave us three small, beautifully woven rattan baskets, a garment and a sheet made of hand-woven hemp, and the horns and hairy skull-front of some musk-ox like creature[29].

---

29 We had no idea what it was, until we saw those same horns and furry head on a live animal at the Edmonton Zoo. It was a takin, a rare, large mountain herbivore.

Finally the day came when we could be introduced to Kinram's wife and family. She couldn't bear to leave anyone behind, so had brought all the children. Also, several of the children had long-standing medical issues, and they were hoping for some help to get them better. We were happy to do what we could, and also slaughtered a piglet someone had given us so that they would have some meat to celebrate their big reunion with! We told them, "this is the deal - we'll provide the piglet if you'll help us with the butchering - we don't know how to do that." They were happy to help us with that! But the situation under which that happened was one which none of us were expecting....

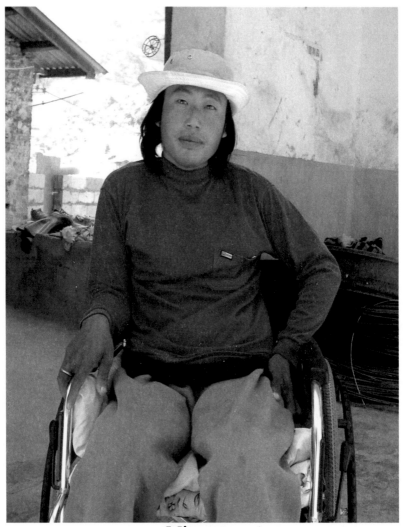

Mingram

Mingram walking!

Insanity

or
A Birth, with Complications

"Dave, are you doing that on purpose, or is it just happening by itself?"

"What?"

"Hon, are you moving your feet up and down on purpose, or are they just moving by themselves?"

After carefully examining his feet, "They're just doing that."

"Can you stop?"

After trying for a few moments, "No."

Sheer panic inside.

Dave had been suffering from constant diarrhea for three months already and was down to skin and bones. In desperation he had made the gruelling overnight bus trip out to the capital to be seen by a Korean specialist and brother in the Lord. Two hours later he had the verdict: medicine resistant parasites. The only medication left for him to try was practically unavailable[30], and rife with unpleasant side effects and risks, at the high dosage he would have to take. However, trying to live with the parasites was also no longer compatible with life. It took many weeks and a lot of tracking down, but finally we had the medicine in hand, along with the concern of a few doctors who wanted to help with Dave's case. The doctors' orders were for at least two weeks of this "chemotherapy". If he could make it to three weeks, eradication of the bug was almost guaranteed. There followed ten days of increasing misery: griping bowel pain, constant, severe nausea and vomiting, foul tastes and foul odours, dizziness, confusion

---

30   If your life doesn't have enough challenges, and you're just looking for one, go ahead and try to buy some quinacrine in China.

and inability to express himself verbally or follow simple directions.

At this same time I was in my eighth month with our seventh child. Dave and I had already been crawling in and out of bed past each other all summer because he was almost incapacitated by his illness, and I was huge, exhausted by the heat and in severe back pain. Day 14, Saturday night, the crisis point came. Dave was acting so strangely that I finally crawled into bed with the children to try and get some sleep.

The next morning, he asked me whether there was a nazgul in the corner. He had battled a ringwraith all night, he said, and could still feel where it's icy blade had entered his chest. It had finally vanished with a scream when he called "Lord Jesus deliver me!" He was convinced that he was dying and had dragged himself to the computer to write emails imploring good friends to come and help me with the children. He was also thankful that his prayer for help had apparently at least delivered the children and I from the monster.

There is no way to adequately describe the next five days except to say that I was carried through. The doctors guessed that Dave was experiencing delirium due to the toxically high doses of medication he'd been on, so I stopped his meds. According to everything they could find on the internet, it should be reversible, but could take anywhere from a few days to a few months for the medication and the psychosis to clear from his system! There was one other sinister possibility, and that was that the medications had damaged his liver, and what we were seeing was brain inflammation brought on by liver failure. "Hepatic encephalitis," it's called. However, Dave did not have any of the symptoms I'd learned to associate with liver failure, like jaundice or abdominal swelling, and liver function tests are only available once a week in our local hospital, so I put that one on the back burner. I had enough to worry about!

Dave was manic, and the children and I had to learn first hand what it's like to live with the mentally ill. The first thing he did once he got out of bed was to help slaughter the piglet the kids had been raising on scraps. Thankfully that's all he did with the knife! It would have been fine, except that he would not let them bleed it properly, nor had he waited for the water to heat, for scalding off the bristles. The kids had to take over, and after a couple of hours of ineffectively scraping at the hair, while the carcass bloated, they were in tears. Thankfully, Kinram, Mingram's older brother, came to the rescue, efficiently scraping and dressing it before the meat went bad. This was the piglet we promised for the occasion of their family reunion, so we gave it to him, and thanked him profusely for rescuing the situation!

Meanwhile Dave was very busy trying to use the computer. Thankfully, for the most part, he was incapable of doing so; his communications were rather bizarre! By this time our friend and neighbour, FangFang, had been alerted to the situation. She just happens to be a psychotherapist, as well as our children's art teacher and confidante. She came over in time to watch Dave tearing in and out of the shower room. He took at least thirty cold showers with his clothes on and could not be convinced that he had not soiled in his pants. He would get me to smell his fingernails caked with soap and insist it was faeces. Once again, we had to give thanks that it was not worse! His obsessions and hallucinations could have been a lot more inappropriate and dangerous than that! Finally, I was able to trick him into eating a cinnamon bun with an anti-psychotic and a sedative hidden in it, and after that he finally settled into a fitful sleep, and I was able to do the same. By this time we had also sent out an urgent plea for prayer. The next morning was such an amazing answer.

Dave woke quietly and softly told me that he'd been to Heaven. He told me he could still see the rough cement walls of our room bathed in a golden light and asked if I could see it too. He described what he'd seen and the people he'd met, the unearthly beauty and the exquisite music. He said he'd been fleeing from demons when he suddenly realized he was being carried swiftly along by a childhood pet, a wonderfully sagacious border collie named Mandy. She whisked him into the gates of heaven, they shut, and immediately he was filled with such a profound sense of peace and joy and ultimate safety. This sensation lingered for awhile, and we could discuss what had been happening, and he was able to process what I was saying. Slowly he grew more tired and confused and started asking me when he could go back to Heaven, and if I'd been there or could go back with him. I'd say no, and he'd ask why we couldn't just buy our tickets! He got so sad and upset.

"You're sure this isn't Heaven? Why can't I go back to Heaven? Why would God do this to me: take me and then bring me back? That's not right. You're sure this isn't Heaven?"

And then when I wouldn't let him eat cheese with his toast (a lactose free diet was doctor's orders) he decided that I was telling the truth after all. If this was Heaven, surely he'd be allowed to have cheese with the rest of us! After awhile he accepted that Heaven was unattainable for the present, and wept like a child. We wept together for Paradise lost. Was this just another hallucination? Well, hallucination or vision, it sure beat the previous nights' hollow! Poor Dave was in such need of peace and reassurance. While he was delirious, of course, he didn't know who he was or where he was or what he was doing. But after each nap or sleep, he'd be lucid for a little while, and experience such fear and humiliation as some of how he'd been feeling and acting came back to him. He felt so utterly vile and would spend most of each time of relative clarity on his face before God, pleading for mercy and forgiveness. Then the confusion would close in again and he'd start asking,

"Where am I? Who am I? Something terrible's happened to me...what are we doing here? Am I really here? Are you really here? Where am I?"

Often I couldn't even finish trying to explain before he'd ask the same question again. Sometimes I would just hold his hand and cry. Sometimes I would explain 200 times, but I was so, so tired...And the Lord gave songs in the night. One was "Trust, trust in the Lord," from Proverbs 3:5-6[31]. Another was "O Sacred King," by Matt Redman:

> "*O Sacred King, O Holy King.*
> *How can I honour you rightly?*
> *Honor that's fit for your Name?*
> *O Sacred friend, O Holy friend*
> *I don't take what you did lightly.*
> *Friendship instead of disgrace*
> *For it's the mystery of the universe*
> *You're the God of holiness*
> *And yet you welcome souls like me*
> *And with the blessing of your father's heart*
> *you discipline the ones you love*
> *There's kindness in your majesty.*
> *Jesus, those who recognize your power*
> *know just how wonderful you are --*
> *That you draw near.*"

I sang these over and over to soothe us both, and that midnight of the soul became a place of worship. I felt His presence, and the uplifting prayers of all those who loved us. We were truly encamped around by angels, and enabled to view the whole experience through the filter of a book both of us had just read called "Repentance - the

---

31   Sung by Jaci Velasquez and Jill Phillips

joy-filled life" by Basilea Schlink. In truth, we both had things to repent of.

Paul commands us in Romans 12, "Never be lacking in zeal, but keep your spiritual fervour, serving the Lord. Be joyful in hope, patient in affliction and faithful in prayer." We had uneasily, slowly slumped from obedience to the first command and become apathetic in our service as a result. How much time we had squandered when we had the health and wits to have used it better! Now the least we could do was try to align ourselves with God's will in the second half of the verse!

By this time Dave was on round the clock sedation, with constricted pupils and a wooden, expressionless face, so unlike his usual affect. FangFang, our psychotherapist friend, told me later that she'd never seen anyone fight the dulling effect of the drugs so hard. Dave never stopped trying to understand what was happening -- it was so brave and so pathetic.

Thursday morning we could finally take Dave in to do liver function and blood clotting tests. I was so worried that he would freak out in the trishaw, or in the lab when they started binding up his arm and poking him, but he just held my hand and did what I said like an automaton. We ran into a few people who knew Dave at the hospital, and they were very nonplussed by his stony stare and inability to recognize or respond to them, but I was just grateful to get the test done and get away without any horrendous incidents. In fact, on the way to the car, we "just happened" to run into a dear Lisu pastor who was attending a conference of over 300 pastors at the time. I explained the situation and asked if they could all pray for Dave's healing. The night before I had sensed God asking me to have the Lisu church leadership intercede for Dave, just as we have interceded for them so many times. It was our turn to humble ourselves and make our neediness known, and God immediately provided the opportunity.

Dave touched my heart deeply that day, because although he was a walking zombie, who did not even know his own name, recognize his children or our home, he still knew me by name and trusted me implicitly. He would go anywhere I led him by the hand, and was a faithful shadow, doing whatever I did. When I hung clothes, he hung clothes. When I went upstairs, he went up stairs. When I hugged him, he hugged me back!

When we got home from the hospital, I finally got around to actually looking up the symptoms for "Hepatic encephalitis" and realized that Dave actually had *all* of them except one - a strange and diagnostic flapping of the hands. His hands were still, but what was going on with his feet? The manual also said that Hepatic encephalitis was 80 % fatal even in advanced hospitals under aggressive therapy...we were at least two days journey away from anything like that. And then we got the lab results, and the Prothrombin time, which the doctors had told me was the crucial indicator for whether Dave's liver had been damaged, was way out of line. Frantically I scanned the results in to the doctors and started waiting for their response. By this time, terror was an acrid taste in my mouth and a throbbing in my belly. Literally a throbbing in my belly; as stress climbed I started feeling the beginning of labour pains. Visions of our family life and life in China ending like a soap opera, with me delivering alone in the local hospital while friends evacuated my husband out to a big hospital in the capital where he would probably die without me invaded my mind and heart.

The response from the doctors was mercifully swift. "Great. Great. His liver's fine. Oh, I see they did a Bleeding time instead of a Prothrombin time, even though I sent them the correct lab name in Chinese." (BT and PT look too alike when written by hand by someone who doesn't know English!)
Light-headed with relief, I had to sit down.

"But what about his feet? Why are his feet paddling?"
"Oh, that's most likely a common side-effect of the anti-psychotic. You should stop that and just use the sedative if necessary."
Well, Hallelujah! A little knowledge is such a stressful thing!

By supper time, my pains had settled down, and Dave was no longer sedated, but still making sense! He ate, and then we went to bed. We slept for 16 hours!! When we woke, he was still "with" us. Our daughter Karen came into the room and asked "Daddy, do you know who I am?" He smiled at her and said, "You're Karen". He'd turned the corner and continued to improve daily from then on.

All that week, our friend FangFang had been coming over twice a day - once to evaluate and advise concerning Dave, and once to bring lunch and an art or craft activity to do with the kids. She helped provide some counsel and comfort and stability at a time when life was on it's head. It's impossible to estimate how much she did to help them (and me) cope with what we were experiencing. The older kids helped, too. Every evening they'd have a "circle the wagons" time in their room, watching "Phineas and Ferb" with the younger kids and laughing off a lot of stress! The children were so tender with their dad during his illness. They would gently repeat themselves many times, offer hugs, and do their best to show respect while quietly not complying with nonsensical commands.

God truly surrounded us, not only with angelic care, but with the care of other ex-pat workers in the county. I was amazed to realize that all but one of them had first hand experience with a mentally ill family member. They not only had good intentions, they really understood what we were going through, and exactly how to comfort and help us. What were the odds that we would have that kind of support in a place as remote as that? Dave's Lisu co-manager, APu, also made himself unreservedly available. He slept over at our place on the night Dave took his many showers, because if Dave had needed to be restrained in any way, it would have been way beyond me to do so. He was also ready to travel with him and be his nurse if he had needed to go to the city. [32] Such a true and faithful friend.

I realized one more beautiful thing through this whole experience. A good marriage is such a powerful thing, and so worth investing in unreservedly. The oneness you build through years of living with each other, serving each other, trying to understand one another, and being there for one another really shines at a time of crisis.   Dave's love for me surpassed his dreadful disorientation. My love for him transcended the loss of him in every role I'd ever known him in, and everything I knew him by. We were still connected at a very deep level, and were still a great comfort to each other, even though we were completely out of control of the situation and in free-fall. Yes, and underneath are the "everlasting arms".

I'll admit that when I first discovered that I was pregnant for the eighth time, it took some getting used to. Haven was already six, and we'd long since given away all our infant clothes, diapers and other paraphernalia. And while six kids can still be squeezed into some "normal" sized vehicles, seven cannot.   There was no getting around the fact that this was going to be an adjustment! The next years were going to be quite different than I'd envisioned. I would have to give up the idea I had of working with Ruth, my midwife friend, to train local women -- and the doctors in the labour and delivery ward -- in the interventions which would promote safe, natural childbirth. I would be unable to start a physiotherapy

---

32   Chinese hospitals do not provide meals or any personal care - just medications and medical procedures. It's up to the family to provide a care giver.

program for children with cerebral palsy, or an intercessory prayer group with young moms for their children who were being sent to boarding school. However, as I lifted all these "dashed hopes" up in prayer, I became convicted that God wanted me to go ahead with them; that He delights in using weak (and tired!) vessels. And I also thought I heard Him say to me, in the words of Pharaoh's daughter, "Take this child and raise him for me, and I will give you your wages." What could I say in return but, "Dear Lord, gladly. Please help us to raise this child up in Your nurture and admonition, for Your honour and purposes."

Ruth was able to make several trips up to Riverbend, and each time spent several days training the hospital staff in how to recognize and prevent many of the complications which led to prolonged labour, avoidable C-sections, still births and birth injuries. Ruth radiated the love of God, and with her seasoned wisdom and grandmotherly warmth and experience, soon had the hospital staff eating out of her hands. With her rosy cheeks, loving smile, and prayers of benediction, she looked like a good fairy godmother, and I so badly wanted her to be the one to welcome my child into the world too! She was more than willing to come, but only had one week-long window where she could make the trip out to Riverbend between other travels and obligations.

In the two weeks between when Dave came out of the "nether-world" and Ruth arrived, I barely moved, not wanting to do anything to start labour before she could come. During that time, she also phoned and told me that she was experiencing some severe back pain of her own, and might not be able to make the trip. We put it in God's hands and hoped for the best. God truly answered prayer on our behalf when our beautiful son, Daniel Judah, was born during the week Ruth came to help -- just an hour and a half before she had to leave! This was three weeks after Dave's turn for the better. By that time he was quite healthy and had the energy to be a wonderful support and birth coach.

Apu and Adu

Apu [Neighbour Apu] impressed Dave right away as a strong and upright young man. This was reinforced when Apu found a man collapsed beside the side of the road. The stranger could not speak any Lisu, and had some kind of running sore on his ankle. Apu picked him up, brought him home and put him to bed, then came to me to see if I had any medicine for the sore. Apu and Adu, his wife, cared for that man, who turned out to be Burmese, just as the "Good Samaritan" cared for the traveller who had been set upon by thieves.

A few weeks later, his wife came to our house, and said that her husband was very ill; could I please give them some medicine? She told me that his urine had turned dark, he'd had no appetite for two weeks, had been unable to keep anything down for a week, and that he had a terrible headache and fever. A doctor friend said, "That sounds like cerebral malaria," and told me the medication to purchase. Since I was seven months pregnant and felt very ungainly and unbalanced on the steep, narrow trails, I sent the medication and IV set-up home with her, and we prayed.

The next day, my house-helper called to me from the path leading up to our house, saying that the neighbours had told her that someone in our village was dying. When I went with her to see who it was, it was Apu. He had refused to let them use the IV medication on him, and was now comatose, jaundiced and still burning with fever. His whole clan had gathered to say goodbye to him, and were wailing and weeping. They had been trying to bring him back to consciousness by beating the backs of his legs with bamboo rods, and had used a form of brutal massage (a traditional healing practice) on him, so that his whole body was covered with purple bruises. Between that and the emaciation from two weeks of vomiting, he looked like a picture out of the Amnesty International newsletter! But, he still had a strong pulse, though very rapid, and I knew we couldn't just let him go.

Thankfully there was one person there who understood Chinese and could translate for me as I tried to convince the room full of people that, with medication and re-hydration, Apu could probably be pulled back from the brink. "He has gone six days without any fluids -- that in itself is life-threatening -- *please* let me take him to the hospital. I can cover the costs." Inwardly praying, I waited for the tide to turn, for the extended family to step back from their rituals associated with death and start to fight for his life. My God-sent translator had already been remonstrating with the villagers, trying to convince them to come up with the money to send Apu to hospital and save his three young daughters from becoming fatherless. By God's grace, we prevailed, and I was soon bundled into a trishaw with the translator and Apu's young wife. She sobbed uncontroll-ably, but began to listen and rally a little as I told her the story of Dave's recovery from Typhus several years earlier. "*Almost* dead is not dead!" By the time we reached the hospital, our hands were welded together, and we went into the hospital side by side.

Some young men carried Apu into the hospital and laid him on a bench while we went to find a doctor. We wandered around for quite awhile and finally, upstairs we found a young woman physician who was galvanized into immediate action when I told her that Apu's pulse was 160 and that I was afraid he was going to die in the corridor! Once he was admitted, I was able to talk with an older doctor who agreed that Apu's symptoms sounded like cerebral malaria, and said she would make sure he was given appropriate treatment. After a couple of hours of IV therapy, he began to move and groan, but the random movements and guttural noises he was making reminded me chillingly of brain-injured patients. I convinced Apu's wife, Adu, to come out for a bite to eat with me, as she had been under constant strain for many days, and would have to continue to nurse him for a long time yet. I was dreadfully afraid that the malaria, un-treated for so long, might have irreversibly damaged his brain, so in my heart, I asked God for a sign that he would heal Apu. I asked that when we returned, he would recognize his wife. When we walked back through the door a few minutes later, he turned his head on the pillow and greeted her!

The next day, he amazed us all by clearly telling me the whole story of how he had become ill, in Chinese, (which he had not spoken for years) not Lisu! His young Burmese guest told him, after several weeks of care, that he had nothing with him, but that if Apu travelled with him back into Burma, his family would reward him for his kindness. Apu believed him, and accompanied him over the mountains into Burma. No sooner had they reached the jungle on the other side, however, than his "friend" was joined by a bunch of ruffians who beat Apu up and stole all the money and supplies he'd brought for the journey! He managed to wrench himself away, fled into the jungle, and made his way home the best he could without any food. Later, he learned there had been a break from a Burmese jail, so he had taken compassion on a jailbird! As I was perusing a photographic encyclopedia of skin diseases, I saw a picture of the sore afflicting the Burmese man, and realized justice would be done, because it was an incurable and eventually terminal fungal infection. In the mean time, however, Apu had come down with cerebral malaria thanks to his nights of exposure in the jungle.

Although he was now lucid, he was still dangerously ill. Cerebral malaria causes clumps in the blood, which do tremendous damage to sensitive organs like the brain, the liver and the kidneys. Apu was terribly jaundiced, to the point that his tears were as yellow as concentrated urine, and his kidneys were basically not functioning. Every day, they put 1500 mL in through his IV, and his bladder drained only about 50 mL, even with strong diuretics. To add to his misery, he was nauseated and would heave up bile every few minutes. All that acid had turned his entire esophagus and mouth into one big canker sore; he was in so much pain he just wanted to die. After two weeks of this, he suddenly became ravenously hungry again -- the body's signal that it was truly starving -- and he still couldn't keep anything down. My heart broke for him, and I knelt by his hospital bed and prayed, with tears, that God would have the same compassion on him that he had had on His own son, who after he had fasted for forty days "was hungry" and was sustained by angels. That same day, his father brought him some especially slippery, slimy kind of "Lisu potatoes", and he was able to keep those down. Was this a sign that God was beginning the healing work and answering our many prayers? For two weeks I had been watching the dismal lab reports on his liver and kidney function and become dreadfully afraid that Apu was going to die all over again from system failure. I also had another concern which I clearly remember "presenting to God" during one of those interminable trishaw rides: at eight months pregnant, with a history of premature labour, I was truly becoming too big to continue safely bumping to town over the rutted roads to visit him in the hospital.

At that point, Apu took a turn for the better and recovered steadily until he could be discharged about ten days later. His wife and little girls were ecstatic. How heart-warming it was to see them cuddled up to him. In Lisu society, when a husband and father dies, the wife is essentially cut off. She has to go find a new husband and a new life. The house, the pigs she raised, the children she bore - all revert to the husband's family. It's a terrible thing to be widowed, and the children also lose both father and mother in one fell swoop. I was so glad this had not happened to them. At the point it became clear that Apu was going to recover, I told him that he should not consider his recovery to be just a matter of medical interventions, and the money which had facilitated them. I reiterated that God had done for him what it looked like treatment would not be able to accomplish. He heartily agreed that God had essentially raised him from the dead, and that for the rest of his life he should consider himself set apart for God's will. His pretty, young wife, Adu, also agreed to become my language instructor. She was overflowing with joy and gratitude, and very motivated to "teach me to talk" so that we could really communicate with one another. She was a cheerful chatterbox, and very innovative in finding ways to help me understand what she meant! For two years we were close companions, and to this day she has an amazing intuitive understanding of what I'm trying to say. She translates from my often butchered Lisu for other Lisu speakers, and interprets their speech into Lisu I can understand! We don't need a Chinese interpreter to understand each other's heart language.

She told me a lot of their story. When they first got married, they were so very poor that everyone kept expecting her to leave him, like his first wife had. There were a number of reasons for their poverty. She was the fourth daughter of a "high country" preacher, and he was the oldest son in a large, blended family. Growing up, Adu did not get to go to school because she was the "goat herd". She didn't even own a pair of flip-flops or clothes without big holes in them until she was a teen ager and almost eligible for marriage. Apu was a teenager when his mom handed him his baby brother to take care of while she crossed the river in a sampan to work a field on the other side. He was standing on the beach, with the hungry, wailing baby on his back, when his mother set out to cross back to nurse him. Half way across, a gust of wind caught the flimsy raft, and it flipped and threw her and another woman into the water. The current pulled them into the rapids, and although he moved as fast as he could over the boulder-strewn shore, life left her as he reached where she'd been washed ashore. His father remarried, and had five more children with his second wife. With six younger children, the older two were very quickly thrown on their own resources to survive. Nevertheless, Apu was tall, strong, a hard worker, a good singer and an upright church-going boy. Adu had never been to school, but she was also a good singer, a hard worker and literate in Lisu. A match was made. They had four children in just under four years. Sadly, the third, a boy, died nine days after birth. Their three girls survived, and so did their parents somehow.

Adu told me about the time just after the birth of one of her babies. Unlike most women, who are fed chicken soup after the birth, they had nothing, not even a bowl of rice. She lay in her bed and bled and wondered how they would survive. Apu was praying that God would somehow help him find something to feed his family. Then he heard a cicada start up near the house. He slipped out to hunt it, (they eat cicadas for the protein) and right under the tree where the cicada was shrilling away, he saw a special kind of mushroom worth a lot of money. He picked it, and in the morning was able to borrow a bike and trade the mushroom in town for enough to buy a bag of rice. They would set off to the fields in the morning with a baby strapped to each of their backs, holding the hand of their oldest. When the girls got a little older, they would be locked into the house with a pot of cold corn gruel to help themselves to when they got hungry. Of course they'd make a huge mess! There was no indoor toilet, and the kids would play in the fire-pit ashes and do whatever they thought up during their long day alone. There was simply no other way for Apu and Adu to get all their field work done.

They continued to work hard to improve their home and farm, and remained active in the church. Adu was an indispensable cook at the tri-annual "jamborees" at Christmas, Easter and Thanksgiving, and at weddings, funerals and other special events. She also proved to have a knack for marketing, and helped make ends meet by buying and selling livestock. Apu bought a tractor, and worked his strong body hard, breaking, loading and transporting rocks, sand and other building materials. Their girls went to school, and life went on. A couple of years ago, Adu started having chronic health issues: pelvic pain, headaches, swelling. As we discussed those things, and tried to help her find some medical help, she also shared that her marriage and spiritual life had become very dry. Shortly before we left, she said that she wished she could leave Apu -- not to get remarried, but just to be freed from all the quarreling.   Their three daughters are in high school, away at boarding school, and highly at risk to delve into all the "peer pressure" scenes of booze, boys and possessions as it is. A divorce would surely compound the pressure. It feels like they're teetering on the brink of total destruction as a family, and I'm tempted to ask myself, "Exactly what good did saving his life do?"

Since writing this, I was able to have a skype call with Adu, arranged through a friend there, and I asked her, "How do you want the end of your story to go?" She responded, praise God, and they have forgiven each other and been reconciled!

Meimei

I first met her when she diffidently came up to our house, seeking medical help for herself and her invalid mother. She became my dearest friend in Lisuland. She was born in the middle of a family of twelve during the Cultural Revolution, the days when it was worth your life to be caught with a Bible, and when the Lisu worked like slaves, going out in the morning to do whatever they were told, not knowing if they would return in the evening. They were hungry, too, and kept themselves alive on wild herbs and roots, insects, and whatever they managed to grow and keep of their rice and corn. Meimei's father eventually became mentally unstable because of the pressure, leaving their mother to somehow keep the ten children alive and fed. She did an amazing job, but they were grindingly poor. One day a baby brother without any pants on accidentally peed into the pot of corn porridge. They had to eat it anyway, as there was nothing else. In spite of their grim situation, their mother was able to keep most of them in school; they were smart kids and did well. To this day, their Chinese is exceptionally good for minority villagers.

Tragedy began to strike once they were grown up. Three of Meimei's older brothers died young: one caught TB, leaving a couple of fatherless children, another was killed in a mining accident, and the third was murdered for his pay cheque in a neighbouring town. An older sister went to work in a noodle shop, and there witnessed the axe murder of her boss's family. She went insane and has never recovered. She was raped during her confused wanderings, and bore a child which her older sister, who was caring for her, also took in. By this time, their mother was also an invalid and living with that sister and her husband and three children. In spite of the extra stress and work, her sister's husband was supportive, and they managed until he was also suddenly killed in a catastrophic land slide which buried the mine he was working in. That slide was so huge it blocked the entire Salween river at flood stage for several hours, and took out houses in a village on the opposite bank. It also buried that big mining operation, killing several hundred people. The disaster was big enough that it provoked national and international relief organizations into action. The families of workers whose bodies were actually found and identified received some compensation. Thankfully, Meimei's brother-in-law was one of these, but it left her sister with four young children, a mentally ill sister and an invalid mother to care for by herself.

Watching all this, Meimei became bitter towards God and questioned what their faith had accomplished: "We pay our tithes, help out with the festivals, attend church, don't drink or smoke and do our best to be 'good'. Doesn't God care about our efforts? Why is He rewarding us with hardship and tragedy?" By this time, she was also married and had two young children. After she'd met us and we realized she lived right in the neighbourhood and had excellent Chinese, I asked her if she'd be willing to come work for me as a translator and patient advocate. I had no idea what a gold mine I had just "stumbled" on, or what an incredible answer to prayer God had just provided!

From the beginning, she displayed a wonderful empathy and sense of humour. I never guessed at the bitter rebellion in her heart or that she was not, in fact, a child of God. She learned quickly, and a little training went a long ways with her. In all the years we worked together, I can't remember one patient complaining about her services as a translator or advocate. She always did her level best to take wonderful care of people, and acted with absolute integrity and truthfulness, whether it came to finances or translating exactly what we'd said without "fudging" it a little. She had such a gift for working with people, such an innate wisdom and winsomeness. Fearful patients, unreasonable drivers, officious hospital personnel -- if Meimei could not bring them around, no one could. In time, this also won her the friendship and respect of a growing circle of "foreign friends". Everyone loved her and wanted to help her and her family. Everyone enjoyed her warm hospitality, and several young women who had come to help with various projects stayed with her many months.

One of her frequent "jobs" working with me, was to translate when we shared Biblical encouragement with patients. She only told us after the fact, but at some point it dawned on her that the reason she had never felt close to God was because she had never put her trust in Christ. She became a radiant and committed Christian, and from then on began sharing her own story and the difference the switch from legalistic religion to a relationship with the Shepherd of her soul had made in her heart. We did not send her often, because she was a mother with home responsibilities, but when she accompanied patients out to the city for surgical outreaches, it was her joy to gather them together in the evenings and go through a devotional book together, praying together over all the concerns people had as they or their loved ones faced or recovered from surgery. In her own home, her children came to love the Bible stories and praise choruses she was learning, and demanded them every night. Her husband also began reading Bible stories to their children, and took great care of them while she was busy caring for patients. They were proud of each other, and worked together to take care of the children, the fields and livestock, his parents, the housework and the patients.

Unfortunately, those contented days did not last. Other men in the village started ribbing her husband about Meimei being the one to bring home the bacon, and he started saying that he wanted to go "out" and get a better paying job. Then she conceived a third child just as their village leader put his thumb print to a document declaring that their village would be a model village and cooperate with authorities to severely punish anyone who tried to have an "illegal" child.[33] What was she to do? After much discussion, she decided to find a place to hide out and have the child far away, and then try to pass it off as her sister's child when she returned. The official in her home town was wise to them, though, so she and her husband decided to just face the music and try to pay off their fine.

They had been separated for six months, and she was recovering from a C-section, but just two weeks after her return home, her husband left for another province to try and earn some quick money. She was so heartsick and distraught that he would do this against her wishes, but did her best to raise the three children and take care of everything at home. Far to the north, her husband found a job sorting large, frozen salt water fish, but he had a problem: his boss was withholding his pay. Finally he made the decision to come home with less than he was owed, because he just couldn't stand being away from his family any longer.

To make matters worse, their fieldstone house had been built with cheap concrete and without a proper foundation, so it was threatening to fall down. Her husband felt even greater pressure to come up with some money, and soon left for a new job: spray painting furniture in a huge factory. When he came back after another three months, he had reverted to some habits which had been very detrimental to their marriage in the early years.

How battered and tired her heart was. Bemused and burnt-out, she still tried to see the right thing to do,

---

33   The Lisu, and other minority tribes, are permitted to have two children as opposed to the "one child policy" which governs the Han Chinese.

to take care of her children, to do what she could for patients. They were still building a big new house together, but she just wanted out: to go sit in a field full of flowers and just *be* until she could sense God's presence again, until she'd healed a bit and found the strength to go on. God felt so far away. Thankfully, although it felt to her like she was barely hanging in there, God still had a firm hold on her. In these past two years she has come through to a place of peace and strength, choosing to focus on her relationship with God and her responses to the circumstances He's allowed in her life. She's learning to accept her husband as he is, trusting God to deal with him in His own time.

Though her job as a health worker developed her faith, life and skills so much, it also complicated their lives a great deal, absorbing much of her time and energy, and causing her to be discontent with the traditional life of a village woman. Typically, a girl is married at about age 17 to a man either her parents or pastors suggest for her. She moves into his parents' home, and begins helping to tend the fields and gardens, gather, chop, and cook pig food, wash the clothes, and do the other housework with her mother-in-law and sisters-in-law. If they are a wealthier family, or if her husband is industrious and able, at some point they move into a house of their own and start to have a little more say in how their children are raised and how they do their work. Many girls have a close relationship to their in-laws and develop friendships in their new village, but it is still a life circumscribed by hard work, poverty and many set-backs.

Meimei did not have the advantage of a loving relationship with her mother-in-law, whose eight sons all have lost, or are on the verge of losing their wives, thanks to their inveterate gambling, infidelity, or dishonesty. Her mother-in-law was an ungrateful, carping, back-stabbing woman who never thanked Meimei for all she did for her, but rather spread lies and complaints about her far and wide. To the best of her ability, Meimei forgave and tried to be patient, uncomplaining and helpful. She strove to see these trials as among those things which would develop Christ-like character. For years she made the gruelling hike up to her in-laws house to check up on them, and dropped everything day or night to take her mother-in-law to the hospital for IV's, which she demanded whenever she felt unwell. At times she spent weeks sleeping at the end of her mother-in-law's bed in the hospital and then welcomed her into their tiny family bedroom so that she could be close at hand to monitor her blood pressure. For all her complaining, the mother-in-law did not want anyone else from that huge extended family to take care of her -- only Meimei.

Recently, Meimei's mother-in-law dropped dead of a stroke while gathering pig food out in her fields. Her death sent the whole family into a tailspin. While all the rest of the family struggled with guilt, blame and regret for the ways they hadn't served her, Meimei was free to grieve, in a very healthy and natural way, the loss of a central person in her life. It is nothing short of miraculous how much she loved that woman, and how fondly she remembers her. Now she is prevailing upon her bereaved father-in-law to come and live with them so she can take better care of him! As I consider her life and the masterpiece she now is, emerging and revealed from out of the dust and darkness of her many trials these past years, I stand in awe at the grace of God.

Entitlement

What exactly is the child of God entitled to? How about an overseas Christian worker? Or western Christians compared to those in developing nations, or the privileged children of the materially wealthy compared to the children of the "poor"? What exactly is poor? How much is enough?   Some people seem blissfully unaware of the discrepancies, or unbothered by them, but most overseas workers struggle with these questions to some extent. We certainly did. While Dave was teaching English, it seemed relatively simple to us: the schools God sent us to teach at paid us the same wage as their native born teachers, and we lived on it, though gifts from overseas helped when we had to travel.

When God asked us, "Would you go to the village for me?" all that changed. Our province had no wealthy villages. This was a call to live among the poor and powerless. The Asian Rural Life Development Foundation in the Philippines, has been equipping people to do just that for some time.   Their vision is taken from Jesus' words, "I have come that they may have life, and have it more abundantly." We resonated with that.

It's a big operation, and beautifully managed. There are dozens of breeding barns filled with sleek goats, the dairy, modern pig barns, teeming fish ponds, acres and acres of lush hedgerows to feed the goats, FAITH (Food Always In The Home) gardens, orchards; even an herbal remedy garden to teach how to make homemade medicine.   The staff were also wonderful, from the attractive receptionist in the main office, to the vet who kept the animals healthy, to the strong, cheerful labourers who took care of the goats. Probably Dave's favourite teacher, though, was Kuya Boni, who taught him how to "story" the Bible.

The American staff, and overseas visitors, lived in nice bungalows with hardwood floors and all the usual amenities like fridges and ovens. Each American family had a Jeep or Land-rover. The local staff lived in wood or cinder block row housing, and the students who came, with their families, to study agriculture and the Bible lived in native huts, with their own garden. Each could have what they were used to. The discrepancies bothered us, though, and we decided that was a pattern we wouldn't follow. We felt that God was calling us to live as close to the level of the local people as was practicable. We thought of Jesus' life: he was not born in the palace, though that would seem to be a more strategic place. He endured all the frustration and delay and condescension which confine the lives of the poor, and so he understood what it was like to be a human being on the bottom rung. If we were being called to incarnational ministry, surely that would be part of it: exposing ourselves to the same context which shaped our neighbours lives.

When we returned to China, we decided not to get a vehicle, but to use public transport, even though we lived in the middle of nowhere, buses were few, and often didn't have seats for us, or would not stop. We did wonder if this was the right decision, and prayed about it. Shortly after that, Dave had to go to the County hospital to buy the kids' immunization shots for me to administer at home. When he got there, the receptionist told him, "We don't have them here -- you'll have to go to the Communicable Disease Clinic." Dave asked her where that was, and she gave him brusque instructions. When she saw he still wasn't clear, she said, "Where are you parked? I'll show you." When Dave said, "I'm not parked; I took the bus," her attitude underwent a huge transformation. "You don't have a car? You're a foreigner doing a project in the village and you take the bus? You're living just like them? That's amazing. Here, I'll take you there myself." She did, and got them to work into their lunch hour so that Dave could catch the afternoon bus home. That same week, the bus driver actually stopped the bus, turned around, and said to Dave, "You're an educated person, probably an engineer or something. We Chinese get an education so we don't have to ride the bus with the common folk. You must really love these people." So we didn't get a vehicle.

We have struggled with both the cost and the compromises which were involved with living in the village. There were days and seasons when all that kept us was the sure knowledge that it was God's will for us to be there, because it definitely felt hard. I sometimes felt like a mole, with no more perspective than the dirt in front of my face. There were so many times when we were all sick and it seemed like life was just all about surviving the rain, the muddy laundry, the diarrhea and runny noses. When my focus was on what we were accomplishing by being there, it was really hard to see the point. But if, by God's grace, I could lift my eyes to Jesus, remember how worthy He is and make an offering of my day, then it all became an act of worship and joy returned to the mix.

Our goal was to be effective mediators, a bridge, between the knowledge and technology, charity and life-saving medical procedures which were "out there", and our village friends. Their isolated, traditional life style is coming to an end, and they need help to transition. We lived as close to their standard of living as we could endure, close enough that we could truly become friends and empathize, yet also living out a commitment to ways and values we hoped they would adopt.[34]

There were compromises or necessary adjustments in our lives, too. We used appliances which many of our neighbours could not initially afford, in order to free up

---

34   Good nutrition, hygiene, aesthetic beauty, discipling our children, domestic skills like baking and sewing which are a part of our families' heritage, etc.

enough time and energy to serve them. Our house was full of books and other educational tools so that our home-schooled children could be equipped to serve in some vocation as well. Once or twice a year, we left the valley for rest, inspiration and necessary shopping. Guilt, defensiveness, justification over these choices and the insurmountable differences between our lives and our neighbours' sometimes sucked a lot of energy. When we left the valley, it was the same thing in reverse; feeling gauche, "country bumpkin" and deprived compared to most other ex-pats!

At those times, it was very helpful to think of Jesus' words to Peter after he had reinstated him at the end of John, and warned him of the hardships and death he would face. Peter saw John, (the disciple whom Jesus loved) and asked, "*Lord, what about him?*"

Jesus said to him, "*...If I want him to remain alive until I return* (have a better job, live more luxuriously, have a more recognized ministry), **what is that to you?** *You must follow me.*"

It was also very helpful to live among sincere Christians who have next to nothing. I will never forget one Grandma who lived near us in Bridgeford. She went barefoot, with old, tattered clothes and a faded head scarf over her thin, grey braids. But she radiated joy. I expect she actually did walk, but she gave the impression of dancing everywhere she went. There was such a holy lightness about her. Her dark eyes shone with incredible love, and her face was just a mass of smile wrinkles. She would always come straight to me, hold both my hands in hers and speak a blessing over me. Then one gnarled, calloused hand would dive into a hidden pocket and come out with candy for the children. At first I thought that in spite of her poverty, she must have had a happy home life, but her sister-in-law enlightened me. "No, she's married to a drunkard and a brute, but her faith sustains her." Wow.

A good friend of ours who grew up in a missionary family in Latin America really helped us to find a perspective we could live with. He said, in essence: "It's all about love." (1 Corinthians 13:3 *"If I give all I possess to the poor ... but have not love, I gain nothing."*) No amount of idealistic self-sacrifice will make up for a lack of true, heartfelt love, and people can sense and respond to genuine loving compassion, even when it comes from someone who lives far away or far above them materially. We know this first hand, because whenever we had to go out to HongKong, we were shown hospitality by a very wealthy family who moved in the highest social circles. Their chauffeur would meet us at the border, relieve all our travel-weary little ones of their back packs, and help us all into the air-conditioned, white leather interior of the Mercedes (or Lexus? One of those fancy brands). Like Cinderella in her enchanted coach, we would be whisked off to another world. When we arrived, Martha would meet us at the door with a kiss to each cheek and a whiff of exquisite perfume, and then she and I would put all the priceless and fragile decorations in the living room out of harm's way so the kids could be themselves. The huge Terracotta horse could stay, and our kids took turns with their grandkids climbing and riding him! One of their wonderful maids would take all our filthy clothes and shoes away to deal with while another served us a sumptuous supper. After supper, our hosts would excuse themselves and leave us to enjoy their luxurious bath rooms before we tucked everyone into bed between crisp white sheets. If we could stay for any length of time, Martha would make sure our kids had a chance to visit Ocean Park and all the exclusive playgrounds and tourist meccas to which she habitually took her own grandchildren. Like their maid, who learned to put a plastic cover over the white fabric dining room chairs before she served our family chocolate muffins for breakfast, Mickey and Martha adapted their life to our needs during our stay with them, and like Jesus, were "not ashamed to call us brothers." We will always thank God for their love and hospitality.

We will always thank God for the privilege of living among the Lisu as well. We gained so much. I have always been struck by that phrase, "*... those who exercise authority ...* **call themselves Benefactors***. But you are not to be like that...*" (Luke 22:25) Living among the Lisu, we were *benefiters*, not benefactors. They are such beautiful people, and there are so many lovely things about their culture and their formation. We became very proud to identify ourselves with them.

I remember catching a ride in a little "mian bao che" [loaf-shaped minivan]. This one was "state of the art", with a little video screen clipped onto the sun visor and plugged into the cigarette lighter. A young rock star in an impeccable white suit was exhibiting a great deal of angst, throbbing about the meaninglessness of his life without his girl friend and throwing himself about in the most affected way. I looked out of the car window to see a group of middle-aged women burdened with heavy back-baskets trudging down the dirt road beside us. Their backs were bent to their loads, but they were laughing together in such a winsome way. As I reflected on the fact that almost all of them would have buried some of their children or a husband or other loved ones, and considered how much of their life was a cycle of heavy toil, the contrast was overwhelming. These people knew how to *live*. They also knew how to die. Their faces were scored by laugh lines, their eyes sparkled -- warmth and cheerfulness emanated from them. Where did they find the strength to be like that with all the daily hardships and set backs, as well as the big griefs which regularly entered their lives? They were so tough, and so tender. So tolerant of one another, so embedded in one another's lives. So very reliant on their Creator's daily mercies, and quick to lean on Him, and each other, in times of trouble.

We often spent time at the bedsides of dying neighbours, and were so impressed by how well they coped even without any analgesic or palliative measures. This was because they were surrounded night and day by concerned relatives who would pray and sing hymns, and take turns on the bed, supporting them in whichever position was comfortable. It was amazing how that physical presence, eternal perspective and constant sensitivity to their need to change position enabled them to make it through severe pain without any dulling narcotics.

We know that brothers and sisters who are very dear to God's heart, to this day, face "*jeers and flogging, while still others are chained and put in prison. They are stoned, they are sawed in two; they are put to death by the sword. They go about in sheepskins and goatskins, destitute, persecuted and mistreated -- the world is not worthy of them. They wander in deserts and mountains, and in caves and holes in the ground.*" (Hebrews 11:36-38)
We have met many of them.
Why are they entitled to that, but we are not?
The simple, truthful answer is that we're not entitled to our comfortable lives and all the privileges of our citizenship or class, and we won't necessarily get to keep them anyway. They were given to us to use, while we have them, for the benefit and respite of those who are suffering greatly on their "earthly pilgrimage", and we selfishly hold on to them at our peril. They are the very things that Jesus warned us could come into our lives like weeds that choke out the Gospel and make us unfruitful. God, save us from that.

Like Jesus said when he was disputing with the Pharisees, "*Now then, you Pharisees clean the outside of the cup and dish, but inside you are full of greed and wickedness. You foolish people! Did not the one who made the outside*

*make the inside also? But **give what is inside to the poor**, and everything will be clean for you."* Luke 11:39-41
That's it, in a nutshell.

A bridge in the valley

Epilogue

Looking back over this book, there are so many births! And in a sense it also feels like this book is something I've been pregnant with for twenty years.

As we've worked on polishing some of these "stones" of witness, I've wondered myself at the stories that somehow made it in instead of others which were equally interesting or revealing. However, life with seven kids goes on, and can't be put on hold indefinitely, at least not for building monuments! There comes a time when you just have to live with what you've chosen. I'm grateful for the refining and processing which has happened in my own memories and understanding as we've gone back over our life. I've been reminded of some things which I'm grateful for as we move back to China in the next few months: that God has always gone before us and never left us "in the lurch"; that He is faithful to speak and lead and provide; that he grants grace, strength and love sufficient for each day and each encounter; that He never tires of lifting up our heads. He is sufficient for the needs, and He is mighty to save. As it says in John, "The Word became flesh and made his dwelling among us. We have seen his glory, the glory of the One and Only, who came from the Father, full of grace and truth...From the fullness of his grace we have all received one blessing after another." As we head into each day, may we be Christ-bearers, that the fullness, the grace, the truth and the blessings may be abundantly shared. This is my prayer. May it be yours. There are a million ways to show Jesus that we love Him as His love is shed abroad in our hearts. He accepts them all. He is so worthy.